ORDNANCE SURVEY

OF

GREAT BRITAIN.

ENGLAND AND WALES.

INDEXES

TO THE

1/2500 AND 6-INCH SCALE MAPS

Reprinted with an Introduction by

Richard Oliver

Published in 1991 by David Archer, The Pentre, Kerry,
Newtown, Montgomeryshire, Wales SY16 4PD
Tel: 068688 382

First published by the Ordnance Survey, Southampton
circa 1905-6

A catalogue record for this book is available
from the British Library

Printed and bound by Dotesios Limited, Kennet House, Kennet Way,
Trowbridge, Wiltshire BA14 8RN

ISBN 0 9517579 1 1

CONTENTS

Diagram of England & Wales showing the pages of the Sections of the Index to the $\frac{1}{2500}$ and 6″ Scale Maps.

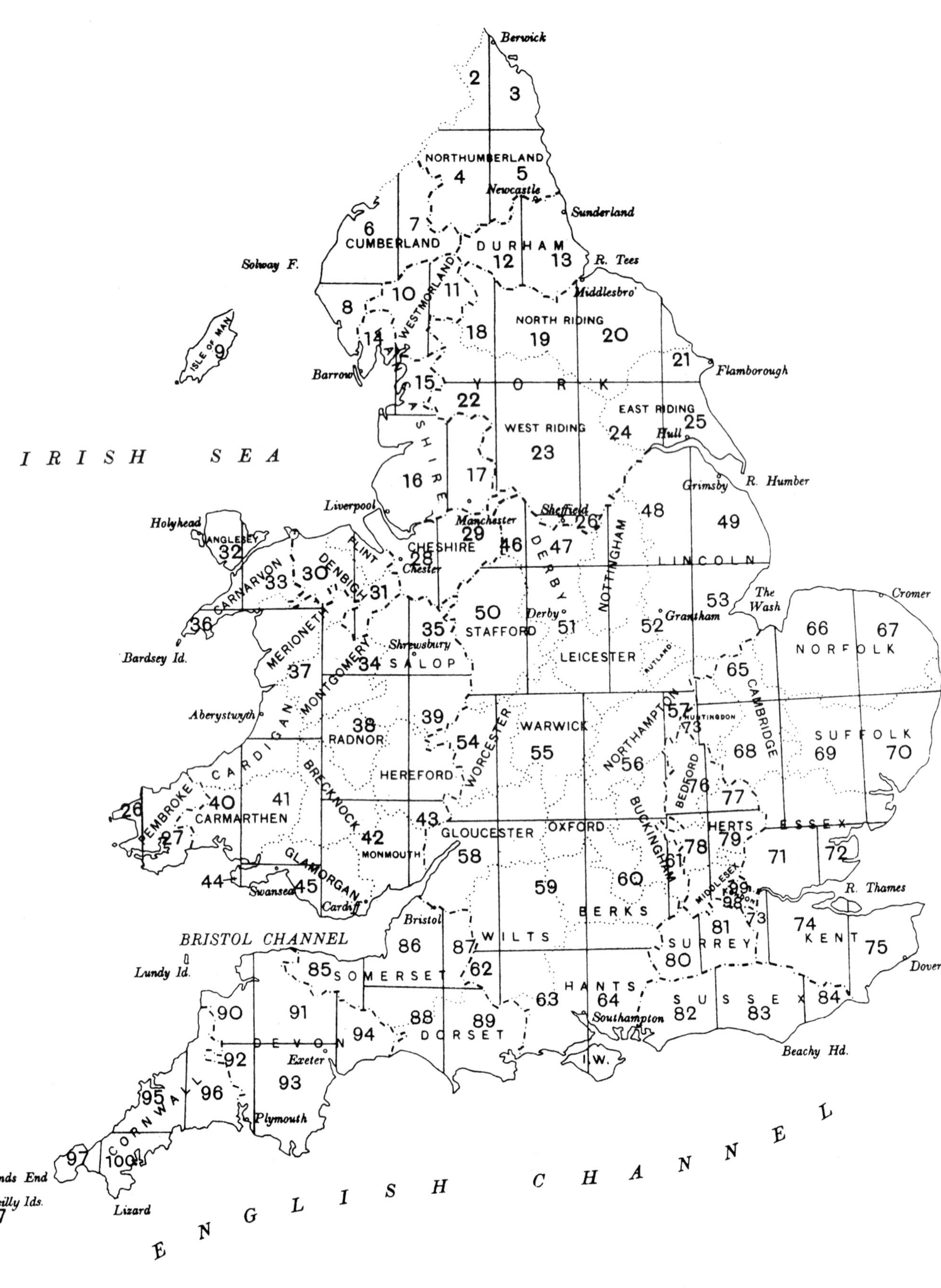

Scale :– 50 Miles to 1 Inch

Miles 25 0 50 100 Miles

Note - *Extent of areas on separate Meridians, encircled thus* –·–·–·–

The Ordnance Survey and its indexes to large-scale plans

It is perhaps both a sign of the continuing growth of interest in old Ordnance Survey maps and of a certain degree of maturity in the facsimile reproduction of them that, I think for the first time, a collection of indexes to some of them should be issued, as a publication in its own right. Indexes have been reproduced in the past, a notable recent example being those in David Archer's reissue of the 1924 Ordnance Survey *Catalogue*, but always as an appendage to something else.

The series of three volumes of indexes to the 1:2500 and Six-inch (1:10,560) county series plans at the Quarter-inch (1:253,440) scale published by the Ordnance Survey *circa* 1905-6, (one each for England and Wales, Scotland and Ireland), were unique, all other indexes to the county series plans being issued in sheet form. They were by no means the first indexes to large-scale OS plans, and they were not the last; we do not know how many were printed, and so there is no real way of judging whether they were successful either as artefacts for sale or as works of reference. By the time the Ordnance Survey issued its last fairly comprehensive *Catalogue* in 1924 the indexes in volume form had come and gone, but the larger story of which they were a part continued, and even now, with their successor in spirit, the 'Plandex', performing a similar function, if less elegantly, it is by no means clear that even a period of consolidation, never mind finality, is in sight. Like everything else about the contemporary Ordnance Survey, the advent of comprehensive digitisation has mean that there is no repose for either map makers or map historians.

It is safe to say that the earliest Ordnance Survey index of all has not survived. It would have been at least partly in manuscript, and would have been used to work out the numbering of the first 33 sheets of the One-inch (1:63,360) Old Series map. As such it might well have been prepared by *circa* 1810, when numbers would have been needed for the group of sheets being published in south-west England. Around 1816, a much more elaborate index to the Old Series was started, at a scale of one inch to ten miles (1:633,600), which could show most villages, main roads, and the more important watercourses and gentlemen's seats, the last a useful consideration from a commercial point of view, serving to 'lead in' the country gentlemen who might undertake to buy all the published sheets. The Ten-mile index was only engraved following the detailed field survey for the parent One-inch map, and was only completed for Great Britain in the 1880s; meanwhile, less elaborate counterparts helped to show potential (sometimes frustrated potential) map users what sheets could be expected to cover a given area in due course. By the early 1830s a foolscap-sized index to sheets 1 to 90 of the Old Series was available, over a decade before the last sheets within it were published, and by 1839 an foolscap index to the Old Series of the whole of England and Wales had been engraved, 35 years in advance of the completion of publication.

By 1839 the mapping of Ireland was developing somewhat differently. The basic scale of survey and publication there was the Six-inch. No doubt rough manuscript indexes were used to work out the sheet numbering, but the indexes which accompanied the completed mapping for each county left even the English Ten-mile index in the shade. A cynic might suggest that the 'scale-free database' was a reality in Irish analogue mapping by 1833, whatever problems its digital realisation might present over a century and a half later, and that the 'Indexes to the Townland Survey' solved the problem of generalisation by dispensing with it, particularly on that of County Dublin. That is not entirely true, but certainly these Irish county indexes were very finely detailed. They were at scales varying from two-thirds of an inch to a mile (1:95,080) to a third of an inch to a mile (1:190,160), depending on what was necessary to fit the whole county onto a landscape-shaped piece of double-elephant paper. Although their primary purpose was to indicate which Six-inch sheets covered which parishes, they enjoyed great popularity as county maps in their own right, particularly as the production of the One-inch map of Ireland was seriously delayed. That of County Kilkenny served as guinea-pig for various cartographic experiments, taking advantage of electrotyping to produce variants of the original plate, and a few were used for geological mapping. Even if one only bought a single Six-inch sheet covering one's estate, it was nice to buy the index and to colour-wash the area of the sheet in question, establishing one's place within at least the county. The Irish indexes were iconographic as well as functional.

The Six-inch came to northern Britain in 1840, and with it came the concept of an elaborately-engraved accompanying index. However, the rate of publication was much slower in Britain, and whereas the indexes were available in Ireland as soon as the sheets they referred to were completed, in Britain there was often a gap of several years. The original plan was to engrave them at a common scale of one inch to four miles (1:253,440), with a view to joining them up on regular sheetlines in due course; the scale was evidently determined by being that at which Yorkshire could just be fitted onto a double-elephant sheet of paper. In the event, this plan had been dropped by the late 1850s, and the indexes followed the example of Ireland, the scale being determined by the fitting of the county onto double-elephant paper. In Scotland electrotypes of the standard One-inch sheets were used for a number of smaller counties, including Fife, which called for two sheets, and sacrificed the convenience of compactness for that of the inexpensiveness of using an existing map. Unlike the Irish indexes, those in Britain not of One-inch parentage were obviously generalised, perhaps, indeed, excessively so; these were indexes, *not* maps.

To judge from the number of surviving examples, the engraved county index was nowhere near as popular in Britain as in Ireland; at such small scales there were plenty of commercial rivals. There were also Ordnance Survey rivals, in the form of cheap, if not free, lithographed sketched indexes, which served the dual purpose of enabling colour tints to be added in illustration of progress in surveying and engraving, and of enabling potential purchasers to locate the desired sheets. In 1853-5 the Six-inch was displaced by the 1:2500 as the basic scale of survey for cultivated land, though the Six-inch would continue to be published as a derived map, by counties. The 1:2500's spiritual parent was the tithe mapping of England and Wales which had been carried on since 1836 on a parochial or township basis, and this no doubt explains, firstly, why until the 1870s the 1:2500 was published by parishes, and secondly, why it was accompanied by sheets or books of reference, giving the acreage of fields and details of land use, which might perhaps have been more conveniently incorporated on the maps. At first there were reference sheets, and indexes to the parish 1:2500 (a number are preserved with the parish sets in the British Library, Map Library) often took the form of leaflets, giving a roughly drawn, usually at 1:63,360, index to the parish, and a list of agents from whom the plans might be purchased, the whole evidently got up with a view to 'mail-shotting' potential purchasers. By 1859-60 the area sheets had been replaced by area books, and these invariably incorporated One-inch indexes to the sheets of the relevant parish, usually rather roughly drawn, though occasionally, where the 1:2500 was being published for districts already covered thus, by the One-inch Old Series, with the 1:2500 sheetlines duly added. It is these indexes to the 1:2500 which have survived for the 1860s and 1870s, and it remains to be ascertained whether the earlier 'mail-shot' style continued to be produced. In the late 1970s the writer saw in a London street-market a collection of these indexes for much of Surrey, of c.1870, which appeared never to have been bound, and so they were presumably sold separately.

Now, aesthetics apart, these indexes were all very well if one knew how the system worked, and, indeed, were prepared to work with it. The desirer of 1:2500 mapping had first to find out which parish the mapping belonged to, (always assuming that the Ordnance Survey had actually got round to mapping it), and whilst those who lived in or owned parishes might know that, it was more difficult for outsiders, such as engineers planning railways. (One also had to find an agent who sold the maps.) The 1:2500 sheets were numbered as divisions of the Six-inch, and in the early 1870s there was a move towards rationality: henceforth the 1:2500 was published by counties, and in due course 1:2500 sheet lines were added to the engraved indexes to the Six-inch. The area books continued to be published by parishes until the mid-1880s, when they were abandoned in favour of putting the acreages of fields where they ought always to have been, in the fields on the maps. The publishing of the land-use information had been jettisoned as an economy measure a few years earlier, though it continued to be collected until 1918, and survived in manuscript, probably unknown even to the organisers of the Land Utliisation Survey, until destruction by bombs in 1940.

The abandoning of the area books was apparently succeeded by the publication of foolscap indexes, showing the sixteen 1:2500 sub-sheets within each Six-inch full sheet. These indexes were at One-inch scale, as before, but the base map was in the style of the 'Advance Edition Published by Photozincography' (*sic*) of the One-inch New Series of 1891-2, and covered counties such as Northamptonshire which the 'Advance Edition' never reached. How many index-leaflets in this style were issued remains unknown; by the 1890s they were clearly 'out', and One-inch parish indexes were back 'in'; they were certainly issued for those counties (Lancashire and Yorkshire in England, and several in Scotland) originally surveyed at Six-inch in 1841-53 and resurveyed or replotted at 1:2500 in 1887-96. They were based on a mixture of existing One-inch engraved mapping and newly-drawn, very generalised, mapping.

In 1896 a Departmental Committee appointed by the Board of Agriculture, which had political charge of the Ordnance Survey, examined, for neither the first nor the last time, the vexed question of how it was that Ordnance Survey maps exhibited a much greater excellence of intrinsic quality than of extrinsic sales. It was no doubt a combination of this committee's proceedings and those of another departmental committee, (the Dorington Committee of 1892), in the course of which it was stated that there was great confusion between Six-inch and 1:2500 sheetlines, that was behind the most lavish of all Ordnance Survey indexes, which began to appear in 1897. This was nothing less than not one but *two* alternative versions of the standard One-inch map of Great Britain, one showing 1:2500 sheetlines, the other (a tautology, anyone might think who had not fallen for the evidence given to the Dorington Committee), those of the Six-inch. Parishes were shown in colour on each, and the series is of importance in Ordnance Survey history for its anticipation of 'process printing' eighty years later by green and orange being obtained by combinations of the primary colours. Sir John Farquharson, the OS Director-General, who had overseen the birth of these series, observed in 1900 that it remained to be seen whether, their obvious utility as indexes apart, they would have any sale as maps. By 1904 it was clear that they did not, and further publication was abandoned, with a quarter of Scotland and a third of England and Wales yet to be produced. Publication had followed the publication of the first revision of the 1:2500, which had entailed some minor alterations to 1:2500 sheet-lines, particularly along county boundaries.

All this while Quarter-inch indexes had been published. Their full history remains to be unravelled, but the basic type consisted of the Six-inch and 1:2500 sheetlines, together with parish boundaries. (On some early issues, pending completion of field survey, the boundaries were obtained, where available, from the (misnamed) 'Index to Tithe Survey' version of the One-inch Old Series.) By the early 1900s the current One-inch sheetlines were being thrown in, as well. It was possibly these Quarter-inch indexes, humble things costing twopence or so, which gave someone the idea for the next Ordnance Survey index wheeze, that of publishing the things in national atlases, in other words the original of the volume you are holding now. In 1905 the Ordnance Survey had just completed coverage of the whole of the British Isles by a new and (by previous standards) excellent Quarter-inch map. Why not use this admirable new mapping as the basis for atlases of large-scale sheetlines? Splendid idea!

As I said earlier, we do not know how many of these atlases were printed; we do know that they were allowed to go out of print. From the vantage point of the 1990s, they appear as neat a solution of the problem of indexing the county series maps as the Ordnance Survey ever hit on. Here is the whole of England and Wales in one compact volume (originally foolscap, slightly reduced in size and scale in this republication), small enough for easy storage, yet just large enough for annotation, by diagonal, vertical or horizontal lines, to show one's holdings, ideally originals, perhaps photocopies, at the least Alan Godfrey's excellent reprints. (Mr Godfrey has himself confessed that a copy of this volume is an excellent companion on a railway journey, enabling possibilities for future reprints to be sized up.) They do have minor disadvantages, (as you have probably bought this republication before reading this, you won't mind my pointing them out?), one being that the arrangement of counties, though fundamentally north to south, is sometimes clearly determined by compactness, so that Sheffield adjoins Fishguard, and Cornwall is interrupted by London, and another being that they record the sheetlines current at the time of publication, rather than later modifications: thus on page 25 1:2500 sheets Yorkshire 257.12 and 269.12 are shown; both were published in the first edition of the 1:2500 c.1890, but not in the second, c.1910. Likewise, on page 90, Lundy is shown as covered by two Six-inch landscape-shaped sheets, whereas c.1908 it was republished on a single portrait-shaped sheet. The sheetlines for Essex and Northumberland are the original ones, before the change of county origin; the later sheetlines for those two counties have been added for this reissue. (Omitted from this reissue are a number of rather routine specimens of various types of Ordnance Survey map.)

I suspect it was this sort of thing which helped a decision not to keep these atlases in publication, though the idea of using the standard Quarter-inch topographical map as a base had come to stay, for a while: versions of this basic type of index were still being produced well into the 1960s. At the same time, a family of Half-inch (1:126,720) county indexes and administrative diagrams was being developed, based on the standard topographical map at that scale; the family was an extended one, as some Half-inch diagrams were also issued as direct photo-reductions at Quarter-inch scale. Unfortunately, the contemplated redrawing of the original Half-inch of 1902-10, started in the 1930s but hindered by one thing after another thereafter, was abandoned in 1961, and the base-maps for the diagrams were clearly living on borrowed time. The answer was a series of 1:100,000 county maps, produced by direct reduction from the One-inch Seventh Series in 1965-72, which were issued in various forms, one having county series large-scale sheetlines overprinted in red. This last version faded away as the county series plans were replaced by those on National Grid sheetlines, an operation which took some forty years and was completed, strangely to no fanfare, in the mid-1980s.

It was the National Grid plans which were the cause of the Ordnance Survey's second most lavish, and arguably most curious, series of One-inch scale indexes. This paralleled the abortive venture of 1897-1904 by attempting national coverage, but not succeeding, (155 of 189 possible sheets were issued), but it seems to have been rather more of a success, or less of a failure, with its users. The National Grid had been adopted in 1938 for a number of reasons, one being that it would serve as a framework for large-scale sheetlines, so that no longer would one have to fiddle about with some beastly index diagram; all one needed was the grid reference of one's point of interest, and Bingo! you had the number of the desired plan. It must have seemed too good to be true. It was. For one thing, it took forty years to publish all these National Grid plans. For another, the scales varied according to whether one's district of interest was larger urban, (basic scale 1:1250), cultivated rural or smaller urban (1:2500), or uncultivated (basic scale Six-inch, later 1:10,000). For a third, though the Ordnance Survey top brass of the period may have been, to quote their Archaeology Officer colleague, 'barmy' about the National Grid, the map-buying public was distinctly less so. After a couple of years of endeavouring to sell Nationally Gridded 1:1250 and 1:2500 plans, it became apparent that special indexes would have to be provided. These were based on the current One-inch map, and fell into two groups. The earlier was based on the One-inch New Popular edition, and though not complete it covered most of the areas intended to be published at 1:1250 scale. This was all very well, except that there was no indication of which sheets had actually been published, and several of these index versions of the New Popular were redundant by the time that publication of the 1:1250 within them commenced. They were replaced by a series of indexes based on the One-inch Seventh Series, most of which were issued in two versions, one showing merely 1:2500 and 1:1250 proposed coverage, by purple overprint, and the other - *mirabile dictu!* - overprinted to show what *had* been published.

If one was prepared to overlook the fact that the purple overprint obscured much of the base-map detail, this must have seemed the answer to a long-standing problem. Alas, it was not. Colour printing is always expensive, and it was unrealistic to republish these one-inch indexes more often than once every two or three years, and agents can hardly have relished adding by hand shadings to record the monthly new publications, on the off-chance that someone might actually express interest in the sheet in question. By the late 1960s the One-inch indexes were on the way out. They were replaced by the Plan Availability Index, or Plandex, which consists of loose-leaf A4 sheets, each covering a quarter of a 100 km National Grid square, reissued quarterly, indicating which sheets are published and whether they are available in digital as well as analogue form. This seems quite wonderful, except that the Plandex is purely a series of little boxes, the only external garnishings being the coastline, and (until recently, anyway), telltale thickenings, showing long-obsolete One-inch Seventh Series sheetlines, a relic of the days of One-inch indexes. In a way, we are back in the 1860s; you have to find out from another map (probably the 1:50,000 or 1:25,000) which National Grid square your area of interest falls in, before you can ascertain what your chances are of obtaining, say, digital 1:1250 coverage of it.

You may feel like staying with the present publication instead.

Richard Oliver
Department of Geography
University of Exeter

Further reading

... is, alas, something of a joke. It can be seen that the Ordnance Survey's index struggles and tribulations are worthy of a scholarly monograph rather than this hasty trifle. References to indexes, or associated things, (such as the area books), can be found in the following:

Andrews, J.H., *History in the Ordnance Map: An Introduction for Irish Readers*, Dublin, Ordnance Survey, 1974. [Non-Irish readers will find it of equal value.]

Andrews, J.H., *A Paper Landscape: the Ordnance Survey in nineteenth-century Ireland*, Oxford University Press, 1975.

Col Sir John Farquharson, 'Twelve years' work of the Ordnance Survey, 1887 to 1899', *Geographical Journal*, vol 15 (1900), pp.565-98.

J.B.Harley, *Ordnance Survey Maps: a descriptive manual*, Southampton, Ordnance Survey, 1975.

J.B.Harley, *The Ordnance Survey and Land-Use Mapping*, Norwich, Geo Books, Historical Geography Research Series, 1979.

Richard Oliver, *A Guide to the Ordnance Survey One-Inch New Popular Edition...*,

Richard Oliver, *A Guide to the Ordnance Survey One-Inch Seventh Series*, London, Charles Close Society, 1991.

There are also brief references in *Sheetlines* no.29 (January 1991), and in no.31 (September 1991). (*Sheetlines* is published three times a year by the Charles Close Society, c/o British Library, Map Library, Great Russell Street, London, WC1B 3DG.)

Survey and revision dates for OS 1:2500 and 1:10,560 mapping of England and Wales

Columns: 1, county; 2, first 1:2500 county series survey; 3, 1st 1:2500 county series revision; 4, 2nd county series 1:2500 revision; 5, 3rd county series revision; 6, initial 1:2500 revision/resurvey on National Grid sheetlines.

Compilation: dates for pre-1945 county series survey have been taken from from unpublished Ordnance Survey 'Revision Progress' diagrams, now held by the Charles Close Society, and from the 1924 Ordnance Survey *Catalogue*; dates for post-1945 National Grid surveys have been deduced from information in OS annual reports. (These dates are not necessarily applicable to those urban parts of counties mapped after 1943 at 1:1250, for which see Richard Oliver, 'The Ordnance Survey 1:1250 National Grid surveys: a preliminary list', *Sheetlines* 24, pp 5-11.)

Abbreviations: * after initial survey date = surveyed at 1:10,560 between 1841 and 1853, and 'replotted' at 1:2500 1887-96; + after initial survey date = parts surveyed for military purposes much earlier than the main body of the county; $ after revision date = incomplete revision of county; ** = some further urban revision c.1936-43; $$ = urban areas only surveyed at this date. e after initial survey date = all 6-inch 1st edition of this county engraved, as was the county index; p after date = some 6-inch engraved. (All other 6-inch were photo- or helio- zincographed quarter sheets, accompanied by similarly produced indexes, except for some published 1920-4.) m after date = county series sheets republished on new county origin.

1	2	3	4	5	6
Anglesey	1886-7	1899	1913-23		1969-76
Bedfordshire	1876-82	1898-1900	1921-4$**		1968-80
Berkshire	1866-83e	1897-9	1909-12	1919-33$**	1964-82
Brecknockshire	1874-88	1903-4	1913-16/27$		1962-82
Buckinghamshire	1867-81e	1897-99	1918-33$**		1960-82
Caernarvonshire	1885-88	1898-1900	1910-14**		1959-82
Cambridgeshire	1876-86	1896-1901	1924-6$**		1969-81
Isle of Ely	[do]	[do]	1924-6$		1968-82
Cardiganshire	1885-8	1900-4**			1964-5$$/72-82
Carmarthenshire	1875-87	1903-6	1913$**		1959-82
Cheshire	1870-5e	1896-98	1904-09	1924-5$**	1953-80
Cornwall	1859-88+p	1905-7	1912/32-3$**		1950-81
Isles of Scilly	1887	1905			1978
Cumberland	1859-65e	1897-1900	1922-4$**		1960-82
Denbighshire	1870-5e	1897-99	1909-12**		1959-80
Derbyshire	1872-83	1896-1900	1912-21**		1956-82
Devon	1855-89+p	1902-5	1912/32-3$**		1948-80
Dorset	1862-89+	1900-01	1923-32$**		1954-82
Durham	1854-7e	1894-7	1912-19	1937-9$	1957-82
Essex	1862-76+e	1893-6	1911-22m	1936-40$	1949-81
Flintshire (main)	1869-72e	1897-9	1909-11**		1960-71
(det portion)	[do]	[do]	[do]		1958-77
Glamorgan	1867-78e	1896-9	1913-16	1935-43$	1957-79
Gloucestershire	1873-84	1898-1902	1912-22**		1950-81
Hampshire	1856-75+e	1894-7	1906-10	1923-33$**	1945-81
Isle of Wight	1860-2e	[do]	[do]**		1970-78
Herefordshire	1878-87	1902-4	1924-8$**		1967-75
Hertfordshire	1863-86e	1895-7	1912-23/34$**		1961-81
Huntingdonshire	1882-7	1899-1901	1924-5$		1969-81
Kent	1858-73+e	1893-7	1905-10	1931-2/7-40$	1955-79

1	2	3	4	5	6
Lancashire (main)	1888-93*p	1904-12	1924-38$**		1954-82
Furness	[do]	[do]	1931-2$**		1959-81
Leicestershire	1879-86	1899-1902	1927-30$**		1954-77
Lincolnshire	1883-8	1898-1906	1914-32$**		1963-82
Holland	[do]	[do]	1929-30$**		1967-79
Kesteven	[do]	[do]	1915-6/28-9$**		1965-82
Lindsey	[do]	[do]	1915-19/30-2$**		1963-80
London	1862-72e	1891-5	1912-14	1935-6$	1948-68
Isle of Man	1866-9e				1968-80$$
Merionethshire	1873-88	1899-1900	1913-14$		1971-82
Middlesex	1862-71e	1891-5	1910-13	1932-6**	1961-73
Monmouthshire	1875-81e	1898-1900	1915-20**		1958-83
Montgomeryshire	1874-87	1900-1			1966-82
Norfolk	1879-86	1900-6	1925-7/38-9$**		1964-82
Northamptonshire	1880-7	1898-1900	1923-8$**		1961-81
S. Peterborough	[do]	[do]	1924-5$		1969-78
Northumberland	1855-64e	1894-7	1912-22m	1936-40$	1956-82
Nottinghamshire	1876-85	1897-9	1912-19**		1953-77
Oxfordshire	1872-80e	1897-99	1910-21$**		1962-80
Pembrokeshire	1860-88+p	1904-6**			1964-82
Radnorshire	1883-8	1901-4	1926-7$		1972-82
Rutland	1883-4	1899-1903	1928$		1962-4
Shropshire	1873-84	1899-1902	1924-6$		1956-82
Somerset	1882-8	1900-3	1927-30$**		1955-80
Staffordshire	1875-86	1897-1902	1912-23	1937-8$	1956-79
Suffolk	1876-85	1900-04	1924-6$		1955-82
Surrey	1861-71e	1891-6	1910-13	1932-4$**	1963-78
Sussex	1869-75	1895-8	1907-10	1925-33$**	1955-79
Warwickshire	1880-88	1898-1904	1912-23$	1936-9$	1953-75
Westmorland	1856-60e	1896-8	1910-13**		1967-81
Wiltshire	1873-85e	1898-1900	1921-4	1939-42$	1956-82
Worcestershire	1880-88	1898-1904	1921-6$	1937-8$	1959-75
Yorkshire	1888-93*p	1901-14	1913-39$**		1952-82
North Riding	[do]	1907-14	1926-8$**		1964-82
West Riding	[do]	1901-8	1913-39**		1952-82
East Riding	[do]	1904-9	1925-9$**		1962-79

INDEX TO THE MAPS OF

ENGLAND AND WALES,

ON THE SCALES OF

25·344 AND SIX-INCHES TO ONE MILE.

PREFACE.

The Index is drawn on the scale of Four Miles to One Inch, and is arranged by counties, or by groups of counties when on the same meridian. Thus, to start from the North of England, Northumberland, Cumberland. Westmorland, Lancashire, Durham, and Yorkshire are all on different meridians, and they are accordingly arranged separately in the Index. All the central counties, on the other hand, are on the same meridian, and they are all on one continuous Index, their sheet lines being all continuous and parallel to one another. Other counties are arranged on the same principle according to whether they are on the same or on different meridians. The number of each 6-inch sheet is shown in its centre. Parts of certain counties are still published in full sheets, but in most cases this map is now published in quarter sheets, and, where so published, the description N.W., N.E., S.W., S.E., is printed in the centre of each quarter sheet. If the quarter sheet has no letters (N.W., &c.) on it, it may be inferred that the quarter sheet lies entirely outside the county, and will be found on the Index of the adjoining county. Every $\frac{1}{2500}$ plan has its number in the centre of it, and where there is no number, there is no $\frac{1}{2500}$ plan of that area. Thus in the diagram the number of the 6-inch sheet is 36, but only 3 quarter sheets are published, viz.:—N.W., N.E., and S.W.

1	2	3	4
N.W.		N.E.	
5	6	7	
	36		
9	10		
S.W.			
13	14		

The S.E. portion is not published because there is no part of it in the county in question. Similarly, there are the following $\frac{1}{2500}$ plans all forming part of 6-inch sheet 36, and described as 36. 1, 36. 2, or 36. 14. It is known that there is no 36. 8, as there is no plan number in it. It has not been published on the $\frac{1}{2500}$ scale either because it is moorland or uncultivated district, or because no part of it falls in the county in question.

In the case of adjoining counties on the same meridian, the 6-inch sheets and $\frac{1}{2500}$ plans crossed by county boundary bear the numerals of both counties, thus:—43 N.E. Wilts and 7 N.E. Hants are one and the same quarter sheet, partly filled up with Wilts and partly with Hants. Similarly the $\frac{1}{2500}$ plan 43. 3 Wilts covers exactly the same area of ground as 7. 3 Hants, and is composed of parts of both counties.

In ordering maps, however, it is better, though not essential, that the numerals used should, as far as possible, be those of the county in which the required area is situated.

CONTENTS.

• The London Index is on a scale of 2 miles to one inch, and that of the Tyneside Survey on a scale of one inch to one mile.

COMBINED SHEETS.

SIX-INCH SCALE.

8A S.E.	*is published on*	9 S.W.
12B N.E.	,,	13 N.W.

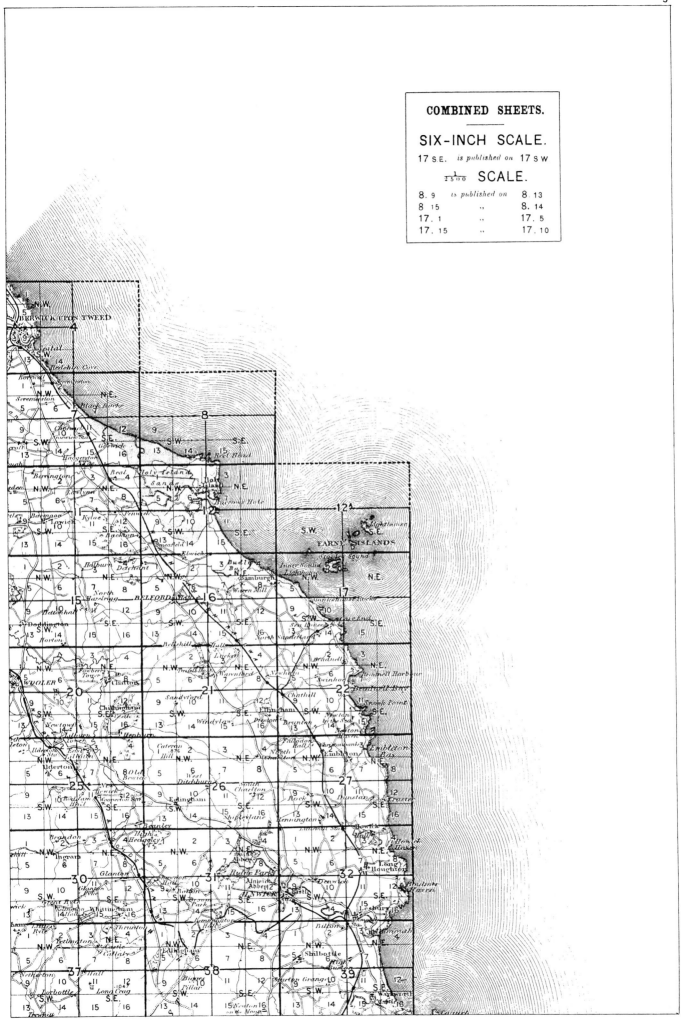

COMBINED SHEETS.

SIX-INCH SCALE.

17 S.E. *is published on* 17 S W

$\frac{1}{2500}$ SCALE.

8. 9	*is published on*	8. 13
8. 15	,,	8. 14
17. 1	,,	17. 5
17. 15	,,	17. 10

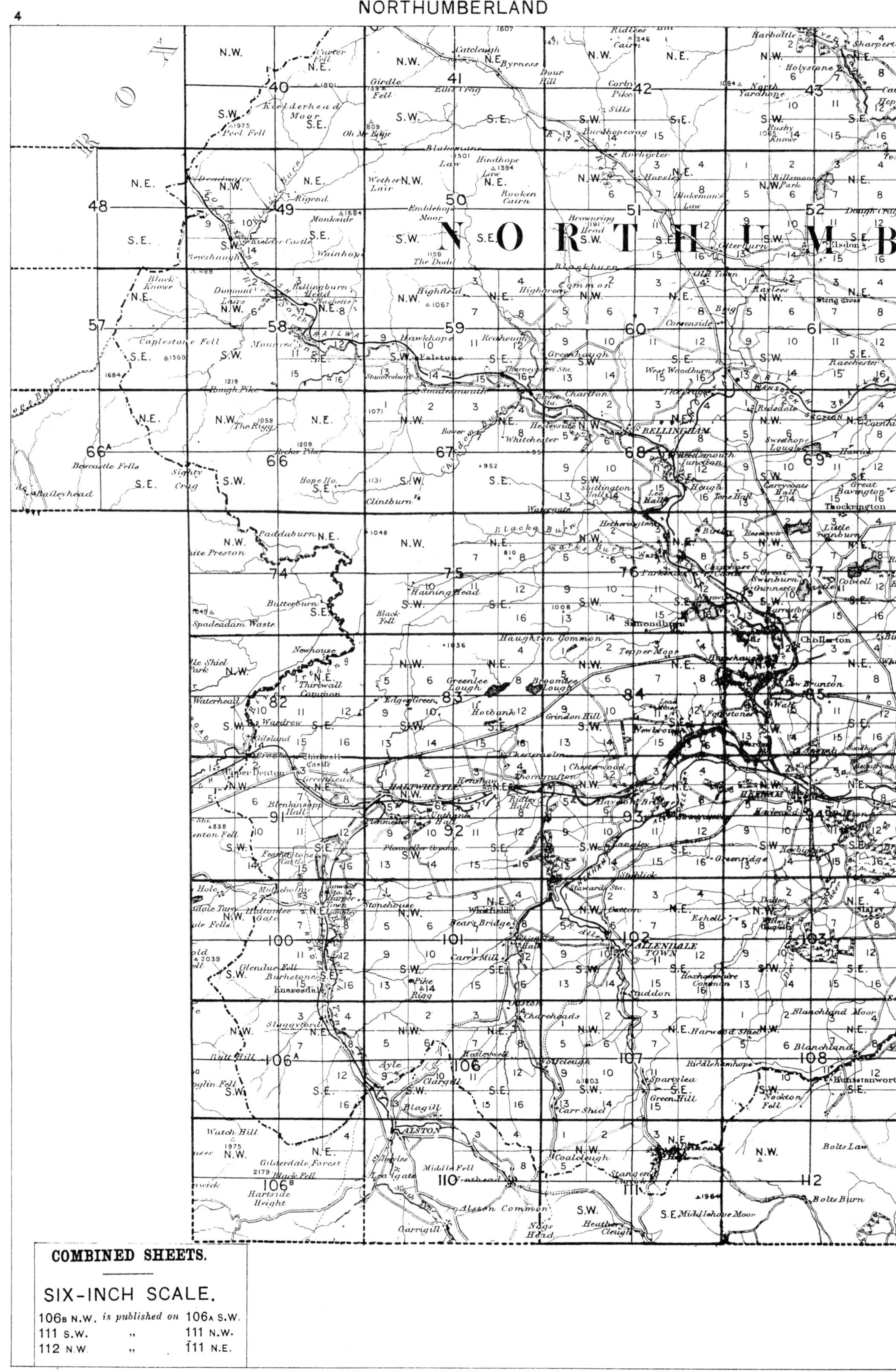
NORTHUMB
COMBINED SHEETS.
SIX-INCH SCALE.
106B N.W. is published on 106A S.W.
111 S.W. " 111 N.W.
112 N.W. " 111 N.E.

Note.—For $\frac{1}{2500}$ scale Maps south of the line shaded thus see Tyneside Index on Page 101.

COMBINED SHEETS.

SIX-INCH SCALE.

2A S.E.	*is published on*	3 S.W.
5A N.E.	,,	6 N.W.
9B S.W.	,,	14 N.W.
9B S.E.	,,	14 N.E.
9A S.W.	,,	15 N.W.
20 S.W.	,,	20 S.E.

$\frac{1}{2500}$ SCALE.

44.11 *is published on* 44.12

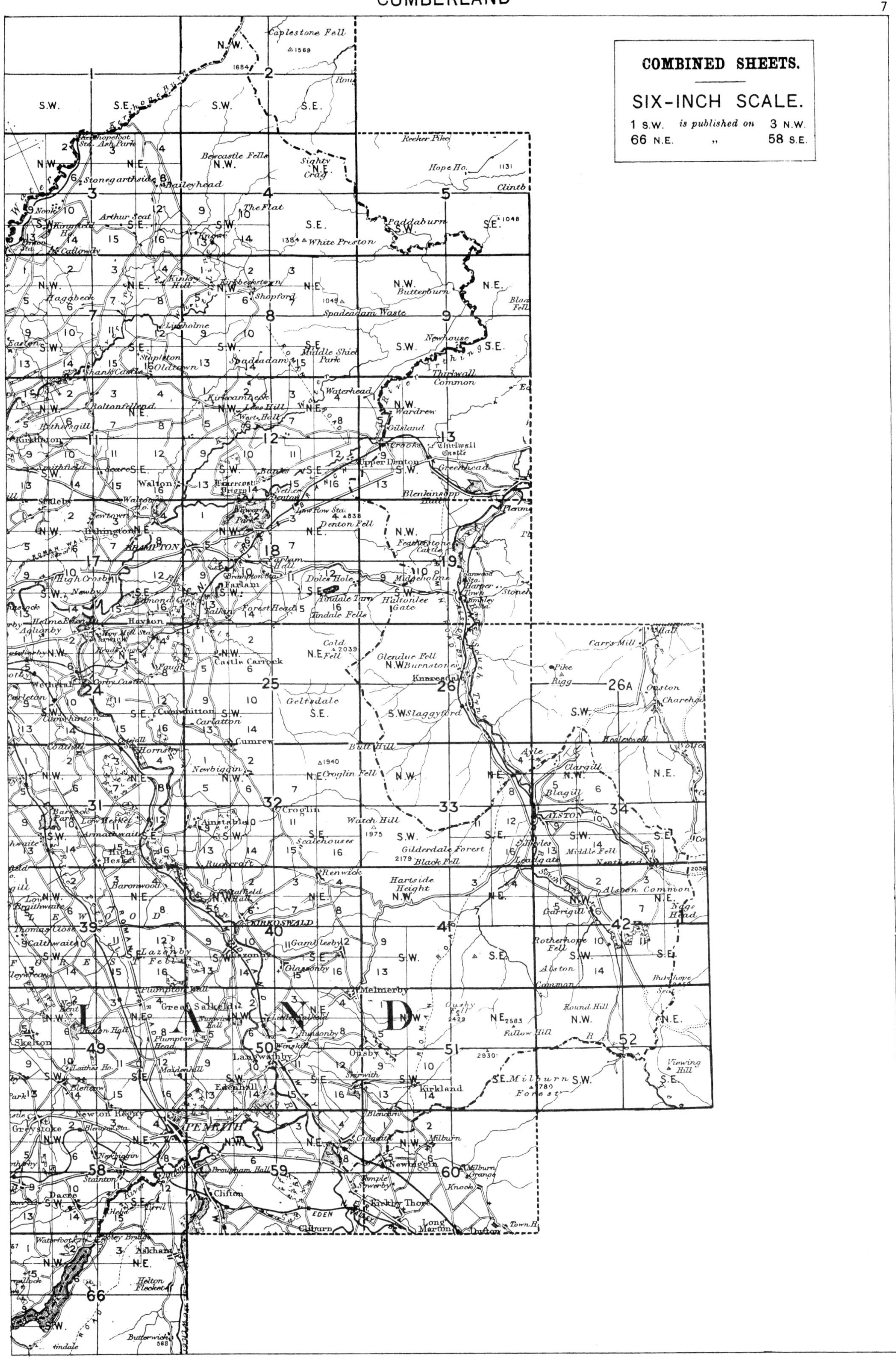
COMBINED SHEETS.
SIX-INCH SCALE.
1 S.W. is published on 3 N.W.
66 N.E. „ 58 S.E.

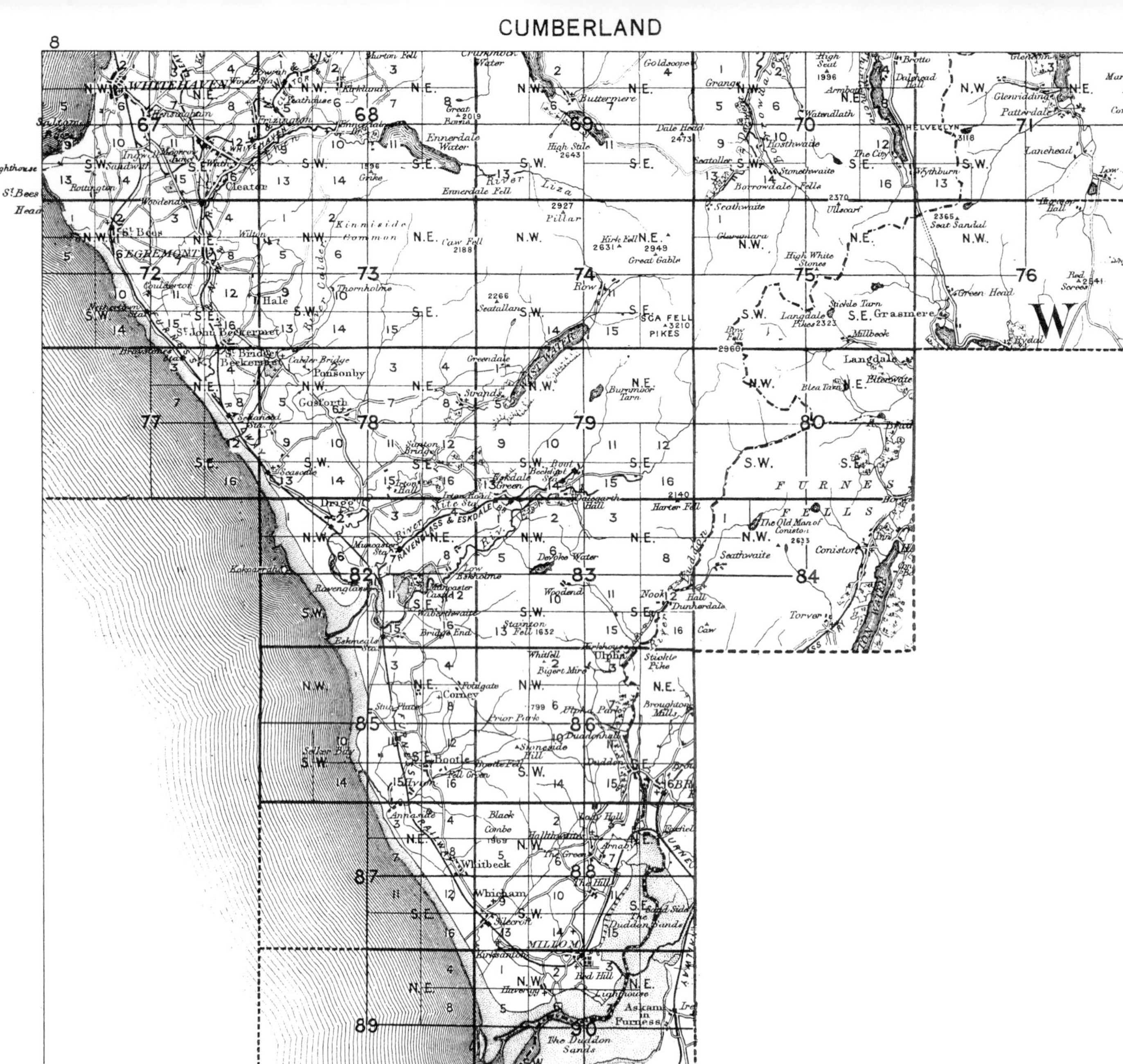

COMBINED SHEETS.

SIX-INCH SCALE.

71 N.E.	*is published on*	65 S.E.
80 N.E.	„	80 N.W.
80 S.E.	„	80 S.W.

$\frac{1}{2500}$ SCALE.

72. 5	*is published on*	72. 1
77. 7	„	77. 3
77. 16	„	77. 12
87. 11	„	87. 16
89. 8	„	89. 4

COMBINED SHEETS.

$\frac{1}{2500}$ SCALE.

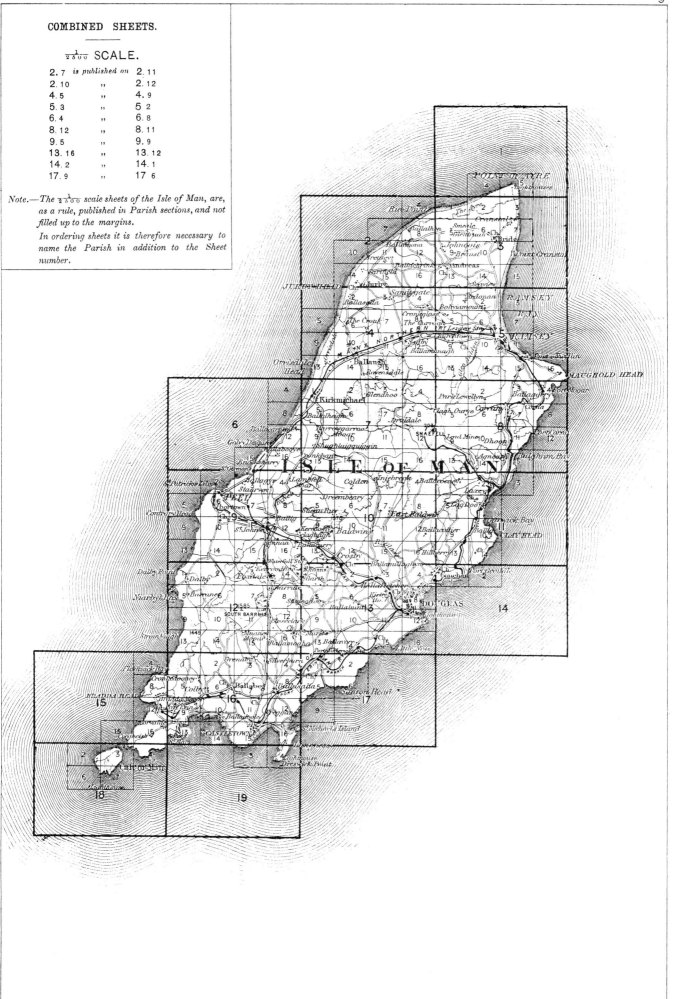

Sheet		Published on
2.7	*is published on*	2.11
2.10	"	2.12
4.5	"	4.9
5.3	"	5.2
6.4	"	6.8
8.12	"	8.11
9.5	"	9.9
13.16	"	13.12
14.2	"	14.1
17.9	"	17.6

Note.—The $\frac{1}{2500}$ scale sheets of the Isle of Man, are, as a rule, published in Parish sections, and not filled up to the margins.

In ordering sheets it is therefore necessary to name the Parish in addition to the Sheet number.

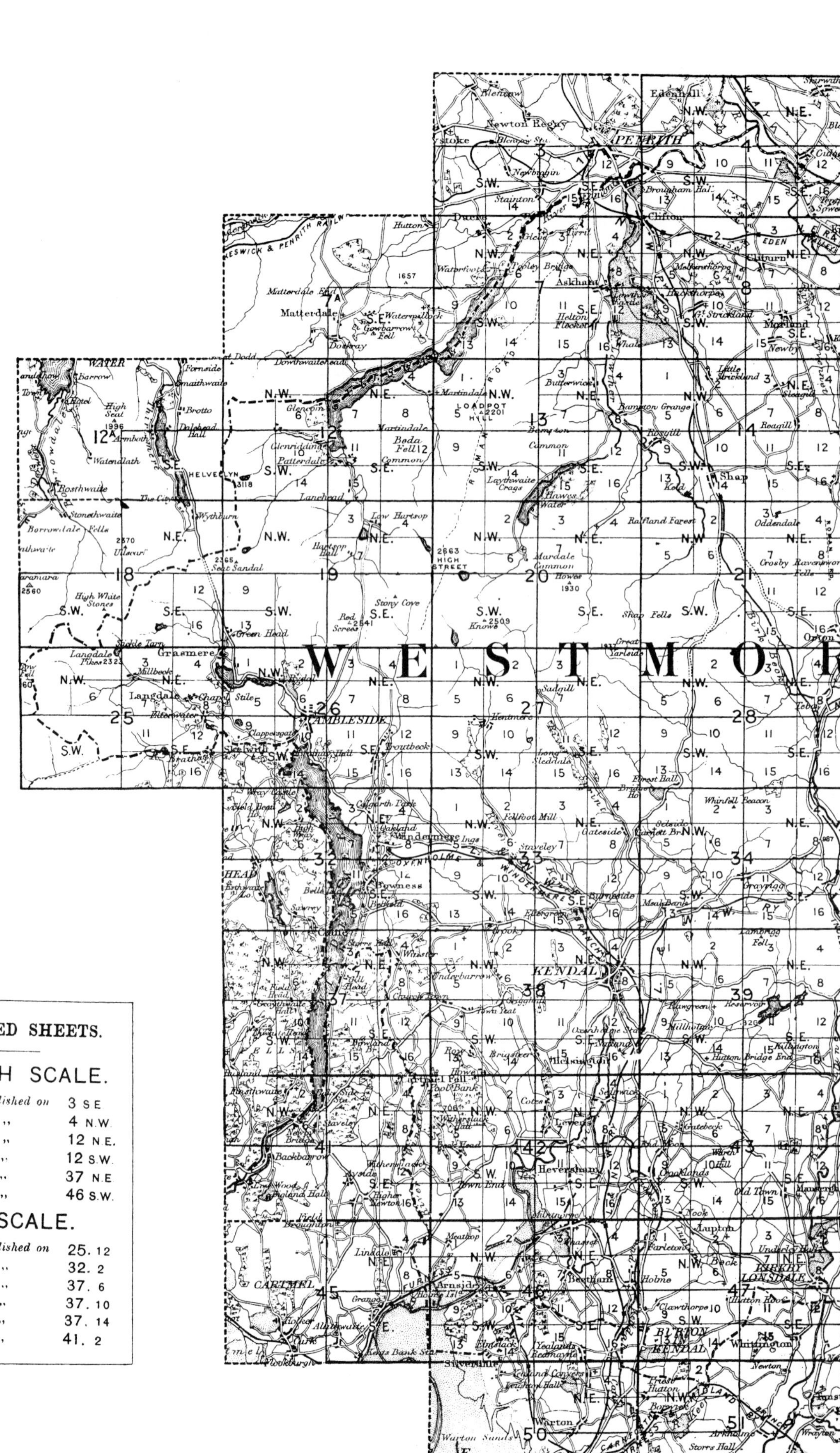

COMBINED SHEETS.

SIX-INCH SCALE.

3 S.W.	*is published on*	3 S.E.
4 N.E.	,,	4 N.W.
7A S.E.	,,	12 N.E.
12A S.E.	,,	12 S.W.
37 N.W.	,,	37 N.E.
45 S.E.	,,	46 S.W.

$\frac{1}{2500}$ SCALE.

25. 16	*is published on*	25. 12
32. 6	,,	32. 2
37. 2	,,	37. 6
37. 11	,,	37. 10
37. 15	,,	37. 14
41. 6	,,	41. 2

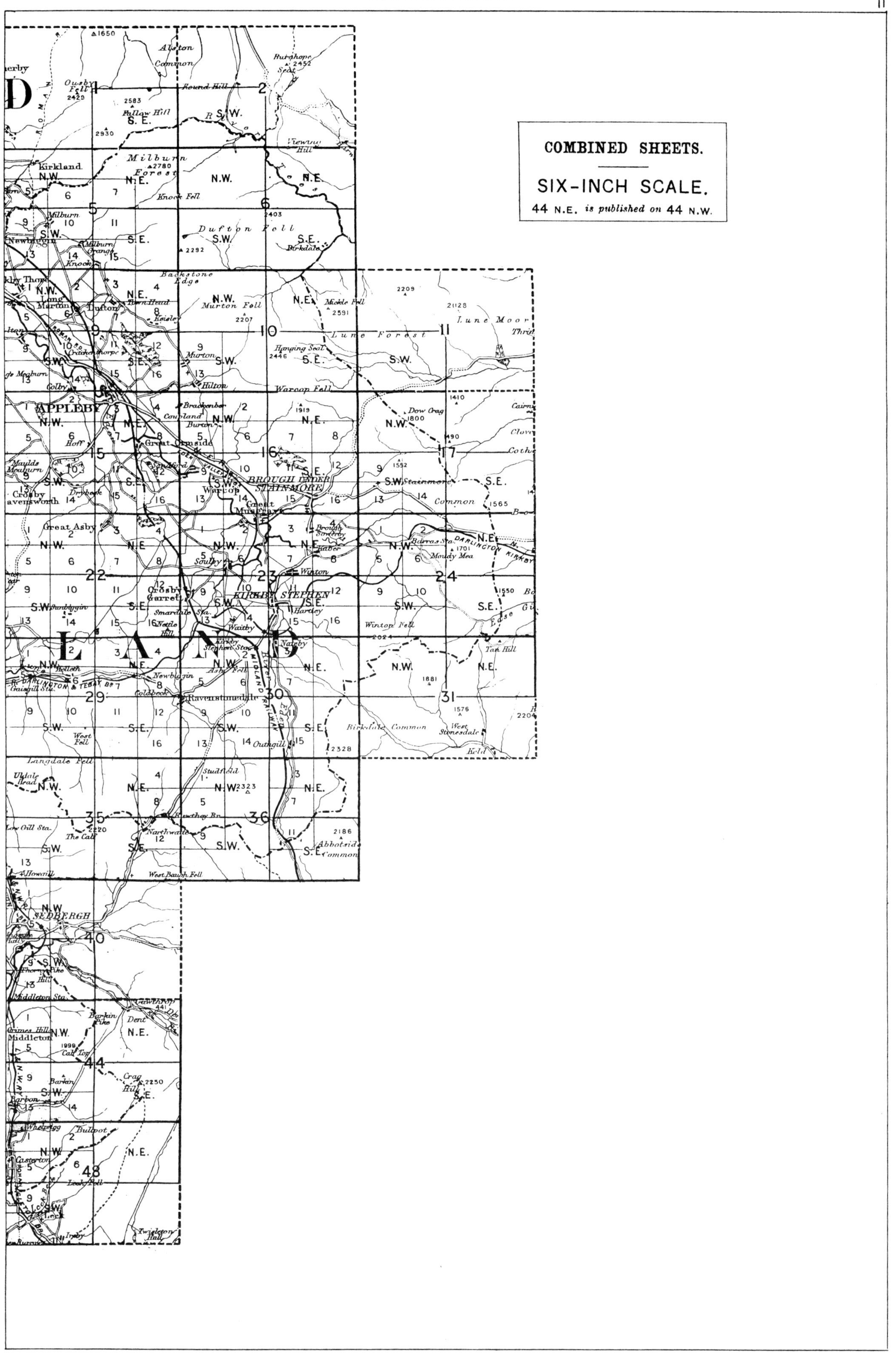
COMBINED SHEETS.
SIX-INCH SCALE.
44 N.E. is published on 44 N.W.
Alston Common
Round Hill
Burnhope Seat
Ousby Fell
Fallow Hill
Kirkland
Milburn Forest
Knock Fell
Dufton Fell
Milburn
Newbiggin
Knock
Backstone Edge
Long Marton
Dufton
Murton Fell
Mickle Fell
Lune Forest
Lune Moor
Hanging Seat
Murton
Hilton
Warcop Fell
APPLEBY
Colby
Brackenber
Coupland
Burton
Hoff
Great Ormside
Dow Crag
Sandford
BROUGH UNDER STAINMORE
Warcop
Great Musgrave
Stainmore
Common
Crosby Ravensworth
Drybeck
Great Asby
Brough Sowerby
Kaber
Barras Sta.
Mouldy Mea
Winton
KIRKBY STEPHEN
Crosby Garrett
Smardale Sta.
Hartley
Waitby
Winton Fell
Nateby
Tan Hill
Newbiggin
Ravenstonedale
Coldbeck
Gaisgill Sta.
MIDLAND RAILWAY
West Fell
Outhgill
Birkdale Common
West Stonesdale
Keld
Langdale Fell
Uldale Head
Low Gill Sta.
The Calf
Northwaite
West Baugh Fell
Abbotside Common
Howgill
SEDBERGH
Middleton Sta.
Barkin Pike
Dent
Middleton
Calf Top
Barbon
Crag Hill
Whelprigg
Bullpot
Casterton
Leck Fell
Leck
Ireby
Twisleton Hall

COMBINED SHEETS.

SIX-INCH SCALE.

9 S.W. *is published on* 16 N.W.

$\frac{1}{2500}$ SCALE.

9. 15 *is published on* 16. 3

11. 5 ,, 11. 6

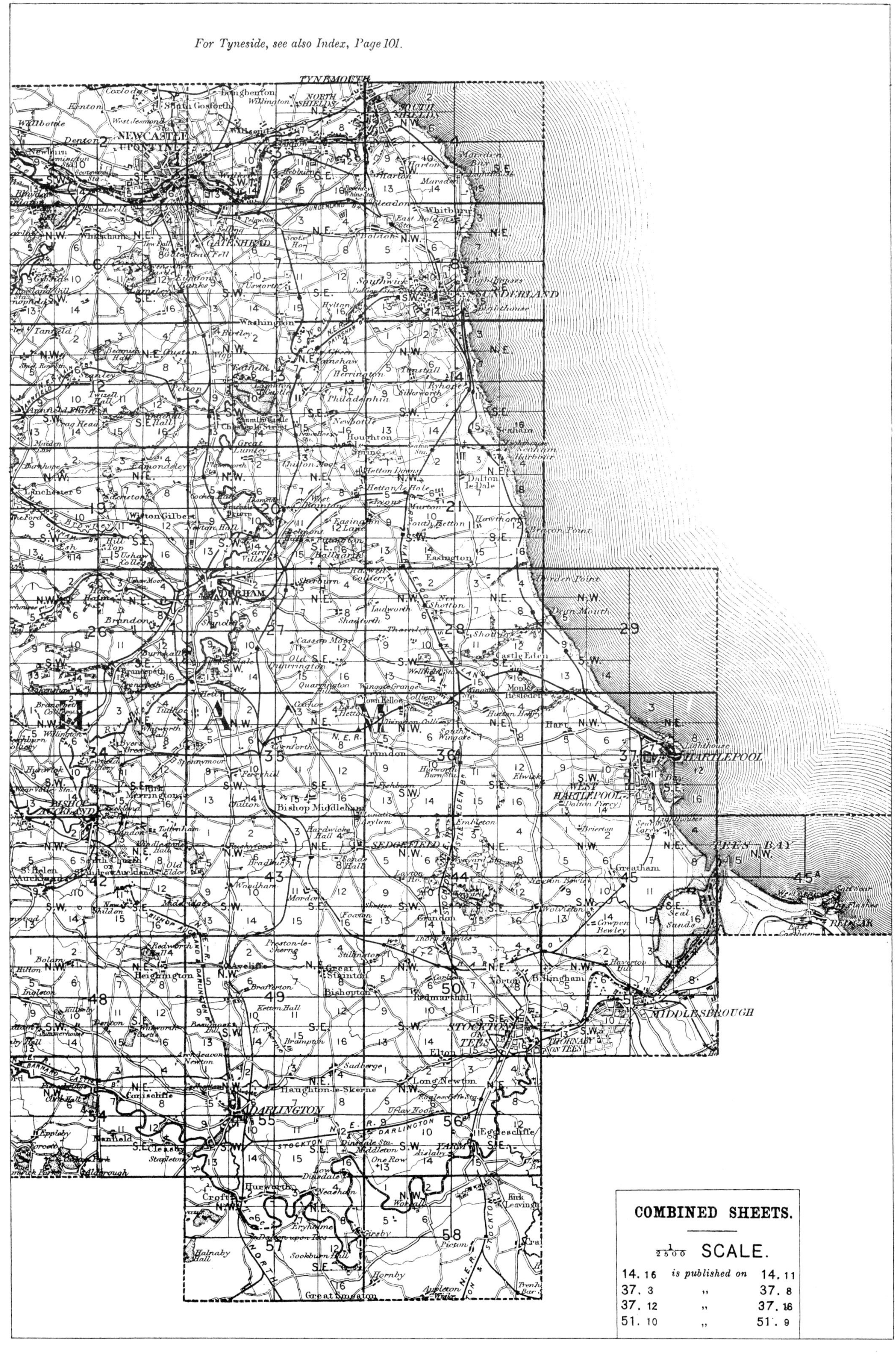

COMBINED SHEETS.

$\frac{1}{2500}$ SCALE.

14. 16	*is published on*	14. 11
37. 3	,,	37. 8
37. 12	,,	37. 16
51. 10	,,	51. 9

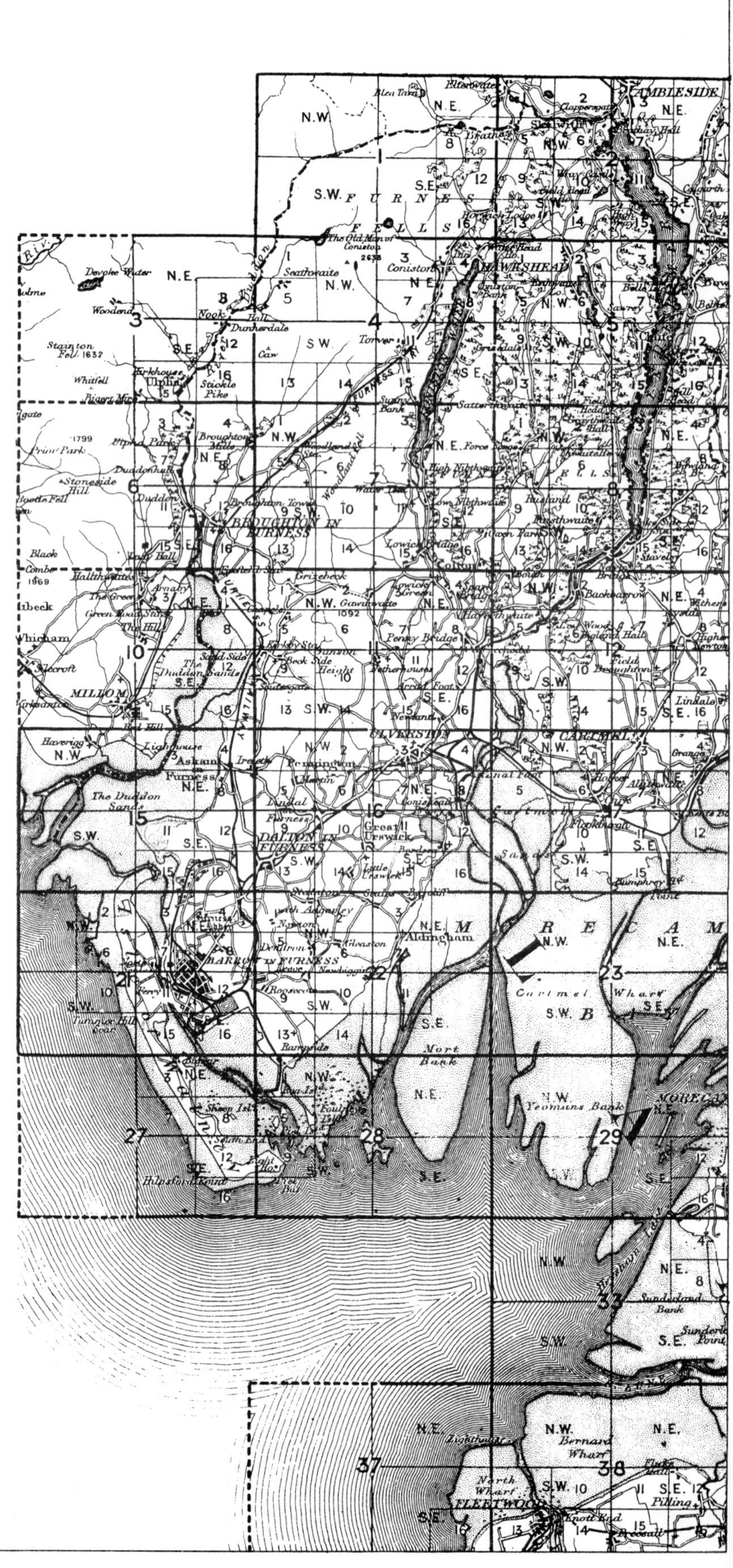
AMBLESIDE
HAWKSHEAD
Coniston
FURNESS
FELLS
The Old Man of Coniston
Devoke Water
Seathwaite
Torver
Stainton Fell 1632
BROUGHTON IN FURNESS
Broughton Mills
Stoneside Hill
Black Combe 1969
Whicham
Silecroft
MILLOM
Haverigg
The Duddon Sands
Askam
ULVERSTON
CARTMEL
Newland
Pennington
DALTON IN FURNESS
Great Urswick
Little Urswick
Aldingham
Gleaston
BARROW IN FURNESS
Roosecote
Rampside
Walney
Piel
Foulney
Mort Bank
Yeomans Bank
Cartmel Wharf
MORECAMBE
Sunderland Point
Bernard Wharf
North Wharf
FLEETWOOD
Knott End
Pilling
Lowick Bridge
Penny Bridge
Grange
Flookburgh
Lindale
Satterthwaite
Rusland
Hulme
Grizebeck
Gawthwaite
Dendron
Newbiggin
Stainton
Humphrey Head Point
Backbarrow

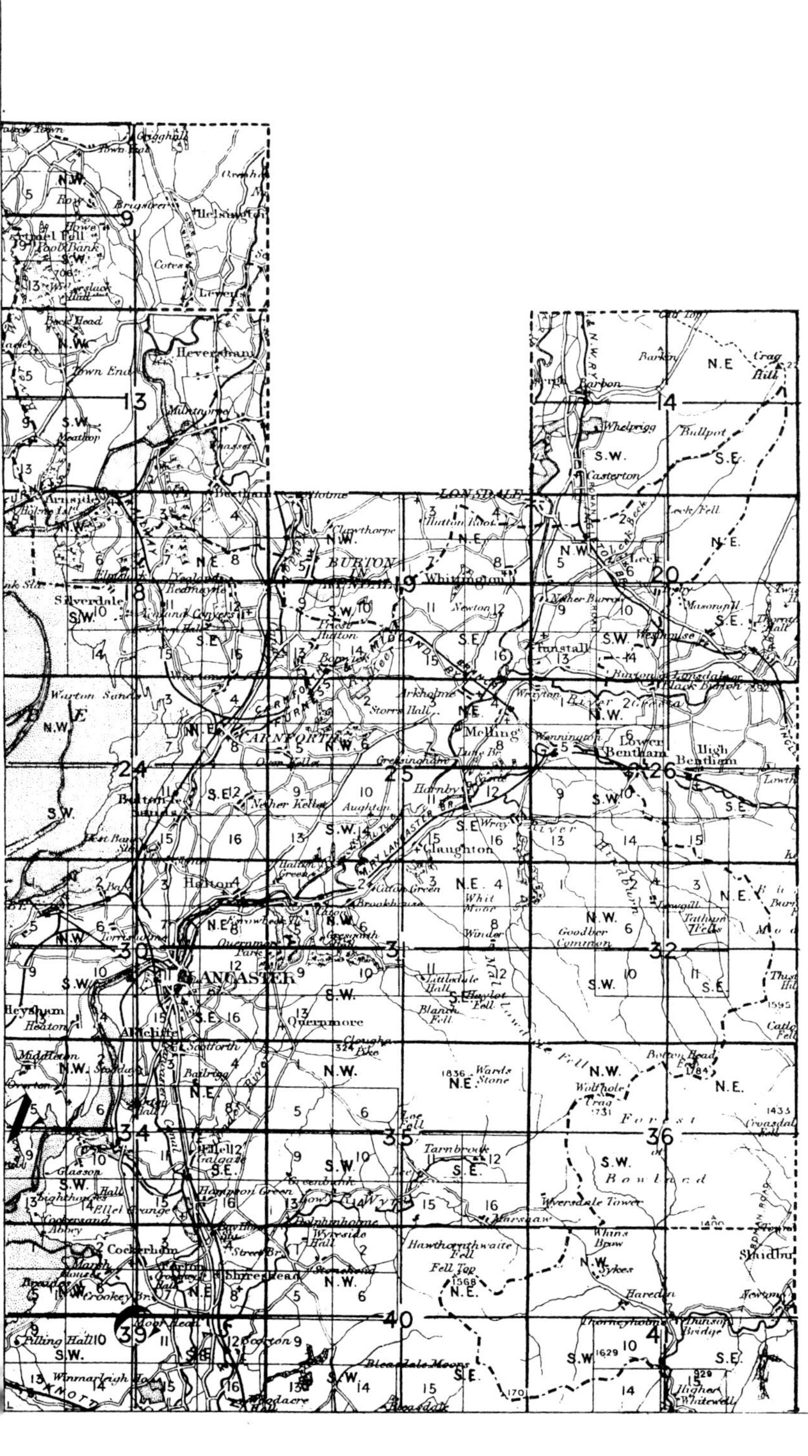
LANCASTER
CARNFORTH
LONSDALE
BURTON
Silverdale
Arnside
Heversham
Milnthorpe
Whittington
Melling
Tunstall
Wennington
Lower Bentham
High Bentham
Barbon
Casterton
Halton
Caton
Brookhouse
Quernmore
Glasson
Cockerham
Garstang
Heysham
Aldcliffe
Scotforth
Galgate
Wyresdale Tower
Hawthornthwaite Fell
Goodber Common
Claughton
Hornby
Arkholme
Borwick
Warton Sands
Bolton le Sands
Middleton
Dolphinholme
Forton
Pilling Hall
Winmarleigh
Bleasdale Moors
Bowland
Forest

COMBINED SHEETS.

SIX-INCH SCALE.

82 S.W. *is published on* 82 S.E.
113 S.W. „ 113 S.E.

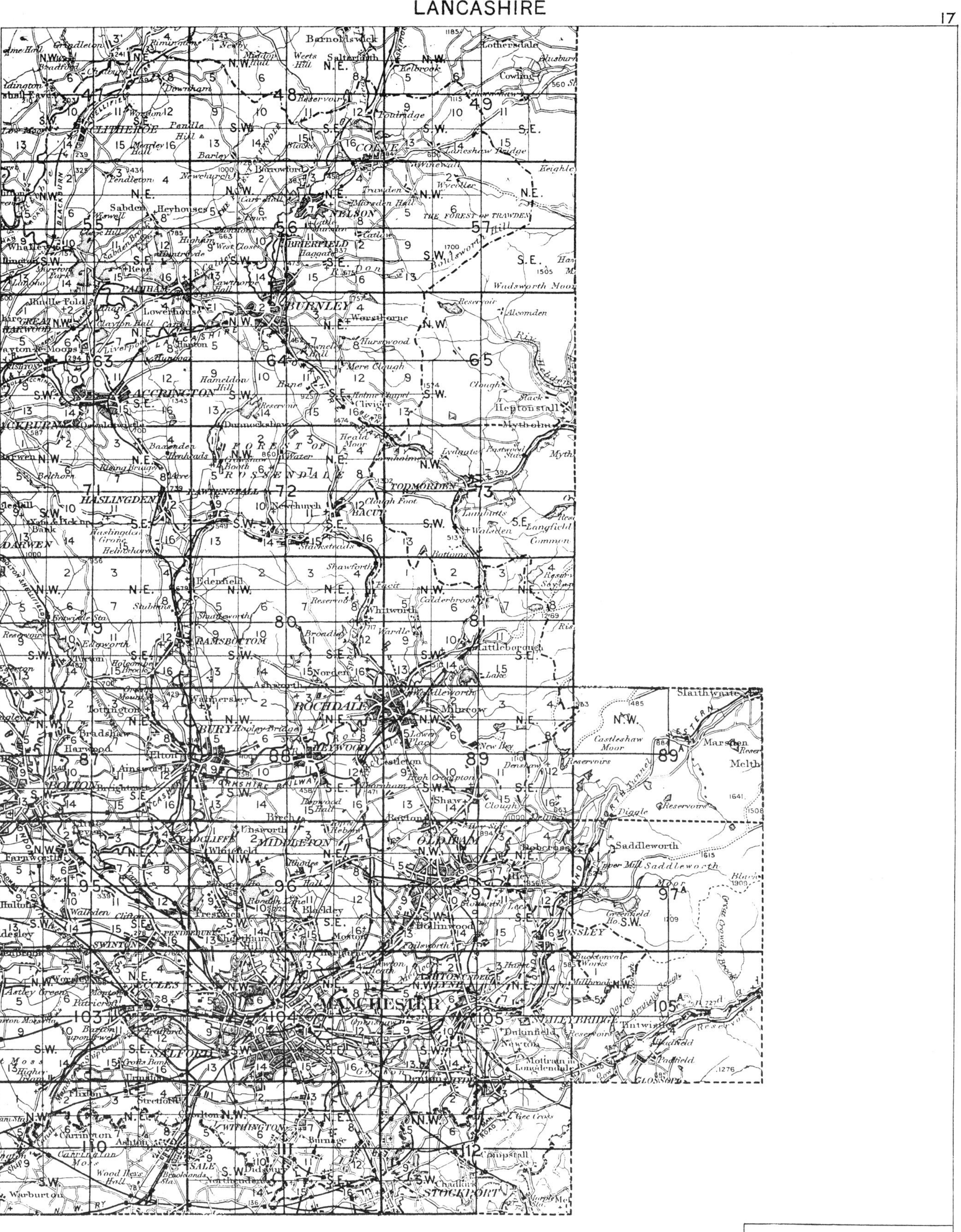

COMBINED SHEETS.

SIX-INCH SCALE.

73 S.E.	*is published on*	81 N.E.
89A N.W.	,,	89 N.E.
112 N.E.	,,	112 N.W.

$\frac{1}{2500}$ SCALE.

48. 1	*is published on*	48. 5
49. 5	,,	49. 9
81. 4	,,	81. 8
89. 16	,,	89. 12
97. 4	,,	97. 3

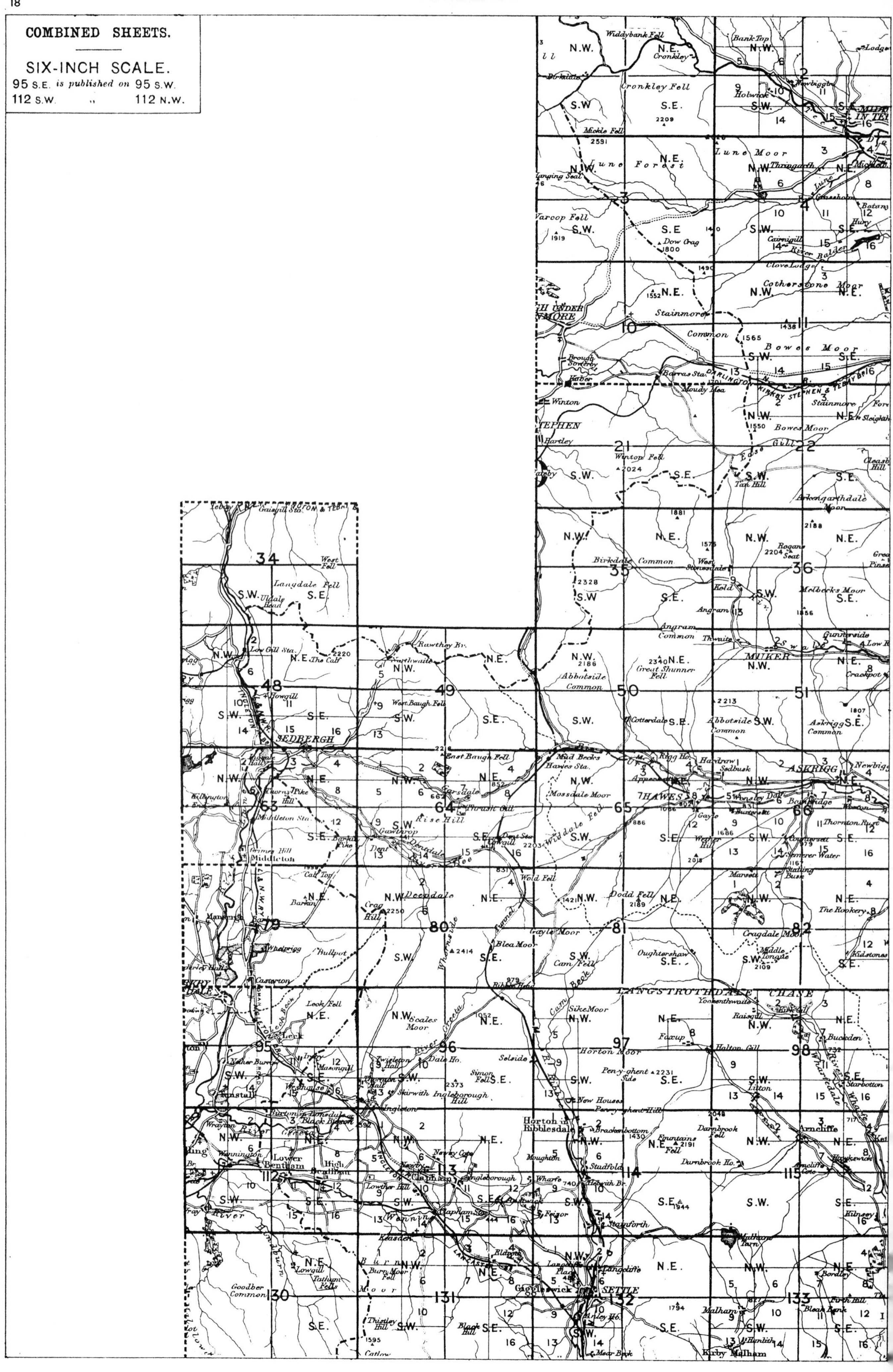
COMBINED SHEETS.
SIX-INCH SCALE.
95 S.E. is published on 95 S.W.
112 S.W. ,, 112 N.W.
Widdybank Fell
Cronkley
Cronkley Fell
Bank Top
Newbiggin
Holwick
Mickle Fell
2591
2209
Lune Moor
Lune Forest
Thringarth
Mickleton
Grassholme
Botany
Hury
Waroop Fell
1919
Dow Crag
1800
Cairnigill
River Balder
Clove Lodge
Cotherstone Moor
Stainmore
Common
Bowes Moor
Brough Sowerby
Kaber
Barras Sta.
Moudy Mea
Winton
Hartley
DARLINGTON KIRKBY STEPHEN & TEBAY Br.
Stainmore
Bowes Moor
Sleightholme
Winton Fell
2024
Tan Hill
Arkengarthdale Moor
Clea Hill
2188
Tebay
Gaisgill Sta.
West Fell
Langdale Fell
Uldale Head
Birkdale Common
2328
West Stonesdale
Keld
Angram
Angram Common
Thwaite
Rogans Seat
2204
Melbecks Moor
Gunnerside
Low Row
MUKER
Crackpot
Rawthey Br.
Low Gill Sta.
The Calf
2220
Howgill
SEDBERGH
Abbotside Common
2186
Great Shunner Fell
2340
Cotterdale
Abbotside Common
Askrigg Common
1807
2213
Mud Becks
Hawes Sta.
Mossdale Moor
Widdale Fell
HAWES
Appersett
Hardraw
Sedbusk
ASKRIGG
Newbiggin
Bainbridge
Thornton Rust
East Baugh Fell
Garsdale
Thrush Gill
Rise Hill
Gawthrop
Dent
Dentdale
Dent Sta.
Middleton Sta.
Middleton
Gayle
Marsett
Semerwater
Stalling Busk
Wold Fell
Dodd Fell
2189
The Rookery
Deepdale
Crag Hill
2250
Barkin
Calf Top
Mansergh
Whelprigg
Bullpot
Casterton
Whernside
Blea Moor
2414
Gayle Moor
Cam Fell
Oughtershaw
Cragdale Moor
Middle Tongue
2109
Kidstones
LANGSTROTHDALE CHASE
Yockenthwaite
Raisgill
Hubberholme
Buckden
Leck Fell
Scales Moor
River Greeta
Sike Moor
Foxup
Halton Gill
Leck
Ireby
Masongill
Twisleton Dale Ho.
Nether Burrow
Selside
Horton Moor
Pen-y-ghent Side
2231
Starbotton
Tunstall
Westhouse
Thornton
Simon Fell
2373
Ingleborough Hill
New Houses
Pen-y-ghent Hill
Litton
River Wharfe
Ingleton
Burton in Lonsdale
Black Burton
Horton in Ribblesdale
Brackenbottom
Fountains Fell
2191
Darnbrook Fell
Arncliffe
Wrayton
River Greta
Wennington
Lower Bentham
High Bentham
Newby Cote
Moughton
Studfold
Darnbrook Ho.
Hawkswick
Clapham
Ingleborough
Wharfe
Helwith Br.
Arncliffe Cote
Lowther Hill
Clapham Sta.
Feizor
Stainforth
Kilnsey
Wenning
Keasden
Malham Tarn
Langcliffe
Lowgill
Tatham Fells
Burn Moor Fell
Goodber Common
Giggleswick
SETTLE
Malham
Bordley
Thistley Hill
Black Hill
1794
1595
Catlow
Kirby Malham
Mear Beck

COMBINED SHEETS.

SIX-INCH SCALE.

2A S.W. *is published on* 5 N.W.

$\frac{1}{2500}$ SCALE.

12.4 *is published on* 12.3
15.7 " 15.8

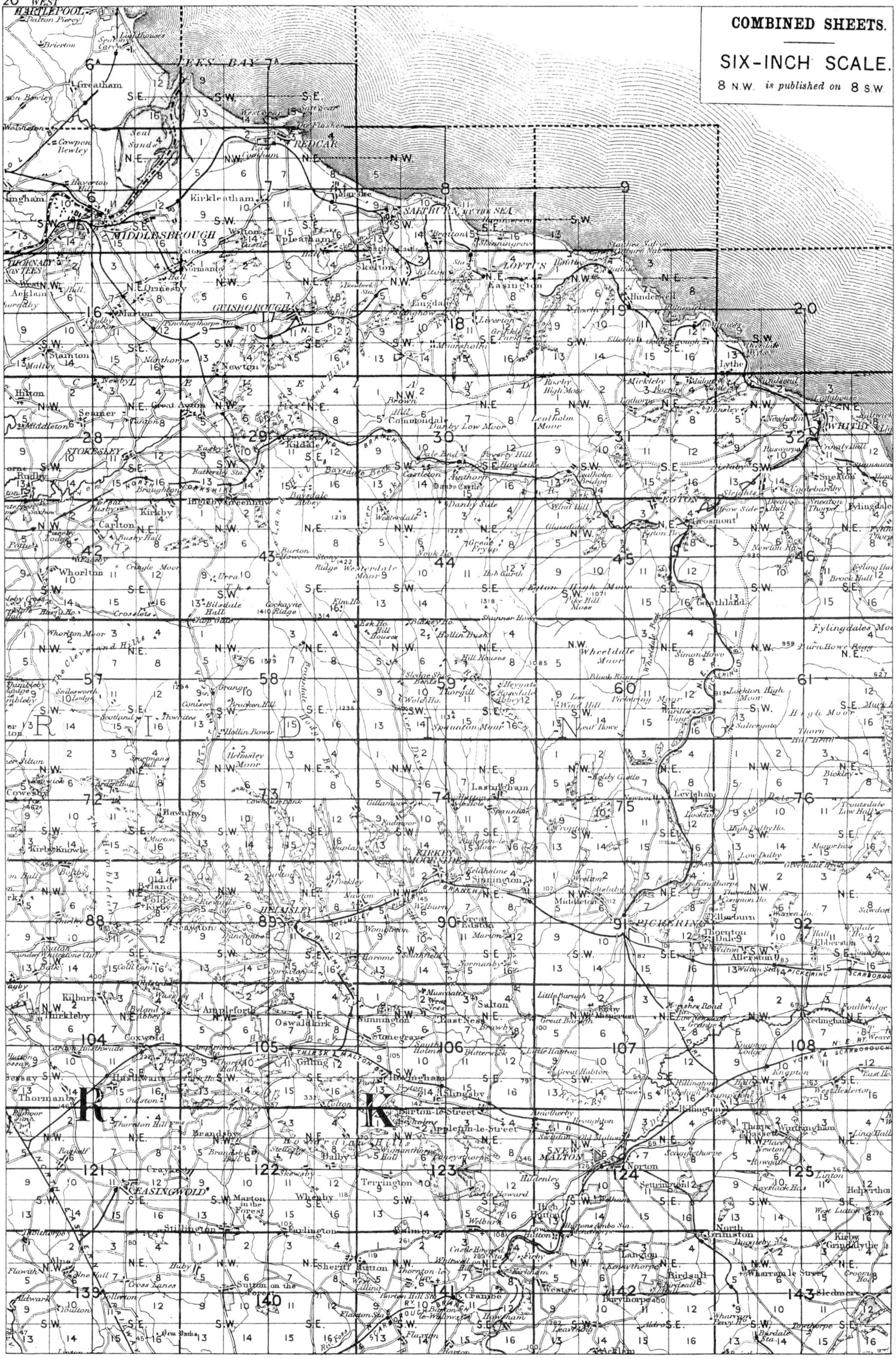
COMBINED SHEETS.
SIX-INCH SCALE.
8 N.W. is published on 8 S.W.
WEST HARTLEPOOL
Greatham
REDCAR
MIDDLESBROUGH
Kirkleatham
SALTBURN BY THE SEA
Upleatham
Skelton
LOFTUS
Easington
GUISBOROUGH
Hinderwell
Lythe
WHITBY
STOKESLEY
Great Ayton
Commondale
Castleton
Danby Castle
Kildale
Ingleby Greenhow
Carlton
Kirkby
Whorlton
Westerdale
Glaisdale
Grosmont
Egton
Goathland
Sleights
Fylingdales Moor
Wheeldale Moor
Hawnby
Lastingham
Levisham
Lockton
KIRKBY MOORSIDE
HELMSLEY
Sinnington
PICKERING
Middleton
Thornton Dale
Allerston
Kilburn
Ampleforth
Oswaldkirk
Coxwold
Hovingham
Slingsby
Gilling
Brandsby
Dalby
Terrington
Castle Howard
NEW MALTON
Norton
EASINGWOLD
Crayke
Stillington
Sheriff Hutton
Whitwell on the Hill
Westow
Birdsall
Langton
Sledmere
Yedingham
Rillington
Settrington
North Grimston
Thormanby
Alne
Flaxton
R
I
D
I
N
G
N
O
R
T
H

COMBINED SHEETS.
SIX-INCH SCALE.
94A S.W. is published on 94 S.E.
1/2500 SCALE.
94A 13 is published on 94. 16
128. 4 " 128. 3
129. 14 " 129. 13
33
47
62
77
78
93
94
94A
109
110
111
126
127
128
129
144
145
146
SCARBOROUGH
FILEY
FILEY BAY
HUNMANBY
BRIDLINGTON
BRIDLINGTON QUAY
FLAMBOROUGH HEAD
Flamborough
Bridlington Bay
North Sea
The Crab Rocks
Cayton Bay
Robin Hoods Bay
Ravenscar
Cloughton
Burniston
Scalby
Seamer
Wykeham
Brompton
Hutton Bushel
West Ayton
East Ayton
Folkton
Flixton
Muston
Reighton
Speeton
Buckton Hall
Bempton
Wold Newton
Foxholes
North Burton
Grindale
Thwing
Boynton
Bessingby
Carnaby
Rudston
Langtoft
Kilham
Cottam
Cowlam
Burton Agnes
Thornholme
Haisthorpe
Fraisthorpe
Sewerby
Marton
Sherburn
Ganton
Willerby
Staxton
Weaverthorpe
Butterwick
Swaythorpe
Buckton
Falsgrave
Newby
Hackness
Harwood Dale
Staintondale
Crowdon
Dry Heads
Thirley Cotes
Octon
Fordon

COMBINED SHEETS.

SIX-INCH SCALE.

182 S.E.	*is published on*	182 S.W.
199 S.W.	,,	199 S.E.
229A N.E.	,,	229 N.W.
229A S.E.	,,	229 S.W.

$\frac{1}{2500}$ SCALE.

229A. 8	*is published on*	229. 5
229A. 12	,,	229. 9

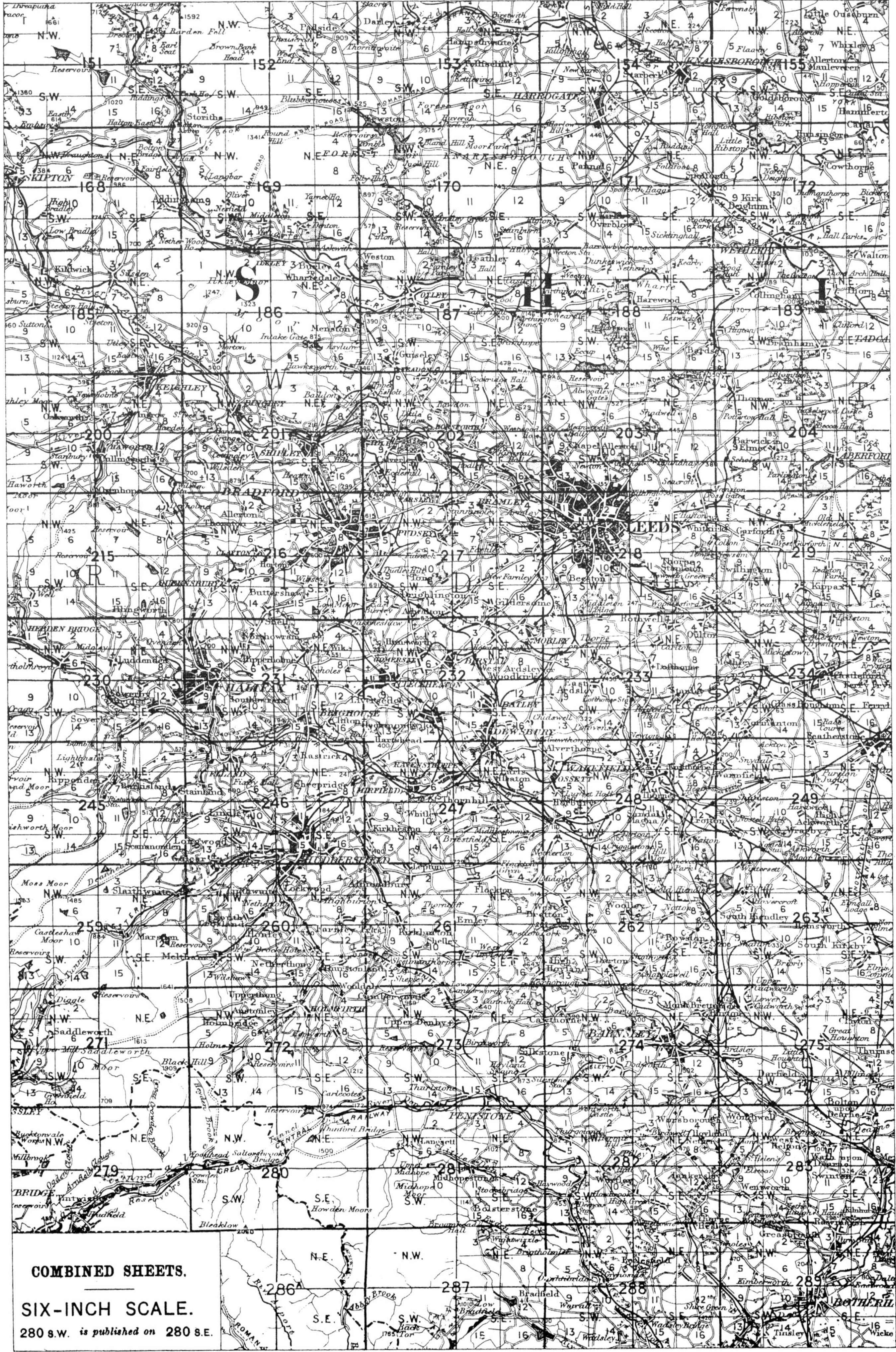
COMBINED SHEETS.
SIX-INCH SCALE.
280 S.W. is published on 280 S.E.
KNARESBOROUGH
HARROGATE
SKIPTON
KEIGHLEY
BINGLEY
SHIPLEY
BRADFORD
LEEDS
PUDSEY
HALIFAX
BRIGHOUSE
DEWSBURY
WAKEFIELD
HUDDERSFIELD
HOLMFIRTH
BARNSLEY
PENISTONE
OTLEY
WETHERBY
BATLEY
MORLEY
ROTHERHAM

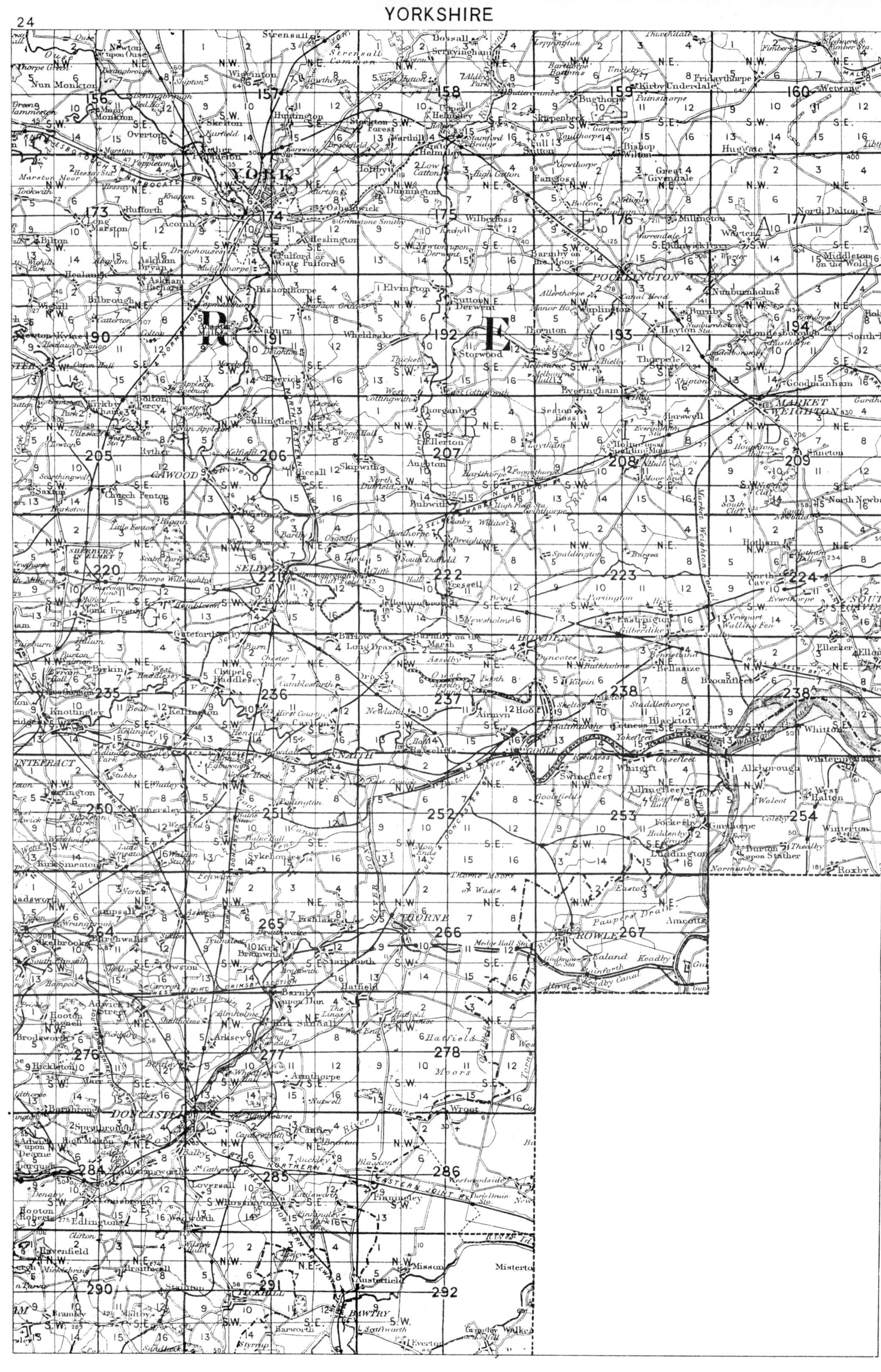
YORK
POCKLINGTON
MARKET WEIGHTON
SELBY
HOWDEN
GOOLE
SNAITH
THORNE
CROWLE
DONCASTER
BAWTRY
TICKHILL
CAWOOD
PONTEFRACT

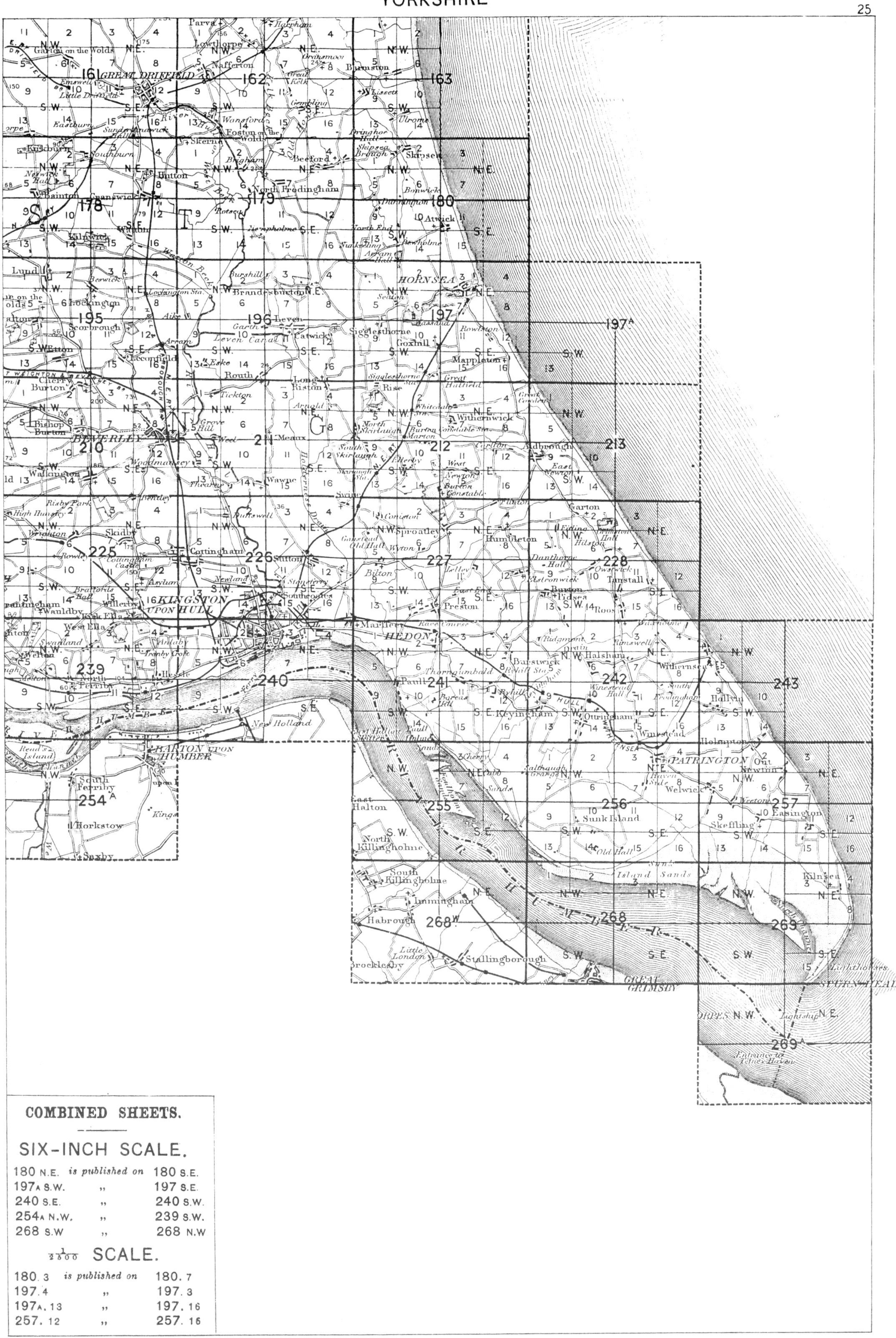

COMBINED SHEETS.

SIX-INCH SCALE.

180 N.E.	*is published on*	180 S.E.
197A S.W.	,,	197 S.E.
240 S.E.	,,	240 S.W.
254A N.W.	,,	239 S.W.
268 S.W	,,	268 N.W

$\frac{1}{2500}$ SCALE.

180. 3	*is published on*	180. 7
197. 4	,,	197. 3
197A. 13	,,	197. 16
257. 12	,,	257. 16

YORKSHIRE

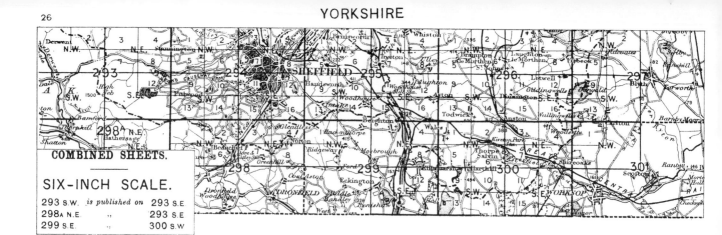

COMBINED SHEETS.

SIX-INCH SCALE.

293 S.W.	*is published on*	293 S.E
298A N.E.	,,	293 S.E
299 S.E.	,,	300 S.W

PEMBROKE

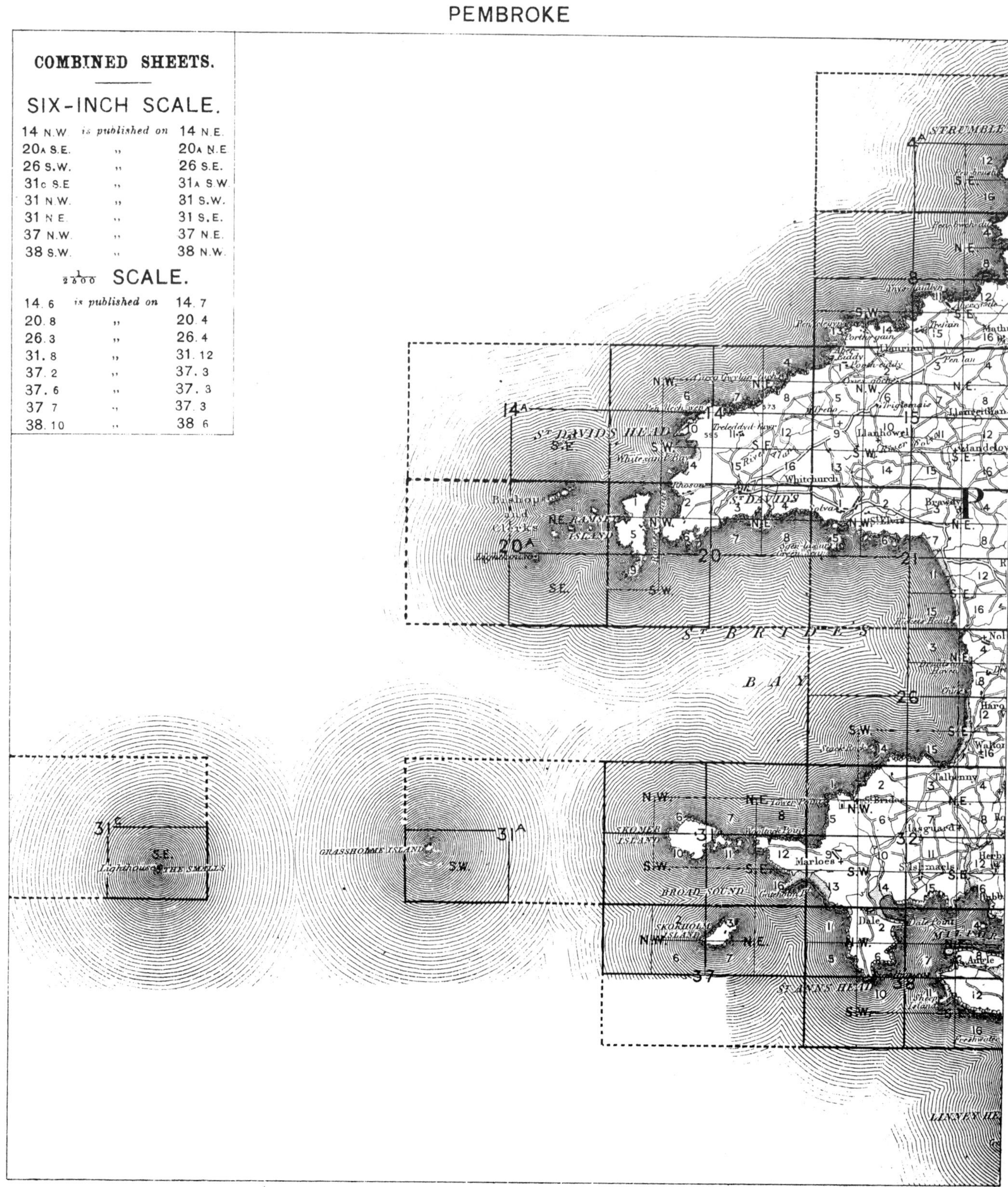

COMBINED SHEETS.

SIX-INCH SCALE.

14 N.W	*is published on*	14 N.E.
20A S.E.	,,	20A N.E
26 S.W.	,,	26 S.E.
31C S.E	,,	31A S.W.
31 N.W.	,,	31 S.W.
31 N.E.	,,	31 S.E.
37 N.W.	,,	37 N.E.
38 S.W.	,,	38 N.W.

$\frac{1}{2500}$ SCALE.

14. 6	*is published on*	14. 7
20. 8	,,	20. 4
26. 3	,,	26. 4
31. 8	,,	31. 12
37. 2	,,	37. 3
37. 6	,,	37. 3
37 7	,,	37. 3
38. 10	,,	38 6

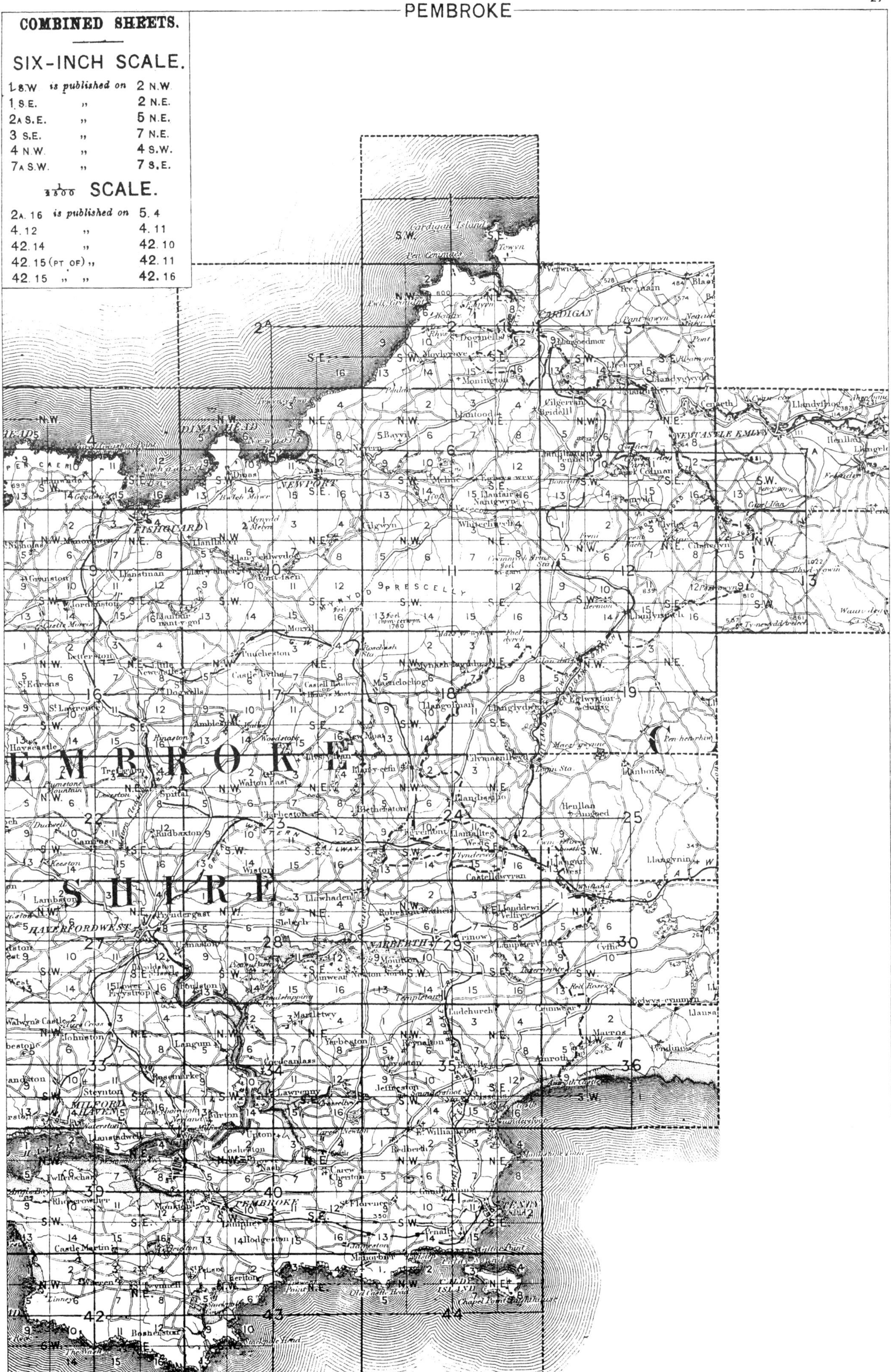
COMBINED SHEETS.
SIX-INCH SCALE.
1 S.W. is published on 2 N.W.
1 S.E. " 2 N.E.
2A S.E. " 5 N.E.
3 S.E. " 7 N.E.
4 N.W. " 4 S.W.
7A S.W. " 7 S.E.
1/2500 SCALE.
2A. 16 is published on 5. 4
4. 12 " 4. 11
42. 14 " 42. 10
42. 15 (PT OF) " 42. 11
42. 15 " " 42. 16
PEMBROKE
SHIRE
CARDIGAN
FISHGUARD
NEWPORT
HAVERFORDWEST
NARBERTH
MILFORD HAVEN
PEMBROKE
TENBY
CALDEY ISLAND
ST GOVANS HEAD
DINAS HEAD
Cardigan Island
NEWCASTLE EMLYN
PRESCELLY

COMBINED SHEETS.

SIX-INCH SCALE.

6 N.E.	*is published on*	6 N.W.
15 S.W.	,,	15 S.E.
30A N.E.	,,	30 N.W.
64A N.E.	,,	64 N.W.

$\frac{1}{2500}$ SCALE.

7. 3	*is published on*	7. 7
15. 12	,,	15. 16
45. 4	,,	45. 8
64. 8	,,	64. 7
65. 15	,,	65. 11

COMBINED SHEETS.

SIX-INCH SCALE.

3A S.E.	*is published on*	3 S.W.
4 S.E.	„	4 S.W.

$\frac{1}{2500}$ SCALE.

3A. 16	*is published on*	3. 13
11. 8	„	11. 4
51. 8	„	51. 4
51. 11	„	51. 7
52. 2	„	52. 1
66. 12	„	66. 11

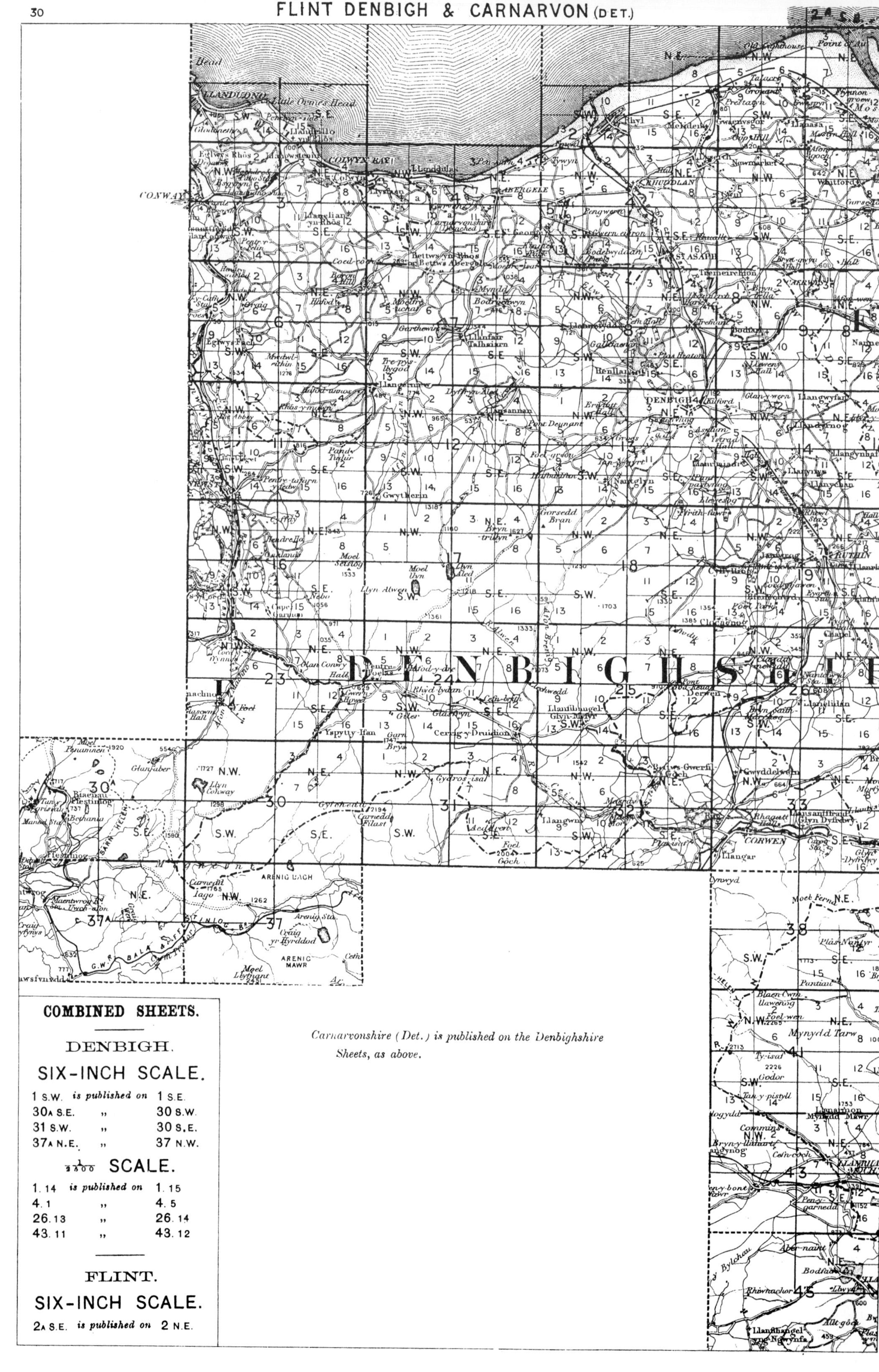

Carnarvonshire (Det.) is published on the Denbighshire Sheets, as above.

COMBINED SHEETS.

DENBIGH.

SIX-INCH SCALE.

1 S.W.	*is published on*	1 S.E.
30A S.E.	"	30 S.W.
31 S.W.	"	30 S.E.
37A N.E.	"	37 N.W.

$\frac{1}{2500}$ SCALE.

1. 14	*is published on*	1. 15
4. 1	"	4. 5
26. 13	"	26. 14
43. 11	"	43. 12

FLINT.

SIX-INCH SCALE.

2A S.E.	*is published on*	2 N.E.

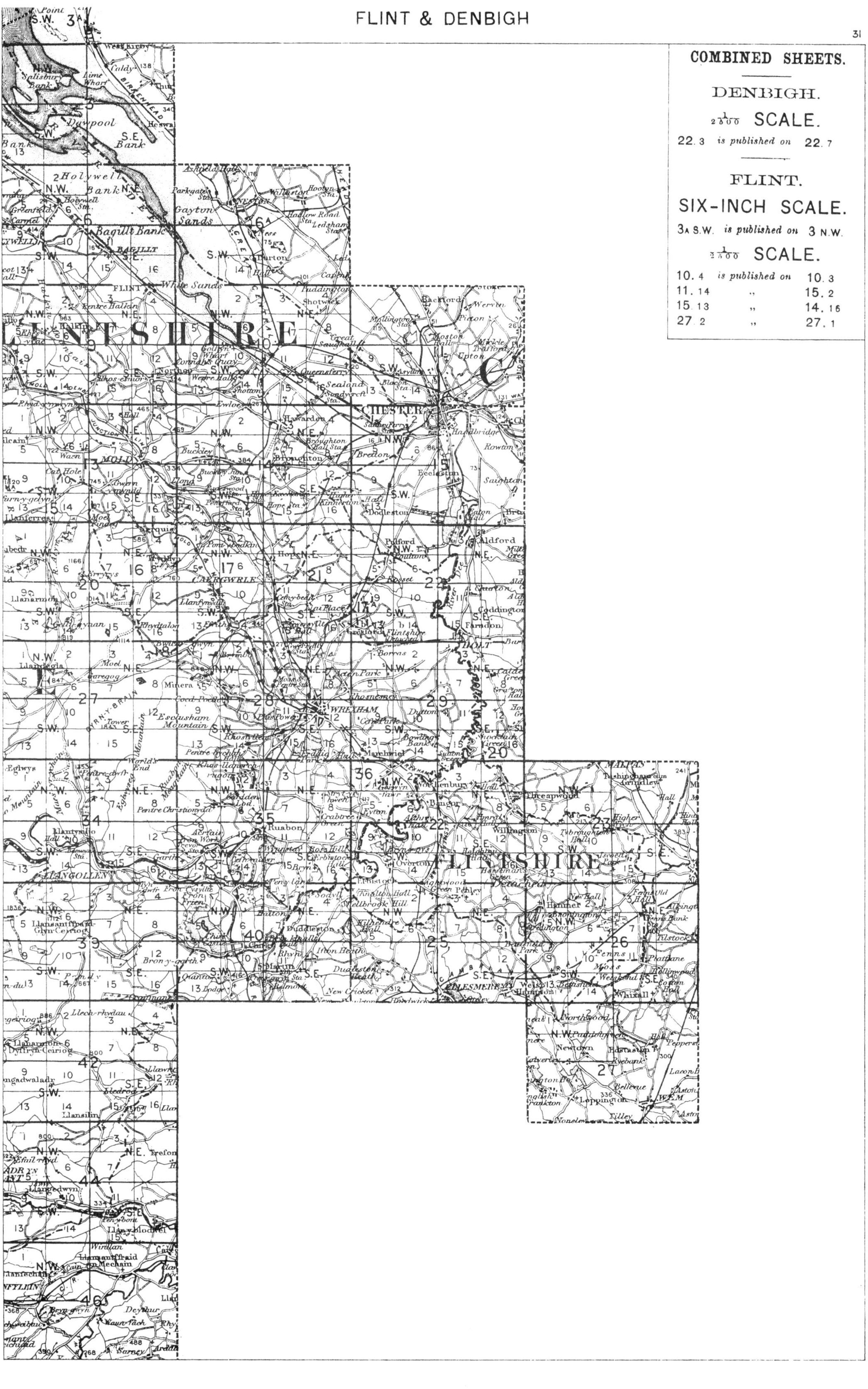

COMBINED SHEETS.

DENBIGH.

$\frac{1}{2500}$ SCALE.

22.3 *is published on* 22.7

FLINT.

SIX-INCH SCALE.

3A S.W. *is published on* 3 N.W.

$\frac{1}{2500}$ SCALE.

10. 4	*is published on*	10. 3
11. 14	"	15. 2
15. 13	"	14. 16
27. 2	"	27. 1

COMBINED SHEETS.

ANGLESEY.

SIX-INCH SCALE.

2A S.E. *is published on* 2 N.E.
10 N.E. ,, 11 N.W.
16 N.W. ,, 16 N.E.

$\frac{1}{2500}$ SCALE.

2. 2 *is published on* 2. 6

CARNARVON.

SIX-INCH SCALE.

25 N.E. *is published on* 26 N.W.

CARNARVON BAY

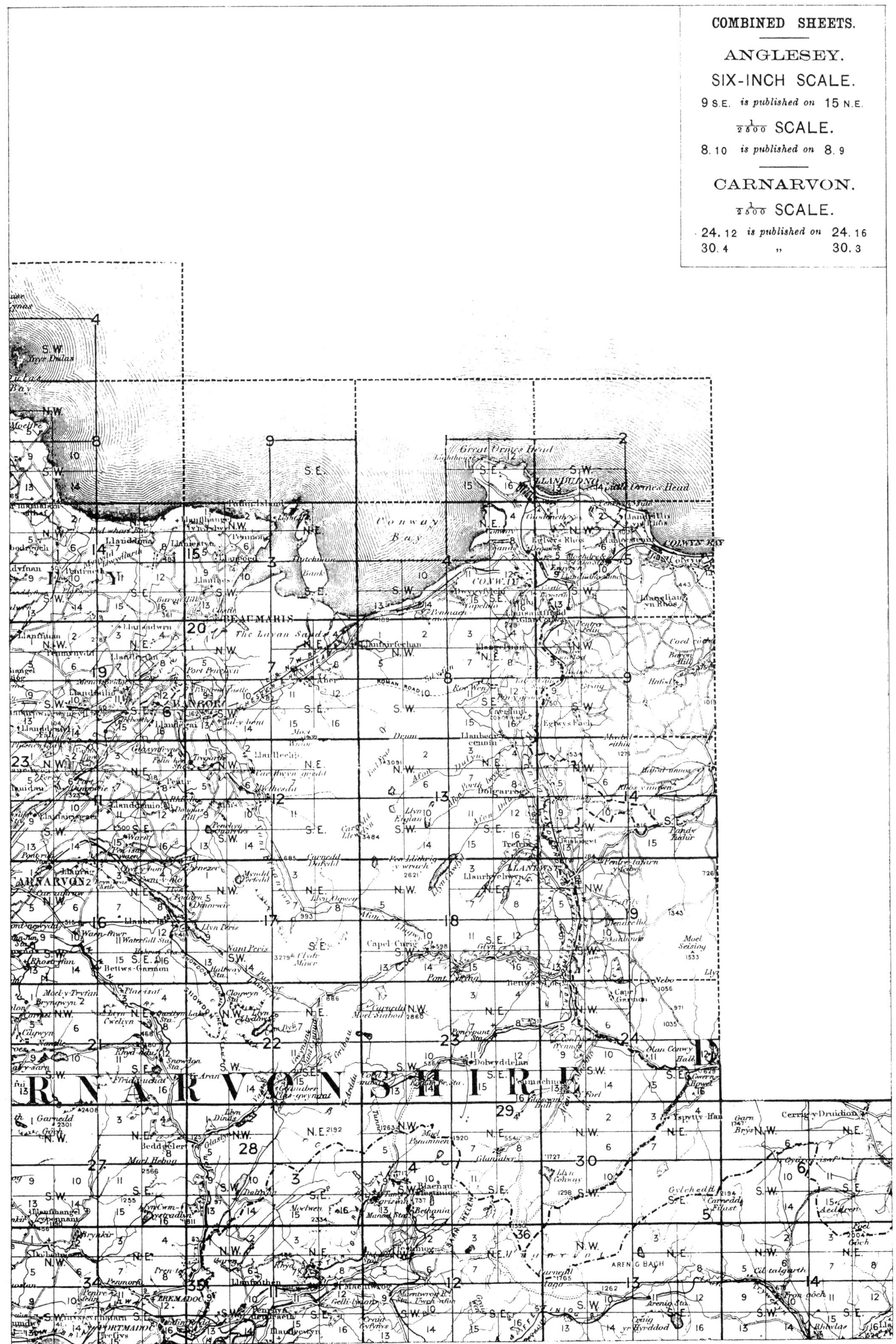

NOTE.—For Carnarvonshire (Det.), see Denbighshire Index, page 30.

MERIONETH

COMBINED SHEETS.

MERIONETH.

$\frac{1}{2500}$ SCALE.

8.12 *is published on* 8.11

SHROPSHIRE.

SIX-INCH SCALE.

5A S.E. *is published on* 5 S.W.

$\frac{1}{2500}$ SCALE.

11.15 *is published on* 11.16

MERIONETH

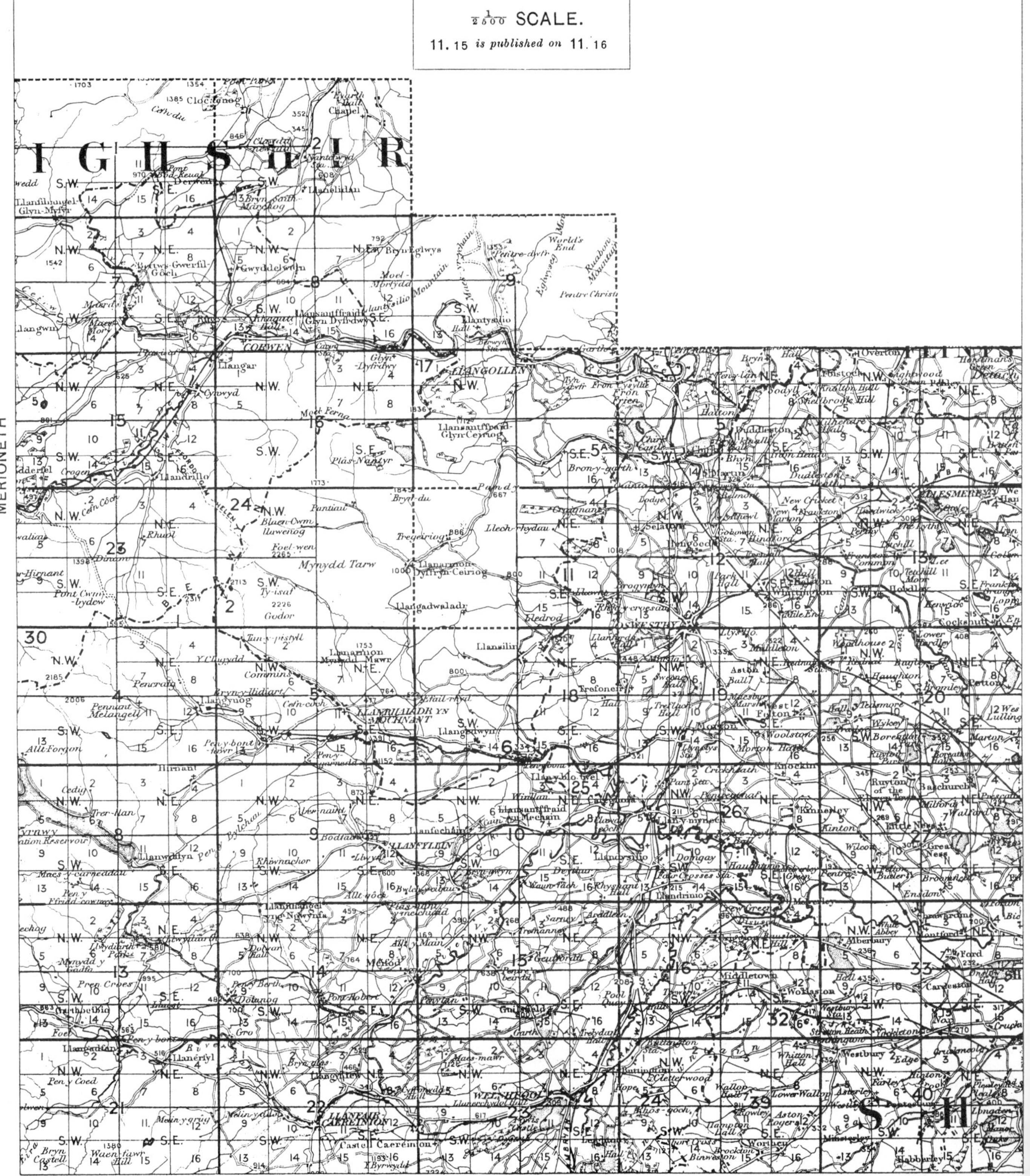

MONTGOMERY

COMBINED SHEETS.

SIX-INCH SCALE.

4 N.W.	*is published on*	4 S.W.
24 N.W.	,,	23 N.E.

$\frac{1}{2500}$ SCALE.

1. 11	*is published on*	1. 12
4. 5	,,	4. 9
16. 3	,,	16. 2
24. 1	,,	23. 4

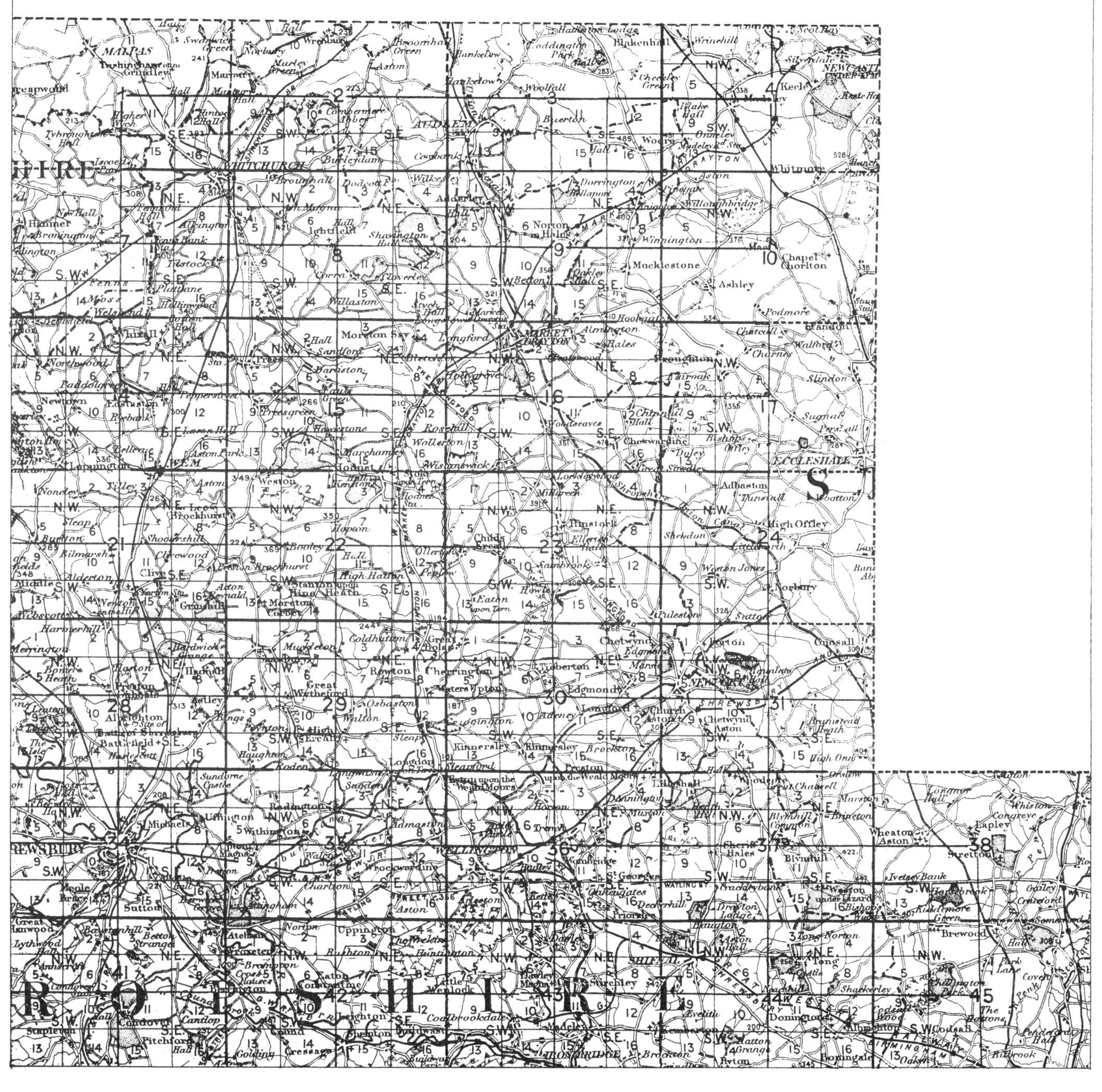

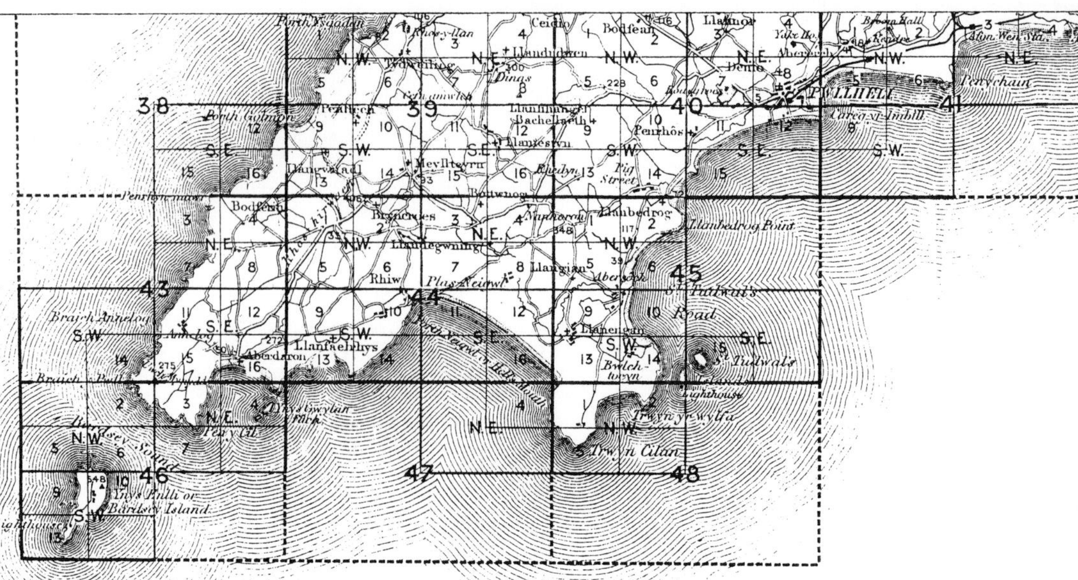

COMBINED SHEETS.

SIX-INCH SCALE.

41 S.W. *is published on* 40 S.E.
47 N.E. „ 48 N.W.

$\frac{1}{2500}$ SCALE.

46. 7 *is published on* 46. 3

CARNARVON

MERIONETHSHIRE

MONTGO

RADNOR

CARDIGAN

BRECKNOCK

COMBINED SHEETS.

MERIONETH.

SIX-INCH SCALE.

31 S.E. *is published on* 32 S.W.

$\frac{1}{2500}$ SCALE.

31.3 *is published on* 31.4

CARDIGAN.

SIX-INCH SCALE.

9 N.E. *is published on* 10 N.W.

$\frac{1}{2500}$ SCALE.

9.4 *is published on* 10.1

14.3 „ 14.7

MONTGOMERY

SHROPSHIRE

BRECKNOCK

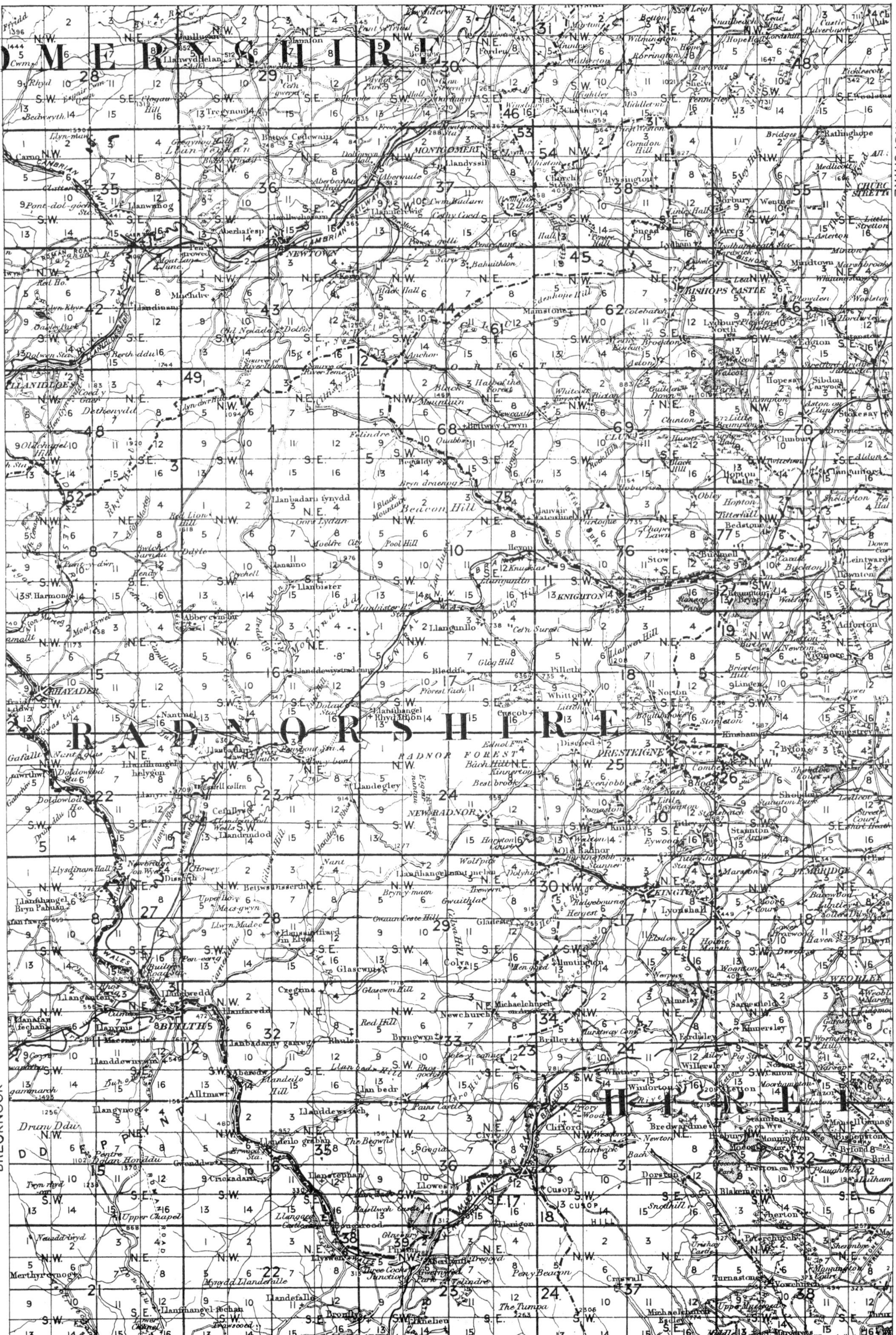

SHROPSHIRE

COMBINED SHEETS.

SHROPSHIRE.

SIX-INCH SCALE.

80 S.E. *is published on* 80 S.W.

$\frac{1}{2500}$ SCALE.

80.11 *is published on* 80.10

HEREFORD.

SIX-INCH SCALE.

36 N.E. *is published on* 36 N.W.
36 S.E. „ 36 S.W.

$\frac{1}{2500}$ SCALE.

13.7 *is published on* 13.11
15.9 „ 15.13
36.11 „ 36.10

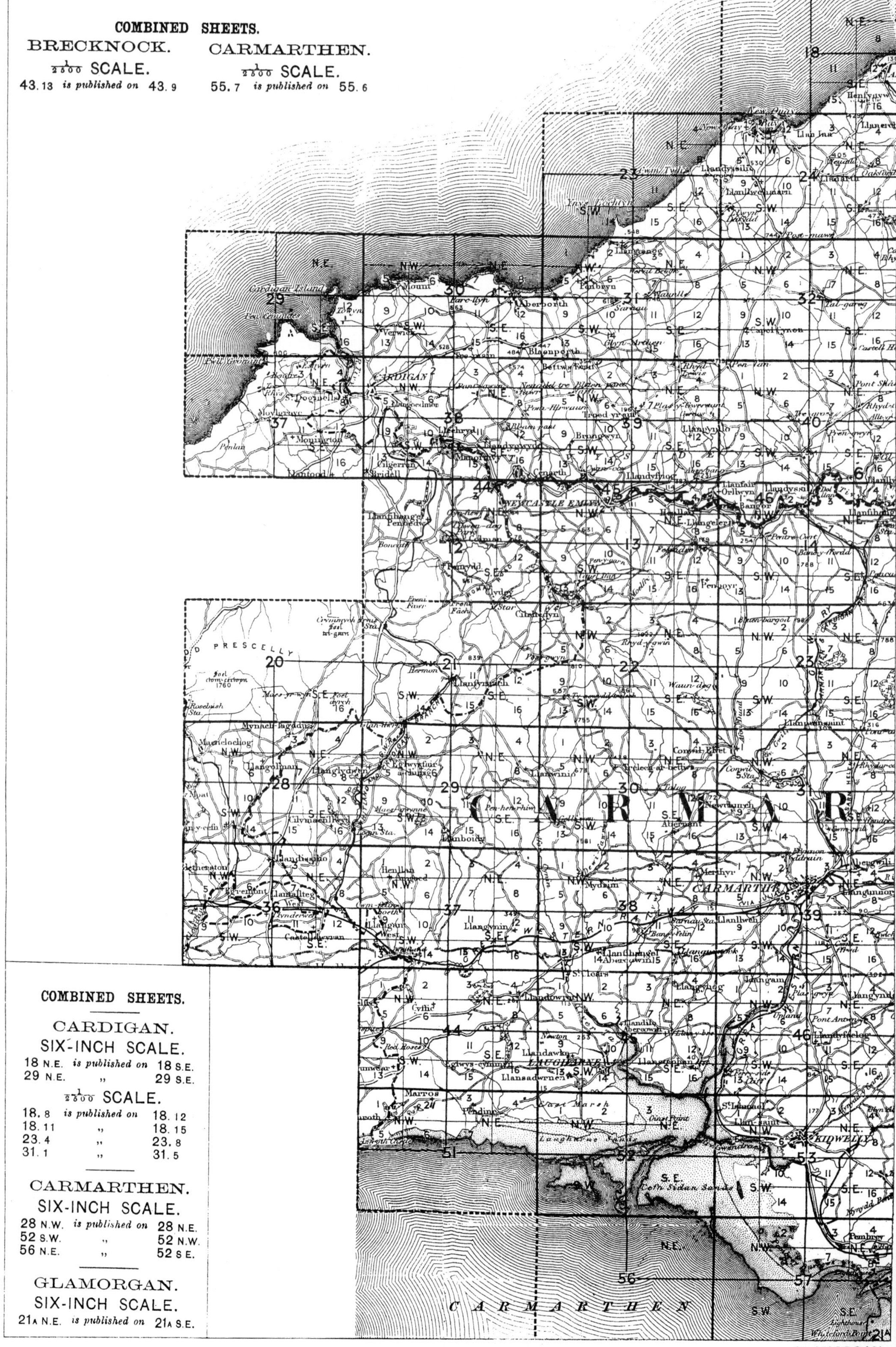
COMBINED SHEETS.
BRECKNOCK. 1/2500 SCALE.
43.13 is published on 43.9
CARMARTHEN. 1/2500 SCALE.
55.7 is published on 55.6
COMBINED SHEETS.
CARDIGAN.
SIX-INCH SCALE.
18 N.E. is published on 18 S.E.
29 N.E. " 29 S.E.
1/2500 SCALE.
18.8 is published on 18.12
18.11 " 18.15
23.4 " 23.8
31.1 " 31.5
CARMARTHEN.
SIX-INCH SCALE.
28 N.W. is published on 28 N.E.
52 S.W. " 52 N.W.
56 N.E. " 52 S.E.
GLAMORGAN.
SIX-INCH SCALE.
21A N.E. is published on 21A S.E.
CARDIGAN
GLAMORGAN
CARMAR
CARMARTHEN
CARDIGAN
NEWCASTLE EMLYN
CARMARTHEN
KIDWELLY
LAUGHARNE
PRESCELLY

RADNOR

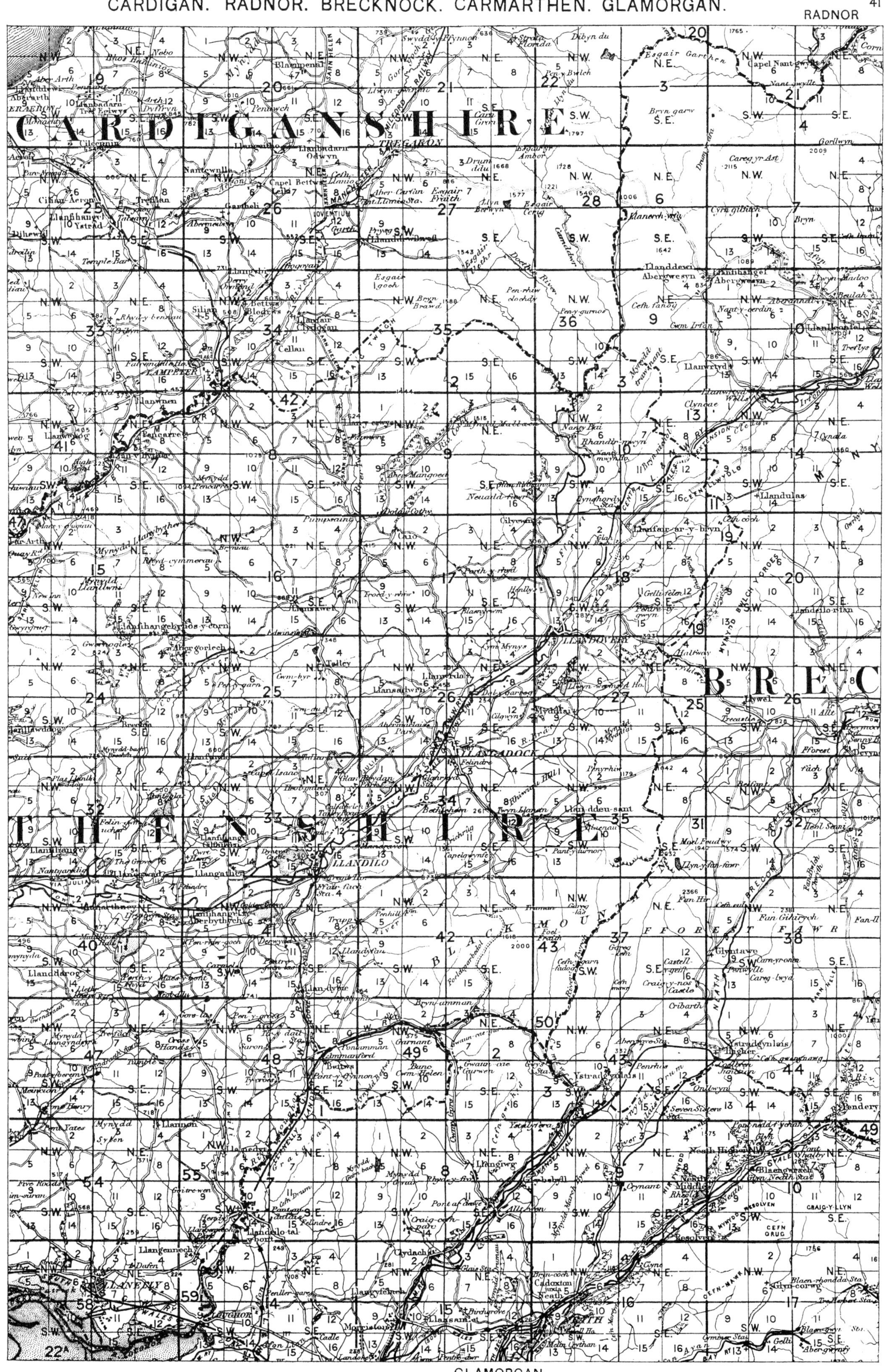
CARDIGANSHIRE
BREC
THENSHIRE
TREGARON
LAMPETER
LLANDOVERY
LLANGADOCK
LLANDILO
LLANELLY
Llanwrtyd Wells
Llandulas
Llansawel
Talley
Ammanford
Ystradgynlais
Neath
Abergwesyn
Llanddewi Abergwesyn
Cilycwm
Myddfai
Trecastle
Llanddeusant
Llangathen
Llanarthney
Llandybie
Llandeilo tal-y-bont
Llangennech
Morriston
Clydach
Cadoxton
Glyn-corwg
BLACK MOUNTAIN
FFOREST FAWR
Fan Hir
Fan Gihirych
Glyntawe
Craig-y-nos Castle
Cribarth
Abercrave Sta.
Seven Sisters
Resolven
Glyn Neath
Pont Nedd Fychan
Crynant
Llangiwg
Ystradgynlais
Pandy
Dafen
Loughor
Llanon
Pontardulais
Cross Hands
Crugybar
Llanfair Clydogau
Cellan
Silian
Llanwnen
Llanybyther
Llanfihangel-rhos-y-corn
Abergorlech
Brechfa
Llanfynydd
Llanwrda
Gwynfe
Llandyfan
Carmel
Porth-y-rhyd
Llanddarog
Tumble
Llangyndeyrn
Pontyberem
Five Roads
Llanedy
Pont Yates
Capel Nant-gwyllt
Llanerch-yrfa
Llanafan
Llangammarch
Llanwrtyd
Crai
Sennybridge
Devynock
Brecon

HEREFORD

BRECKNOCK

GLAMORGAN

COMBINED SHEETS.

BRECKNOCK

$\frac{1}{2500}$ SCALE.

50.7 *is published on* 50.6

GLAMORGAN.

SIX-INCH SCALE.

50 S.E. *is published on* 50 N.E.

51 S.E. ,, 52 S.W.

$\frac{1}{2500}$ SCALE.

50.11 *is published on* 50.7

51.8 ,, 52 9

51.12 ,, 52.9

MONMOUTH.

SIX-INCH SCALE.

11A S.W. *is published on* 10A S.E.

$\frac{1}{2500}$ SCALE.

3.10 *is published on* 3.6

34.16 ,, 34.15

38.4 ,, 38.3

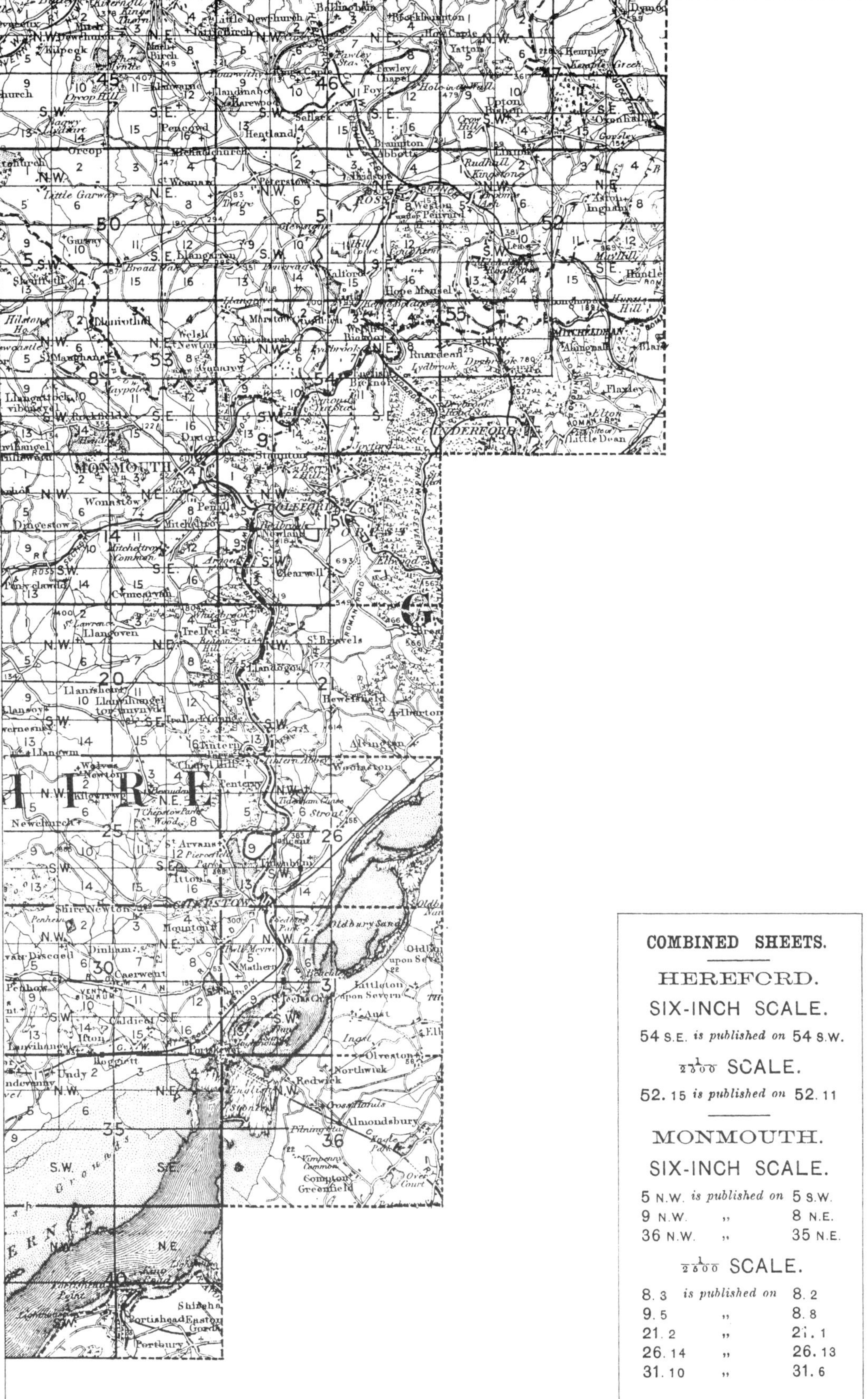

COMBINED SHEETS.

HEREFORD.

SIX-INCH SCALE.

54 S.E. *is published on* 54 S.W.

$\frac{1}{2500}$ SCALE.

52. 15 *is published on* 52. 11

MONMOUTH.

SIX-INCH SCALE.

5 N.W. *is published on* 5 S.W.
9 N.W. „ 8 N.E.
36 N.W. „ 35 N.E.

$\frac{1}{2500}$ SCALE.

8. 3 *is published on* 8. 2
9. 5 „ 8. 8
21. 2 „ 21. 1
26. 14 „ 26. 13
31. 10 „ 31. 6

N.E.
7
8
21
Llangenydd
11
12
S.W.
S.E.
15
16
G
Rhossili Bay
3
4
Rhossili
N.W.
N.E.
WORMS HEAD
7
8
30
12
S.E.

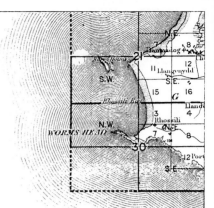

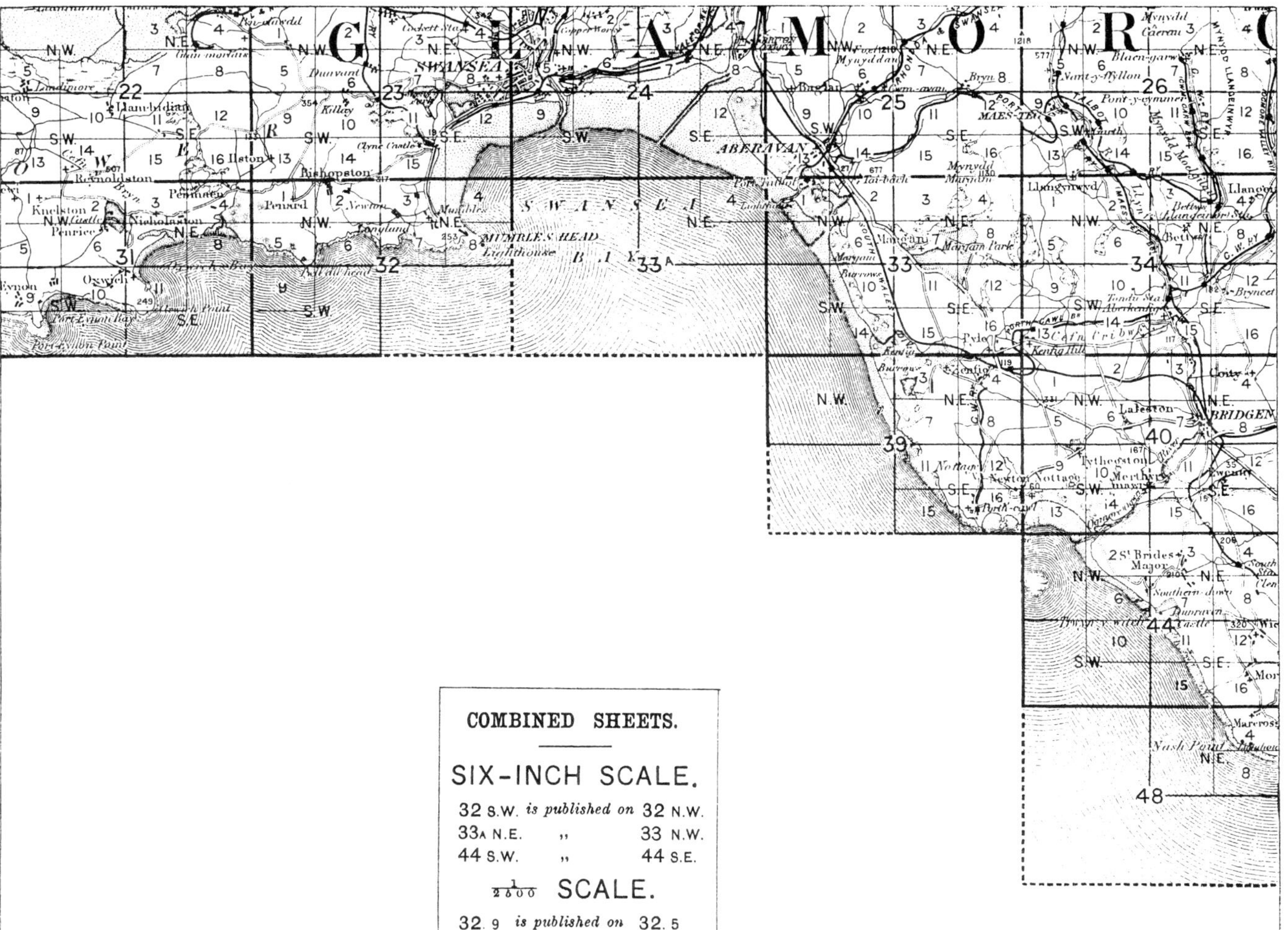

COMBINED SHEETS.

SIX-INCH SCALE.

32 S.W.	*is published on*	32 N.W.
33A N.E.	,,	33 N.W.
44 S.W.	,,	44 S.E.

$\frac{1}{2500}$ SCALE.

32. 9	*is published on*	32. 5
33A. 4	,,	33. 1
44. 10	,,	44. 11

COMBINED SHEETS.

DERBY.

$\frac{1}{2500}$ SCALE.

8. 1 *is published on* 8. 2

STAFFORD.

$\frac{1}{2500}$ SCALE.

1. 13 *is published on* 4. 1

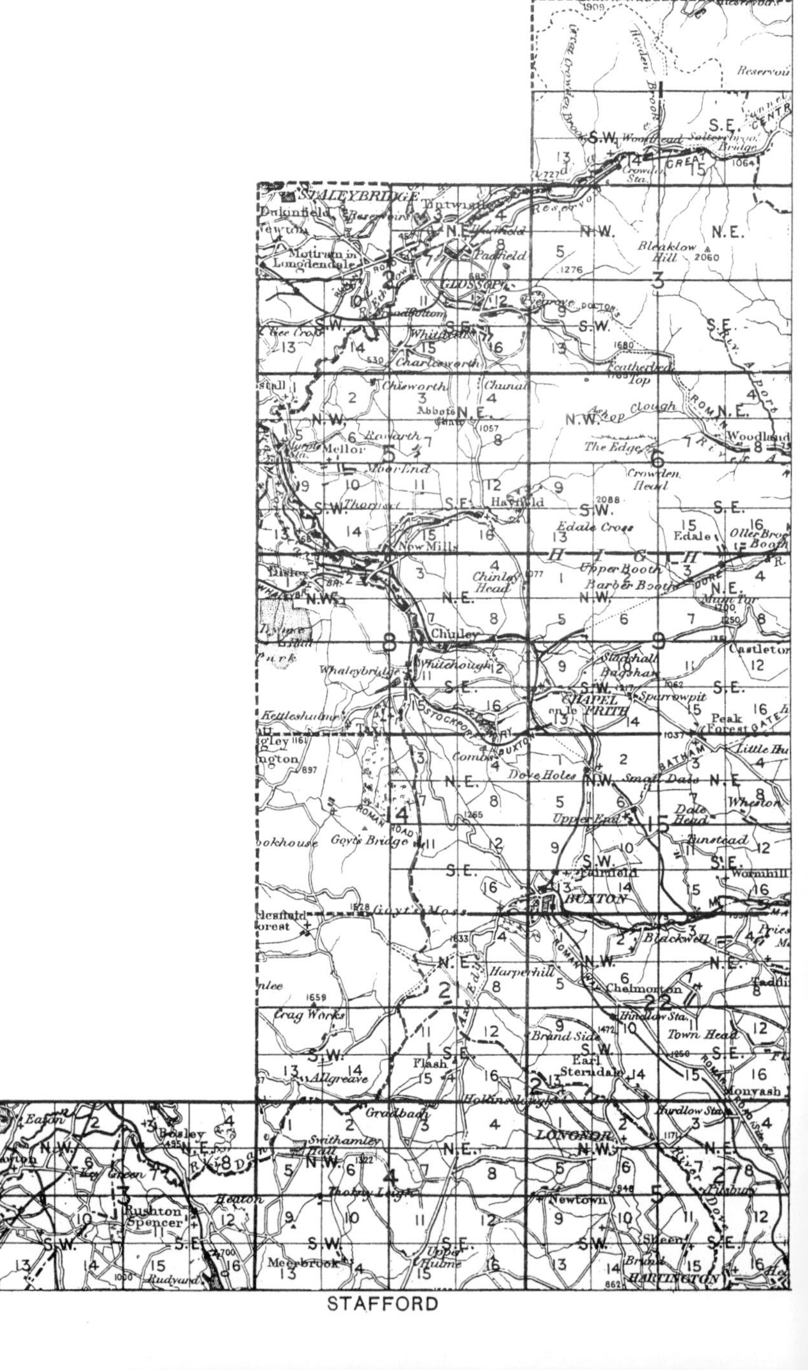

STAFFORD

COMBINED SHEETS.

NOTTINGHAM.

$\frac{1}{2500}$ SCALE.

8. 1 *is published on* 8. 2

8. 5 ,, 8. 6

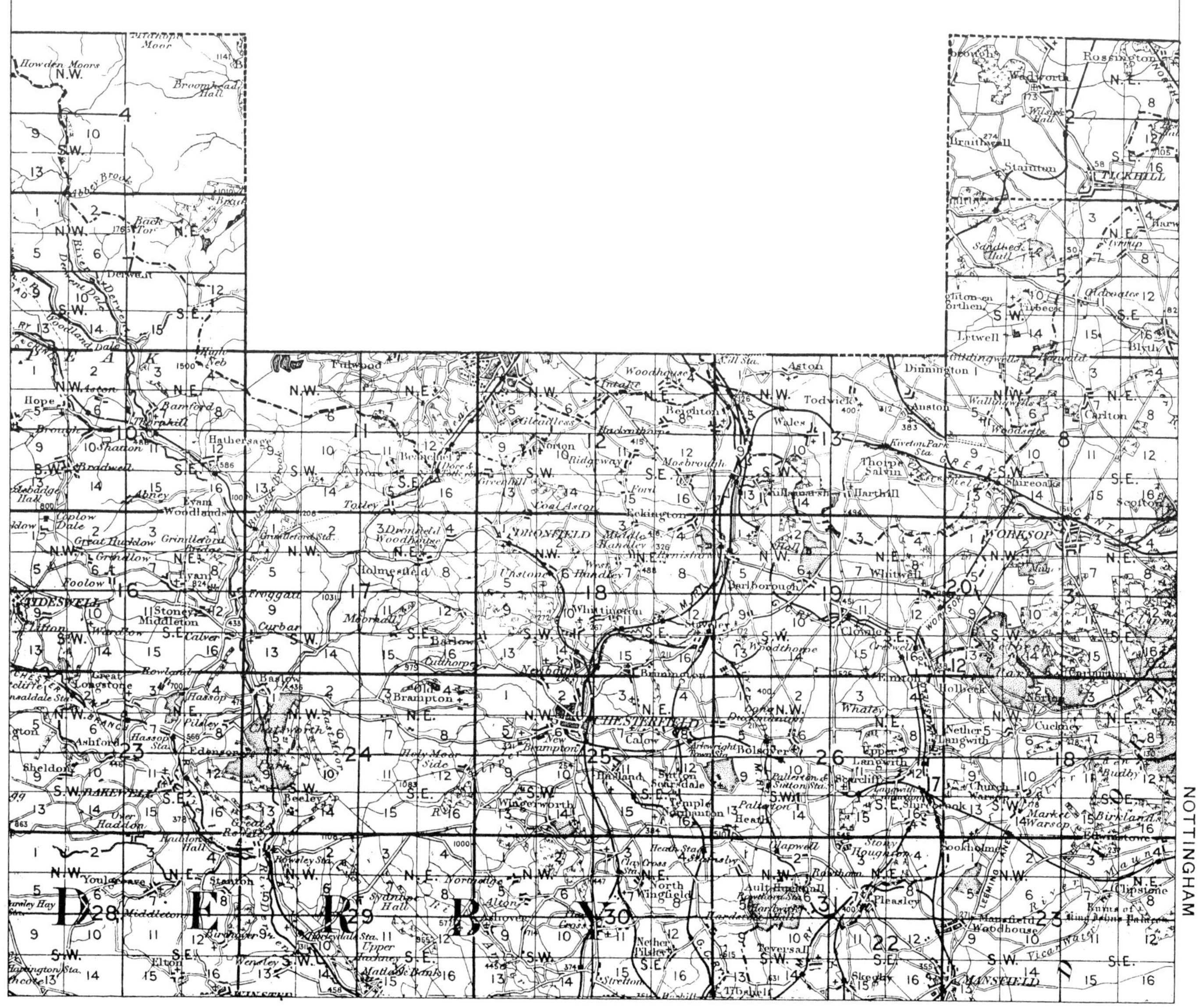

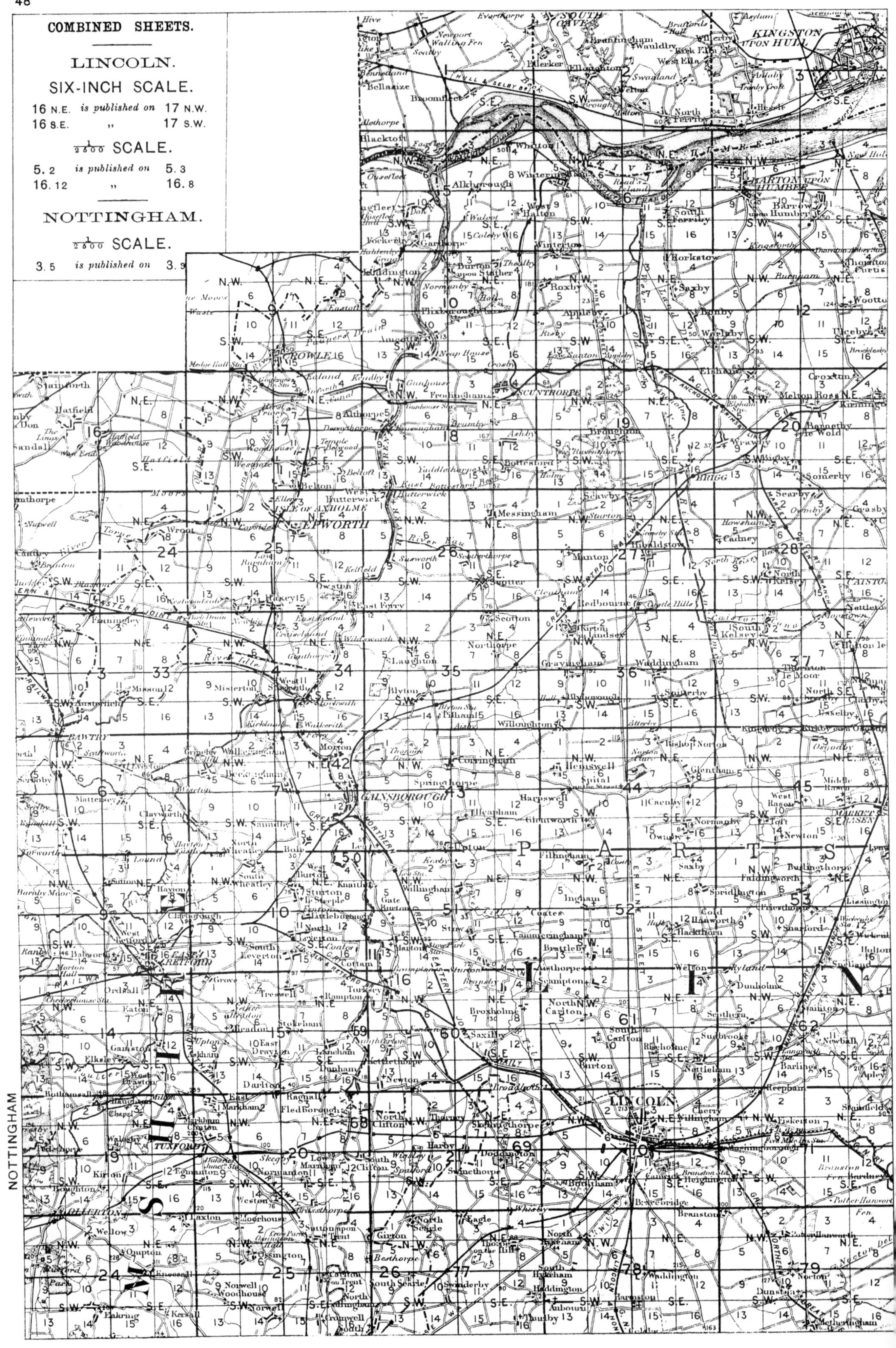
COMBINED SHEETS.
LINCOLN.
SIX-INCH SCALE.
16 N.E. is published on 17 N.W.
16 S.E. " 17 S.W.
1/2500 SCALE.
5. 2 is published on 5. 3
16. 12 " 16. 8
NOTTINGHAM.
1/2500 SCALE.
3. 5 is published on 3. 9
NOTTINGHAM
KINGSTON UPON HULL
BARTON UPON HUMBER
SCUNTHORPE
EPWORTH
ISLE OF AXHOLME
GAINSBOROUGH
LINCOLN
BRIGG
BAWTRY
TUXFORD
EAST RETFORD
MARKET RASEN
CAISTOR
OLLERTON

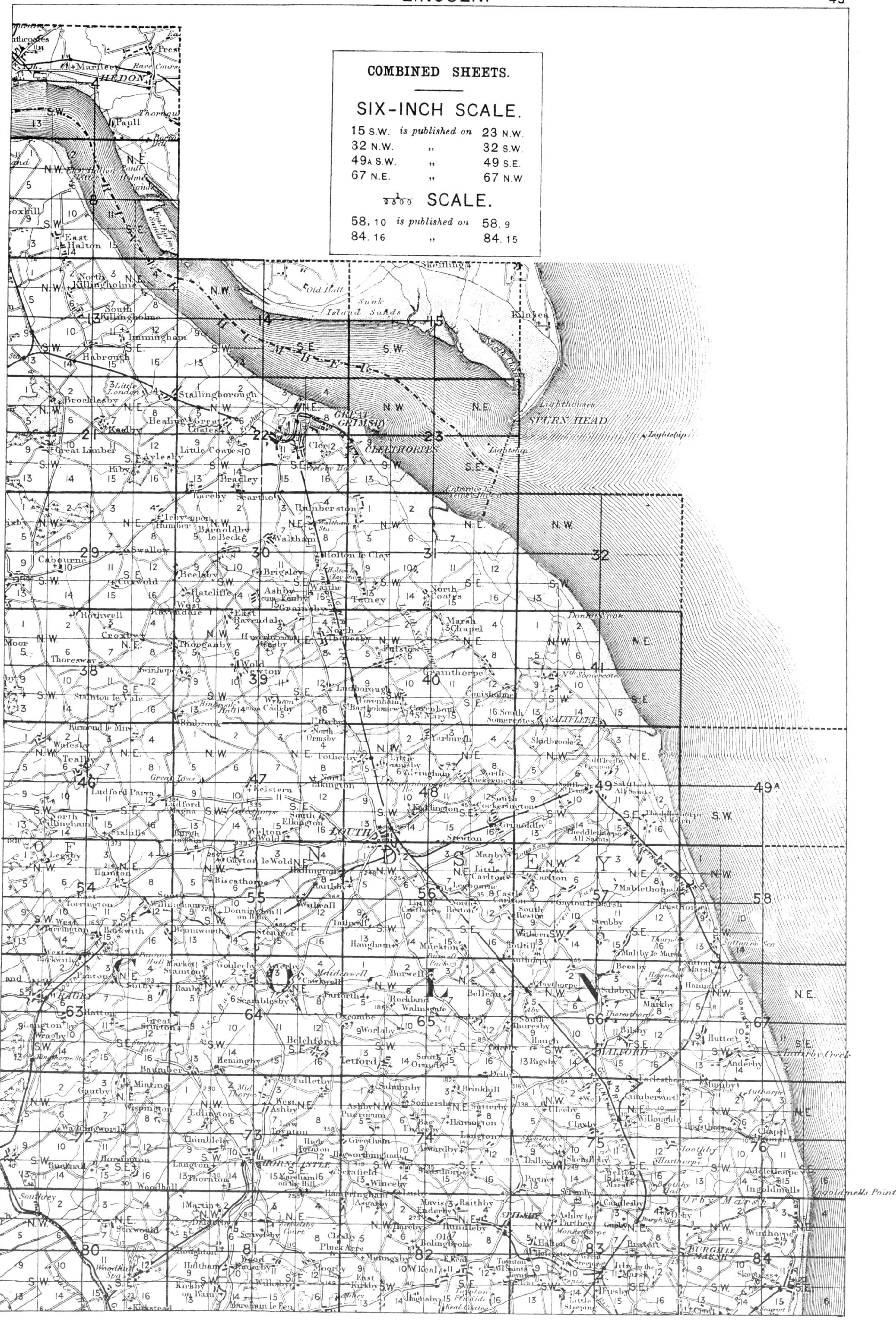
COMBINED SHEETS.
SIX-INCH SCALE.
15 S.W. is published on 23 N.W.
32 N.W. ,, 32 S.W.
49A S.W. ,, 49 S.E.
67 N.E. ,, 67 N.W.
1/2500 SCALE.
58.10 is published on 58.9
84.16 ,, 84.15
GREAT GRIMSBY
CLEETHORPES
SPURN HEAD
LOUTH
HORNCASTLE
SPILSBY
ALFORD
SALTFLEET
BURGH LE MARSH
HEDON
Skegness
Ingoldmells Point

COMBINED SHEETS.

STAFFORD.

$\frac{1}{2500}$ SCALE.

42.3 *is published on* 42.4

DERBY

27

STAFFORDSHIRE

COMBINED SHEETS.

NOTTINGHAM.

SIX-INCH SCALE.

52 N.E. *is published on* 49 S.E.

WORCESTER

WARWICK

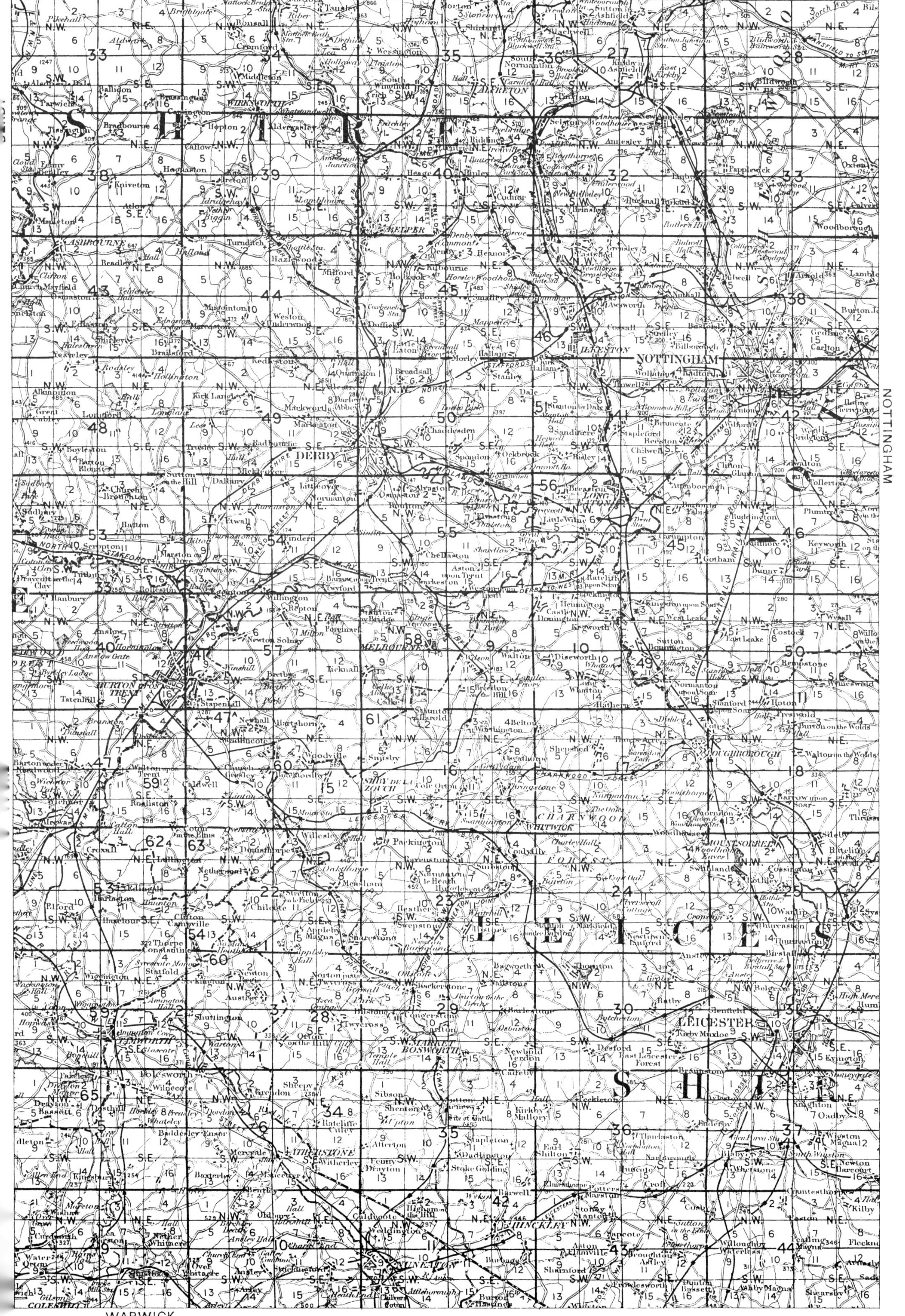
NOTTINGHAM
DERBY
NOTTINGHAM
LEICESTER
ASHBOURNE
BELPER
ILKESTON
BURTON UPON TRENT
LOUGHBOROUGH
MOUNTSORREL
MELBOURNE
ALFRETON
WIRKSWORTH
ATHERSTONE
NUNEATON
HINCKLEY
MARKET BOSWORTH
TAMWORTH
CHARNWOOD
WHITWICK
ASHBY DE LA ZOUCH
COLESHILL

WARWICK

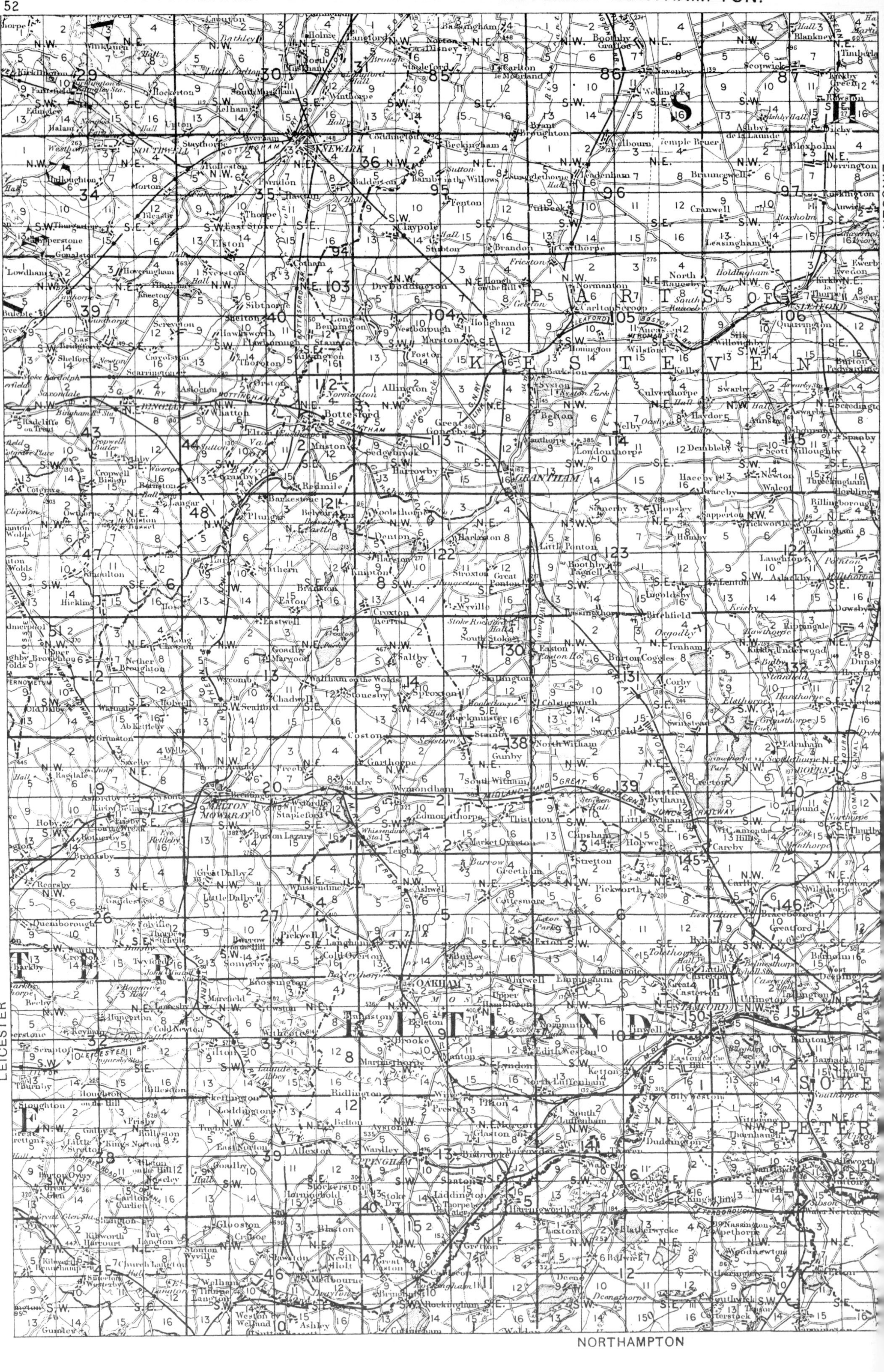
NOTTINGHAM
LEICESTER
NORTHAMPTON
KESTEVEN
RUTLAND
SOKE
PETER
NEWARK
SOUTHWELL
GRANTHAM
SLEAFORD
BINGHAM
MELTON MOWBRAY
OAKHAM
UPPINGHAM
STAMFORD
BOURN
Bottesford
Navenby
Ancaster

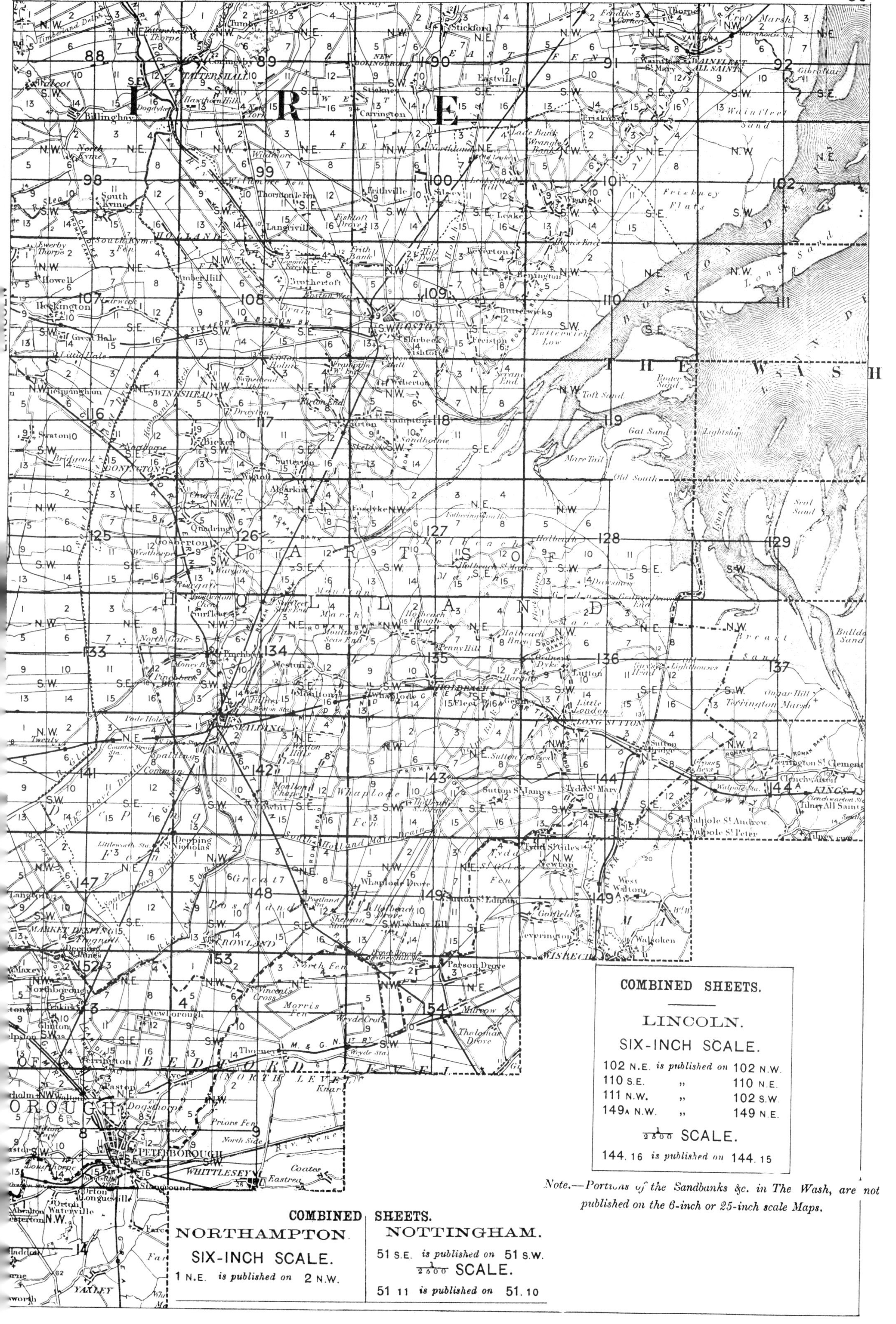
COMBINED SHEETS.
LINCOLN.
SIX-INCH SCALE.
102 N.E. is published on 102 N.W.
110 S.E. " 110 N.E.
111 N.W. " 102 S.W.
149A N.W. " 149 N.E.
1/2500 SCALE.
144.16 is published on 144.15
Note.—Portions of the Sandbanks &c. in The Wash, are not published on the 6-inch or 25-inch scale Maps.
COMBINED SHEETS.
NORTHAMPTON.
SIX-INCH SCALE.
1 N.E. is published on 2 N.W.
NOTTINGHAM.
51 S.E. is published on 51 S.W.
1/2500 SCALE.
51.11 is published on 51.10
THE WASH
BOSTON DEEPS
PARTS OF HOLLAND
BEDFORD LEVEL
PETERBOROUGH
BOSTON
SPALDING
HOLBEACH
WHITTLESEY
LONG SUTTON
TATTERSHALL
DONINGTON
CROWLAND
WISBECH
YAXLEY

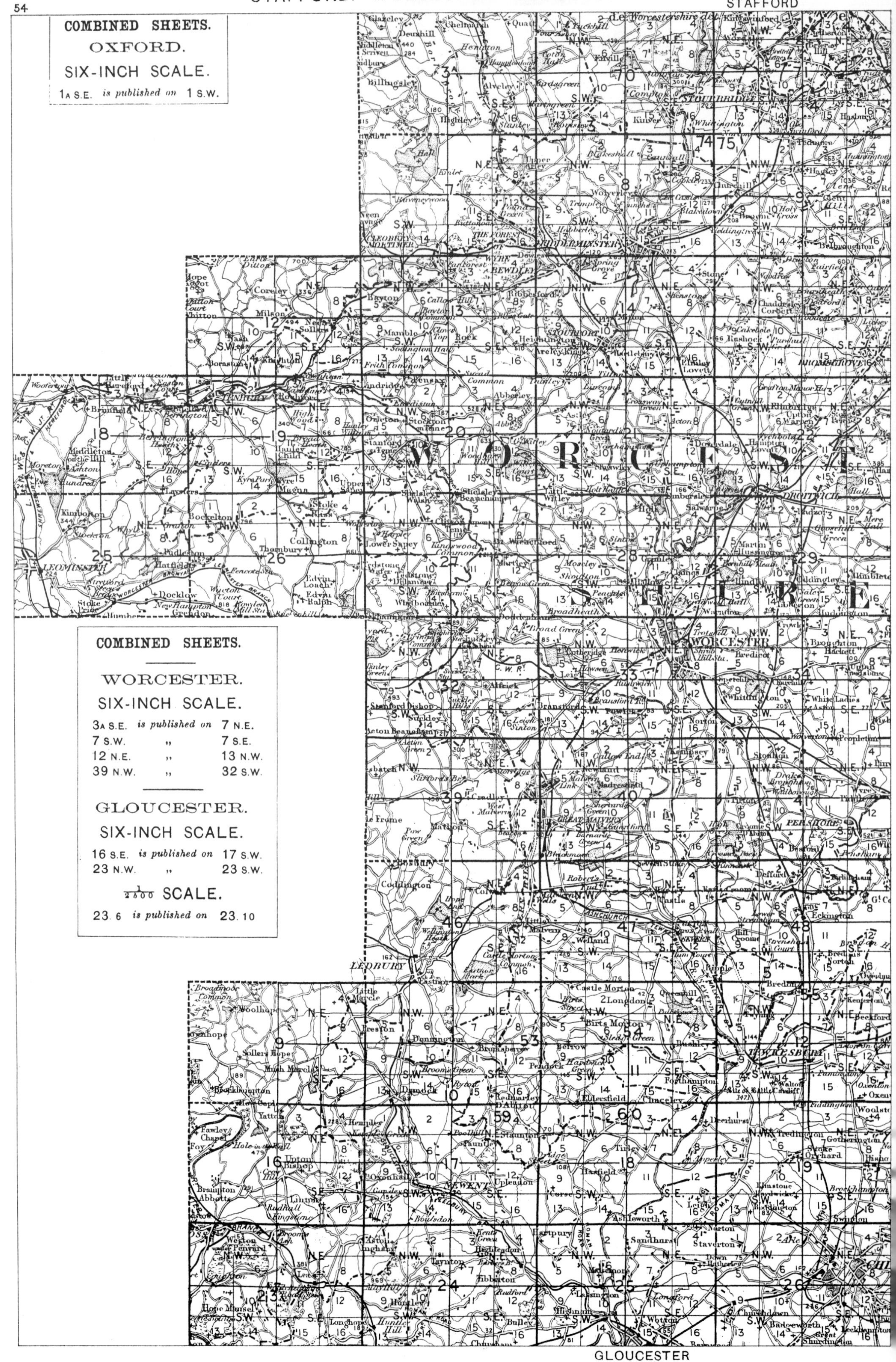
STAFFORD
COMBINED SHEETS.
OXFORD.
SIX-INCH SCALE.
1A S.E. is published on 1 S.W.
COMBINED SHEETS.
WORCESTER.
SIX-INCH SCALE.
3A S.E. is published on 7 N.E.
7 S.W. ,, 7 S.E.
12 N.E. ,, 13 N.W.
39 N.W. ,, 32 S.W.
GLOUCESTER.
SIX-INCH SCALE.
16 S.E. is published on 17 S.W.
23 N.W. ,, 23 S.W.
1/2500 SCALE.
23.6 is published on 23.10
WORCESTERSHIRE
GLOUCESTER

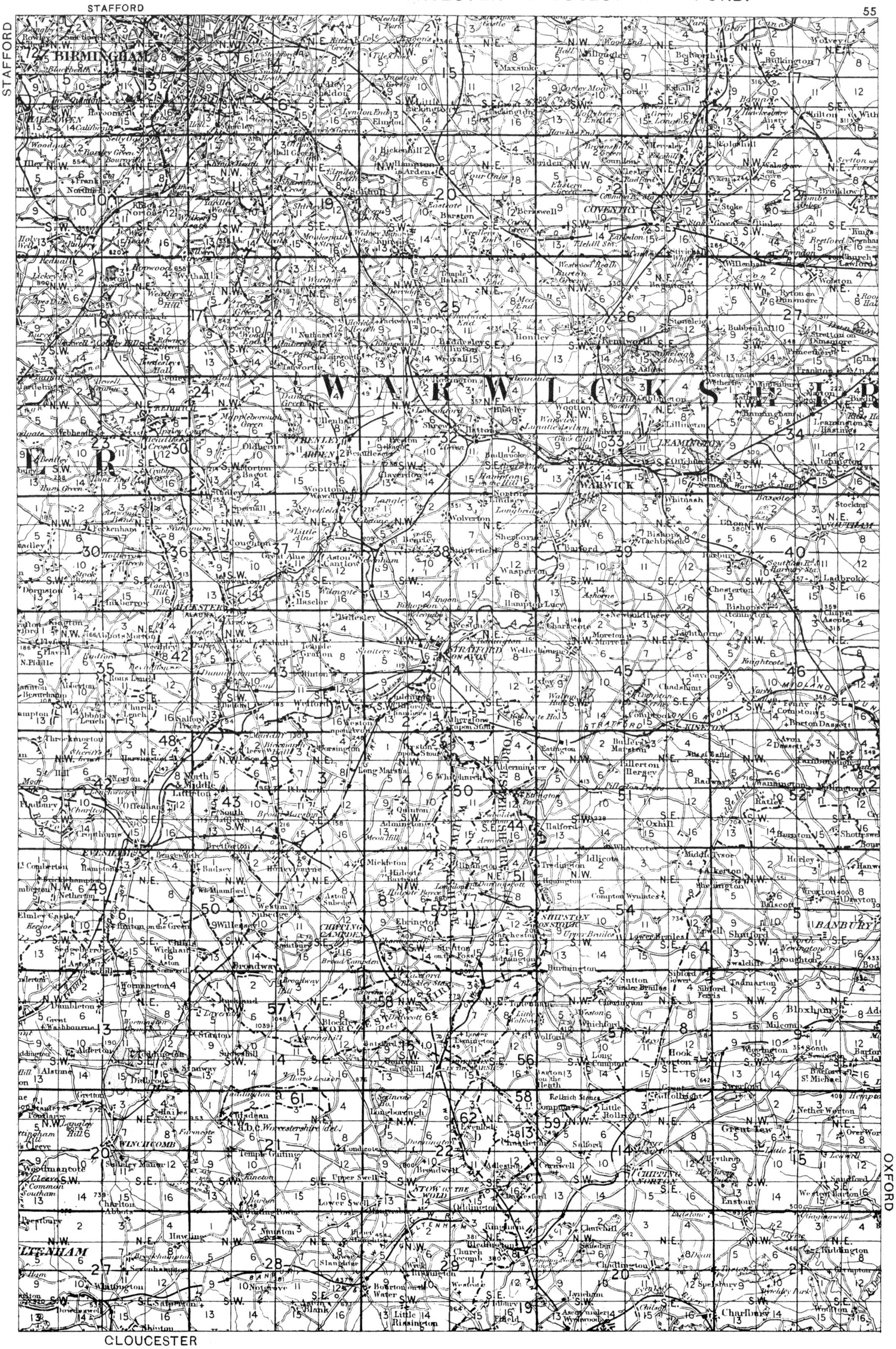
STAFFORD
STAFFORD
OXFORD
GLOUCESTER
WARWICKSHIRE
BIRMINGHAM
COVENTRY
Kenilworth
LEAMINGTON
WARWICK
STRATFORD ON AVON
ALCESTER
EVESHAM
BANBURY
SHIPSTON ON STOUR
CHIPPING CAMPDEN
WINCHCOMB
CHIPPING NORTON
STOW ON THE WOLD
Broadway
Charlbury
Bedworth
Meriden
Henley in Arden
Kineton

LEICESTER

WARWICK

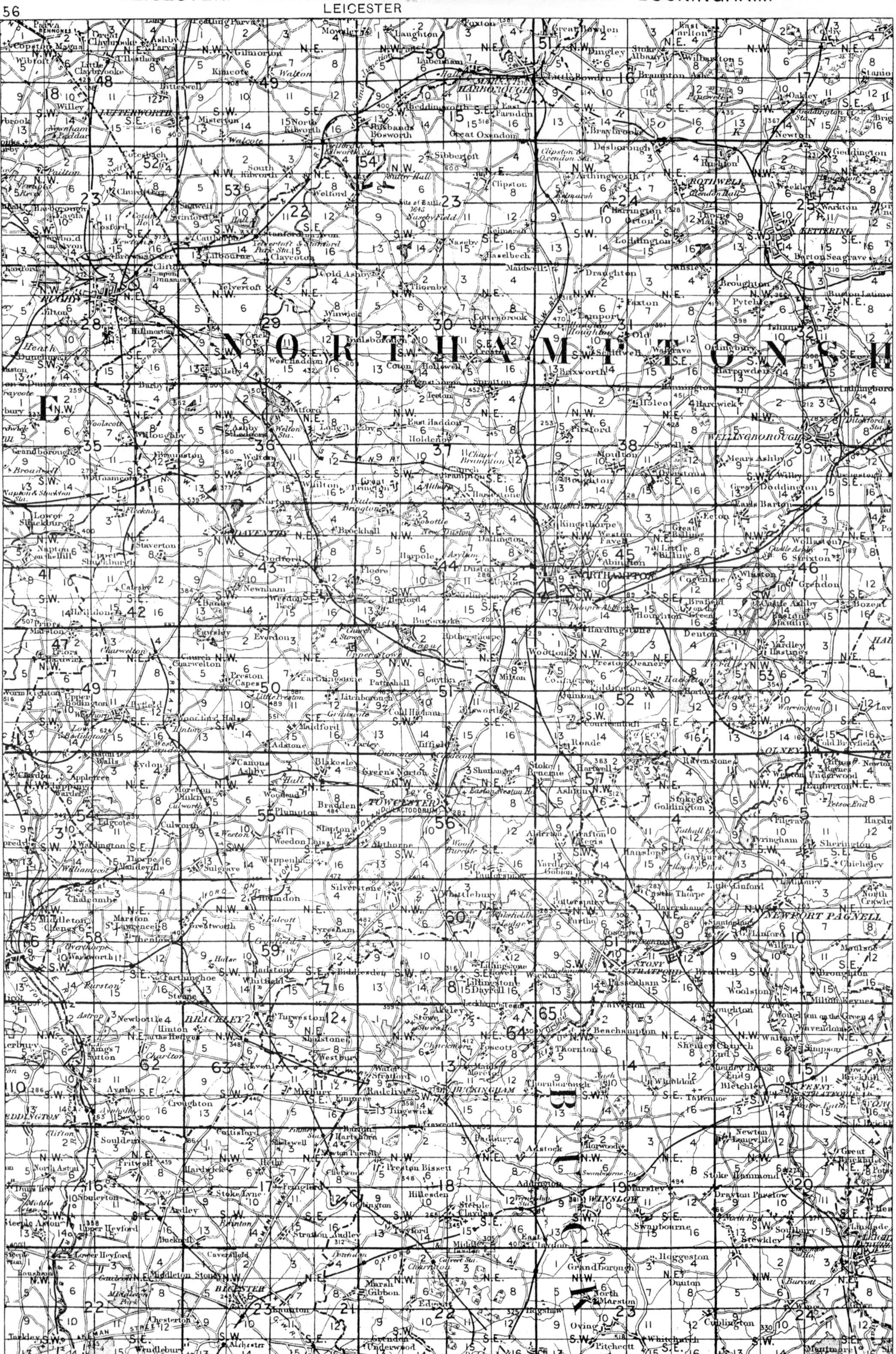

NORTHAMPTONSH

OXFORD

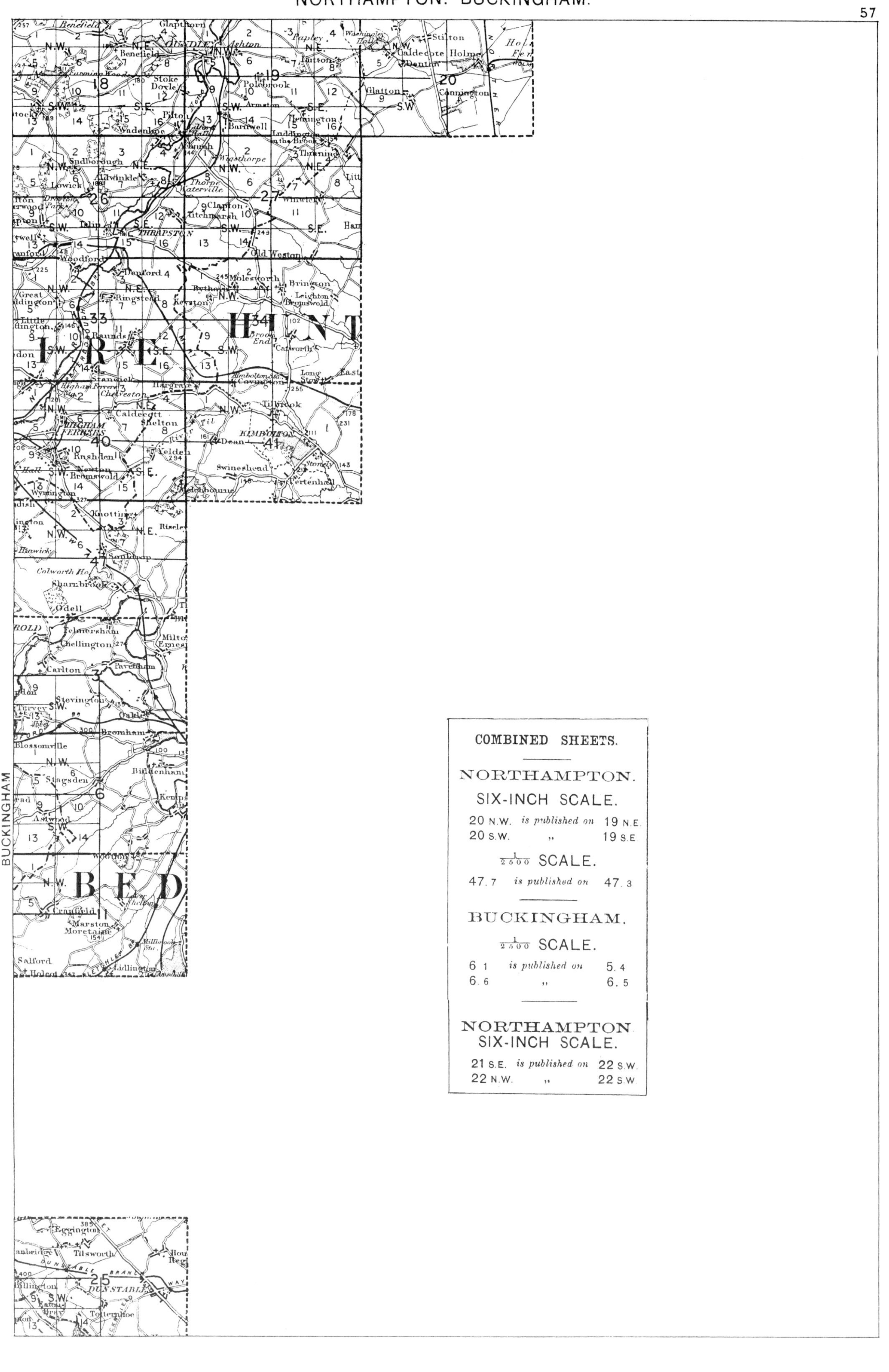
Benefield
Glapthorn
Ashton
Papley
Stilton
Caldecote
Holme
Denton
Stoke Doyle
Polebrook
Glatton
Conington
Pilton
Barnwell
Wadenhoe
Hemington
Luddington in the Brook
Sudborough
Aldwinkle
Thurning
Lowick
Thorpe Waterville
Clapton
Titchmarsh
Winwick
THRAPSTON
Old Weston
Woodford
Denford
Molesworth
Brington
Bythorn
Keyston
Ringstead
Leighton Bromswold
Raunds
Catworth
Kimbolton
Covington
Stanwick
Hargrave
Tilbrook
Chelveston
Caldecott
Shelton
HIGHAM FERRERS
Dean
Rushden
Yelden
Swineshead
Newton Bromswold
Pertenhall
Knotting
Riseley
Souldrop
Colworth Ho.
Sharnbrook
Odell
Felmersham
Chellington
Milton Ernest
Carlton
Pavenham
Stevington
Oakley
Turvey
Bromham
Blossomville
Biddenham
Stagsden
Kempston
Astwood
Wootton
Cranfield
Marston Moretaine
Salford
Eggington
Tilsworth
DUNSTABLE
Billington
Totternhoe
BUCKINGHAM
HUNT
BED
COMBINED SHEETS.
NORTHAMPTON.
SIX-INCH SCALE.
20 N.W. is published on 19 N.E.
20 S.W. „ 19 S.E.
1/2500 SCALE.
47.7 is published on 47.3
BUCKINGHAM.
1/2500 SCALE.
6.1 is published on 5.4
6.6 „ 6.5
NORTHAMPTON
SIX-INCH SCALE.
21 S.E. is published on 22 S.W.
22 N.W. „ 22 S.W.

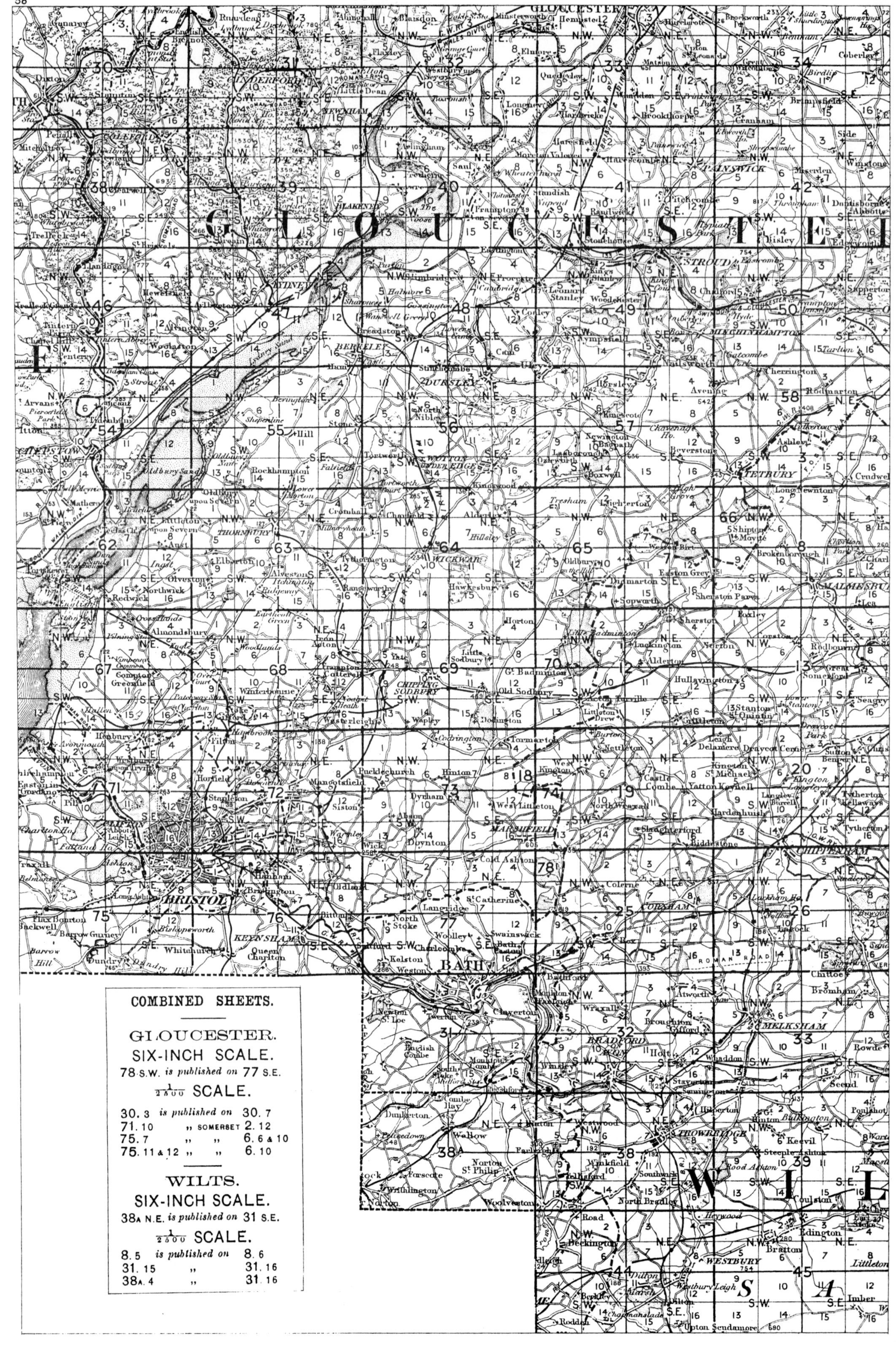
COMBINED SHEETS.
GLOUCESTER.
SIX-INCH SCALE.
78 S.W. is published on 77 S.E.
1/2500 SCALE.
30. 3 is published on 30. 7
71. 10 „ SOMERSET 2. 12
75. 7 „ „ 6. 6 & 10
75. 11 & 12 „ „ 6. 10
WILTS.
SIX-INCH SCALE.
38A N.E. is published on 31 S.E.
1/2500 SCALE.
8. 5 is published on 8. 6
31. 15 „ 31. 16
38A. 4 „ 31. 16
GLOUCESTER
WILTS
BRISTOL
BATH
CHEPSTOW
STROUD
TETBURY
MALMESBURY
CHIPPENHAM
MELKSHAM
TROWBRIDGE
WESTBURY
BERKELEY
THORNBURY
DURSLEY
KEYNSHAM
CORSHAM
SYDNEY
NEWNHAM
CINDERFORD

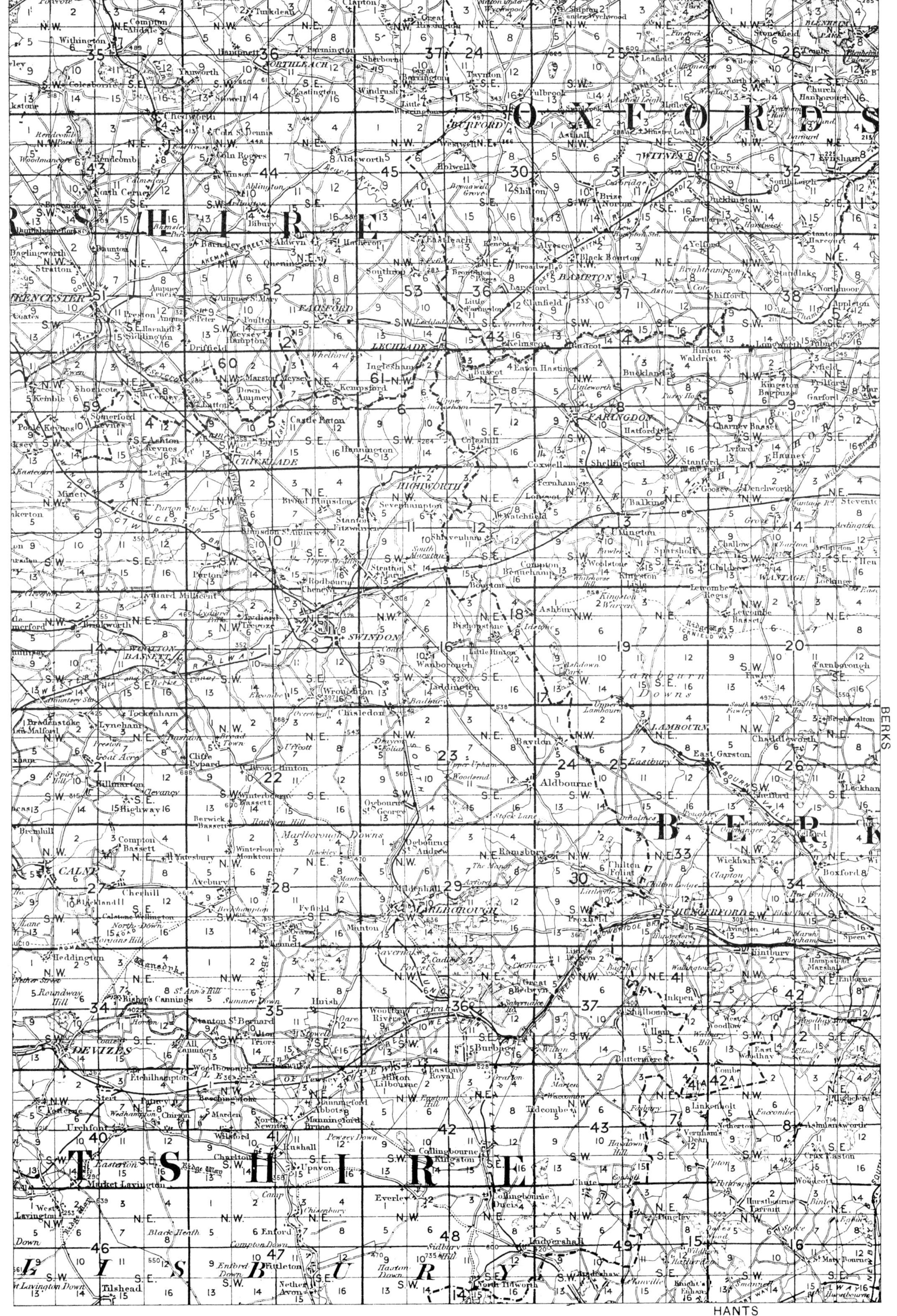
OXFORDS
SHIRE
BERK
TSHIRE
LISBURY
BERKS
NORTHLEACH
BURFORD
WITNEY
BAMPTON
CIRENCESTER
FAIRFORD
LECHLADE
CRICKLADE
FARINGDON
HIGHWORTH
SWINDON
WANTAGE
WOOTTON BASSETT
LAMBOURN
CALNE
MARLBOROUGH
HUNGERFORD
DEVIZES
Aldbourne
Ludgershall
Chedworth
Bibury
Kempsford
Shrivenham
Ashbury
Avebury
Burbage
Pewsey
Upavon
Market Lavington
Tilshead
Kingston Bagpuze
Blenheim Park
Stonesfield
Woodstock

BUCKINGHAM

BERKS

HANTS

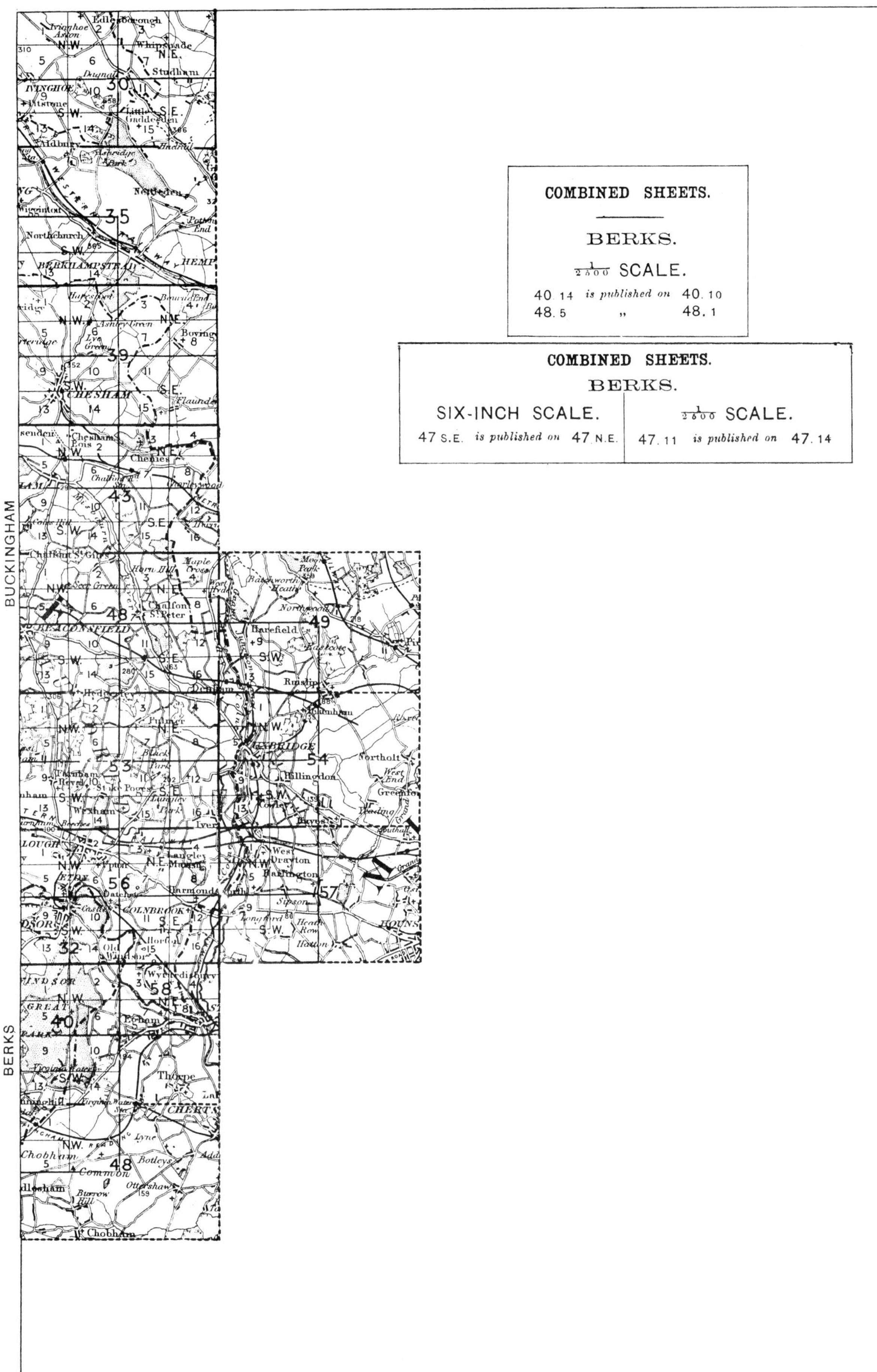

COMBINED SHEETS.

BERKS.

$\frac{1}{2500}$ SCALE.

40.14	*is published on*	40.10
48.5	„	48.1

COMBINED SHEETS.

BERKS.

SIX-INCH SCALE.	$\frac{1}{2500}$ SCALE.
47 S.E. *is published on* 47 N.E.	47.11 *is published on* 47.14

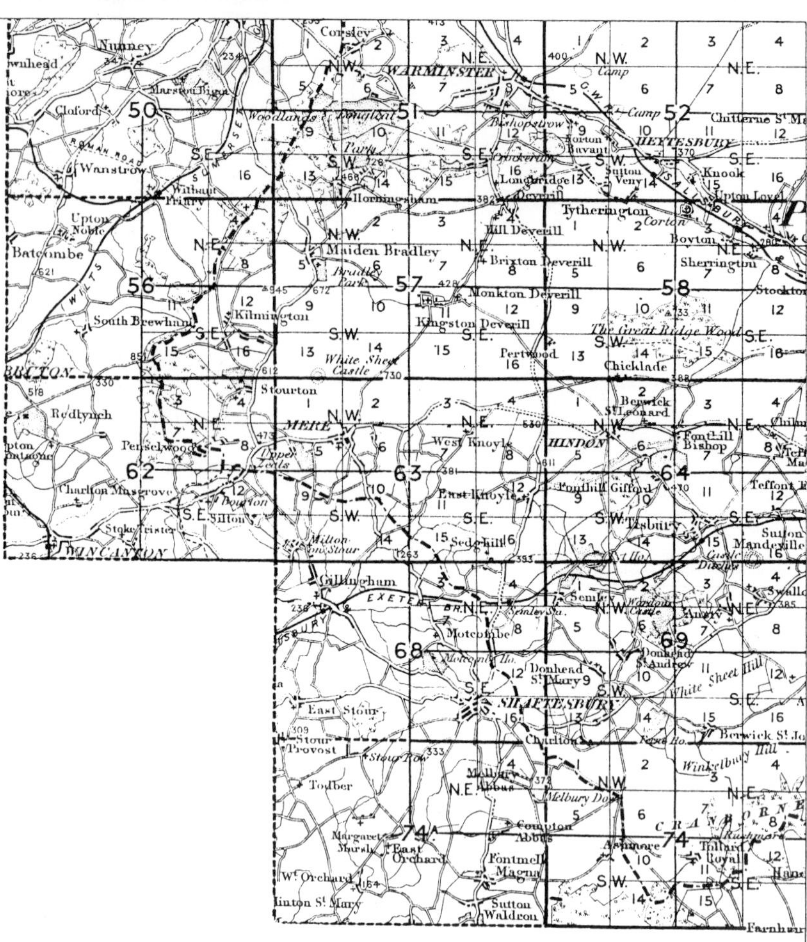

COMBINED SHEETS.

SIX-INCH SCALE.

50 S.E.	*is published on*	56 N.E.
62 S.E.	,,	62 N.E.
74A N.E.	,,	74 N.W.

$\frac{1}{2500}$ SCALE.

51. 1	*is published on*	51. 2
74A. 4	,,	74. 1

COMBINED SHEETS.

WILTS.

$\frac{1}{2500}$ SCALE.

75.6 *is published on* 75.5

HANTS.

SIX-INCH SCALE.

22 S.W. *is published on* 22 S.E.

$\frac{1}{2500}$ SCALE.

54A. 6	*is published on*	54A. 11
62. 6	,,	62. 10
70. 1	,,	70. 5
81. 16	,,	81. 15
85. 4	,,	85. 8
88. 16 [PT. OF.]	,,	89. 13
89. 4	,,	89. 8
89. 7	,,	89. 8
89. 9	,,	89. 10
93. 13	,,	93. 14

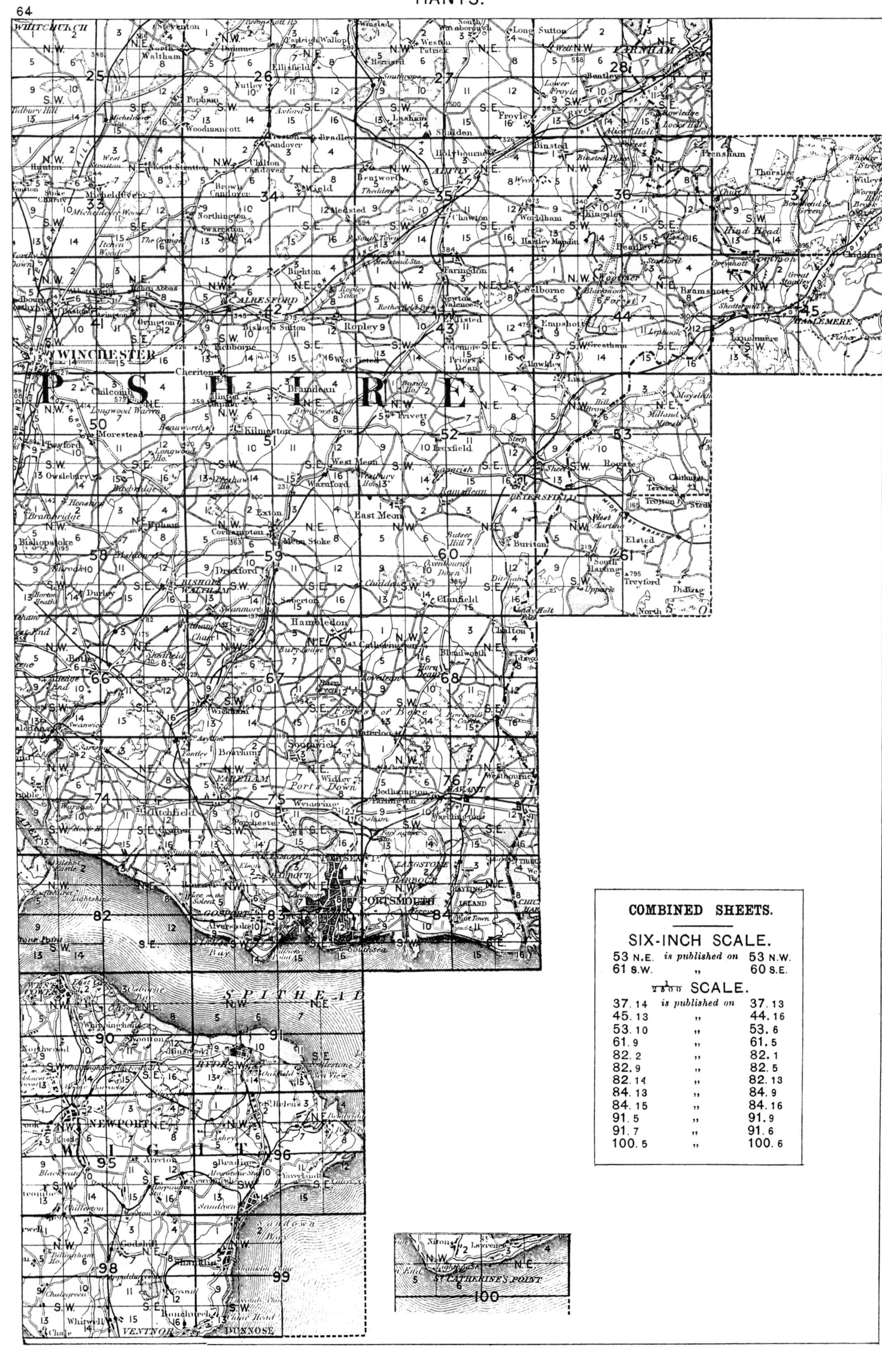

COMBINED SHEETS.

SIX-INCH SCALE.

53 N.E.	*is published on*	53 N.W.
61 S.W.	,,	60 S.E.

$\frac{1}{2500}$ SCALE.

37. 14	*is published on*	37. 13
45. 13	,,	44. 16
53. 10	,,	53. 6
61. 9	,,	61. 5
82. 2	,,	82. 1
82. 9	,,	82. 5
82. 14	,,	82. 13
84. 13	,,	84. 9
84. 15	,,	84. 16
91. 5	,,	91. 9
91. 7	,,	91. 6
100. 5	,,	100. 6

COMBINED SHEETS.

CAMBRIDGE.

SIX-INCH SCALE.

3 S.W. *is published on* 6 N.W.

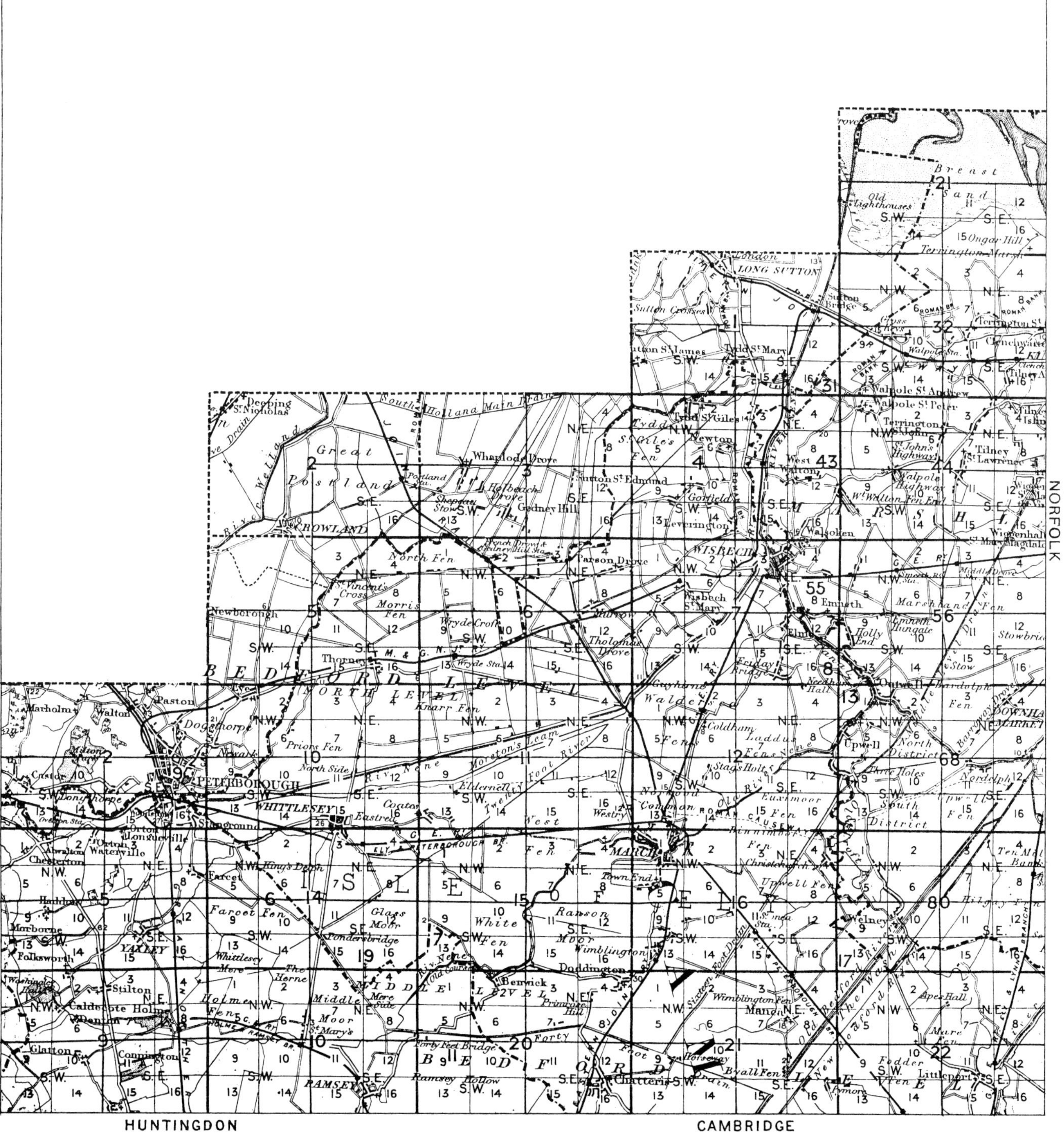

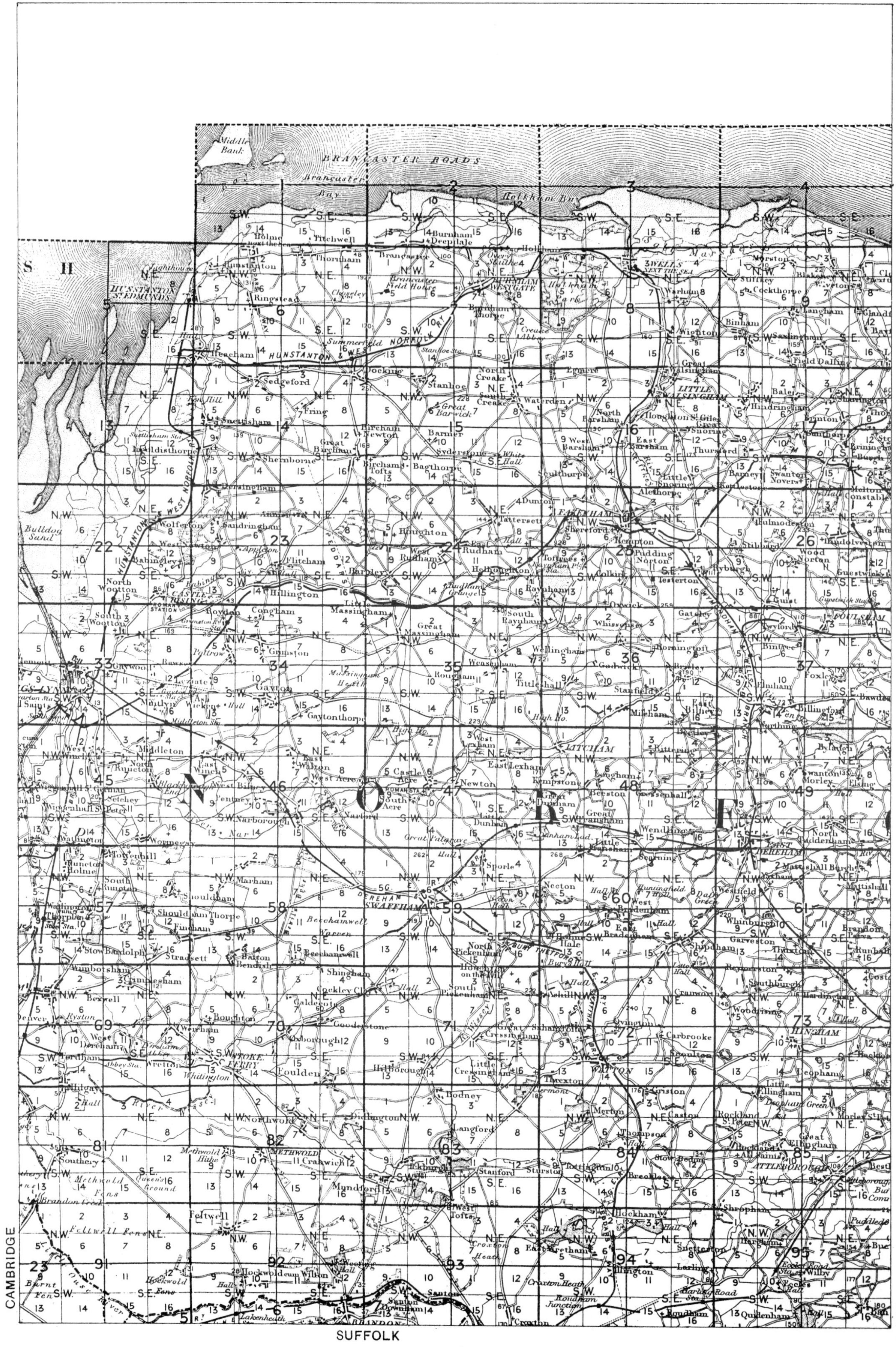
BRANCASTER ROADS
Brancaster Bay
Holkham Bay
Hunstanton
Titchwell
Thornham
Brancaster
Burnham Deepdale
Holkham
Wells next the Sea
Ringstead
Docking
Sedgeford
Stanhoe
Snettisham
Heacham
Fring
Bircham Newton
Great Bircham
Shernborne
Dersingham
Sandringham
Wolferton
Tatterset
Fakenham
Houghton
Flitcham
Hillington
Congham
Grimston
Gayton
Gaytonthorpe
Middleton
West Acre
Castle Acre
Newton
Narborough
Swaffham
Marham
Shouldham
Fincham
Stradsett
Stow Bardolph
Boughton
Wereham
Stoke Ferry
Whittington
Foulden
Gooderstone
Hilborough
Bodney
Northwold
Methwold
Cranwich
Mundford
Feltwell
Hockwold cum Wilton
Lakenheath
Brandon
Southery
Hilgay
Denver
Downham
Stanford
Sturston
Tottington
Thompson
Merton
Caston
Watton
Carbrooke
Scoulton
Hingham
Attleborough
Shropham
Snetterton
Larling
Quidenham
East Wretham
Croxton
Roudham
Illington
Bridgham
Great Ellingham
Little Ellingham
Deopham
Shipdham
Cranworth
Whinburgh
Garveston
East Dereham
Mattishall
Swanton Morley
North Elmham
Litcham
Beeston
Wendling
Scarning
Necton
Sporle
Mileham
Stanfield
Tittleshall
Wellingham
Weasenham
Great Massingham
Little Massingham
Rudham
Helhoughton
Raynham
Colkirk
Pudding Norton
Tofttrees
Hempton
Shereford
Dunton
Sculthorpe
Barsham
Walsingham
Houghton St. Giles
Great Snoring
Little Snoring
Thursford
Barney
Binham
Warham
Wighton
Langham
Cockthorpe
Stiffkey
Morston
Blakeney
Hindringham
Bale
Field Dalling
Saxlingham
Melton Constable
Hindolveston
Wood Norton
Guestwick
Foulsham
Twyford
Bintree
Foxley
Bawdeswell
Billingford
Elsing
Hoe
North Creake
South Creake
Waterden
Burnham Thorpe
Creake Abbey
Egmere
Syderstone
Barmer
Great Barwick
Bagthorpe
Bircham Tofts
CASTLE RISING
North Wootton
South Wootton
Babingley
West Newton
Appleton
Roydon
Gaywood
Bawsey
Leziate
Ashwicken
Mintlyn
East Winch
West Winch
West Bilney
Pentney
East Walton
Narford
South Acre
Great Palgrave
Little Dunham
Great Dunham
East Lexham
West Lexham
Kempstone
Longham
Gressenhall
Bittering
Beetley
Gateley
Brisley
Horningtoft
Whissonsett
Oxwick
Kettlestone
Fulmodeston
Stibbard
Ryburgh
Testerton
Wormegay
Tottenhill
Runcton Holme
South Runcton
North Runcton
Setchey
Wiggenhall St. Germans
Watlington
Barton Bendish
Beechamwell
Shingham
Cockley Cley
Caldecote
Oxborough
Cressingham
South Pickenham
North Pickenham
Houghton on the Hill
Holme Hale
Bradenham
Threxton
Saham Toney
Ovington
Griston
Rockland
Breckles
Stow Bedon
Hockham
Wretham
Croxton Heath
West Tofts
Santon Downham
Ickburgh
Langford
Didlington
Cranwich
Wilby
Eccles Road
Harling Road
Brandon Creek
Methwold Fens
Feltwell Fens
Burnt Fen
River Ouse
HUNSTANTON & WEST NORFOLK RY.
CAMBRIDGE
SUFFOLK

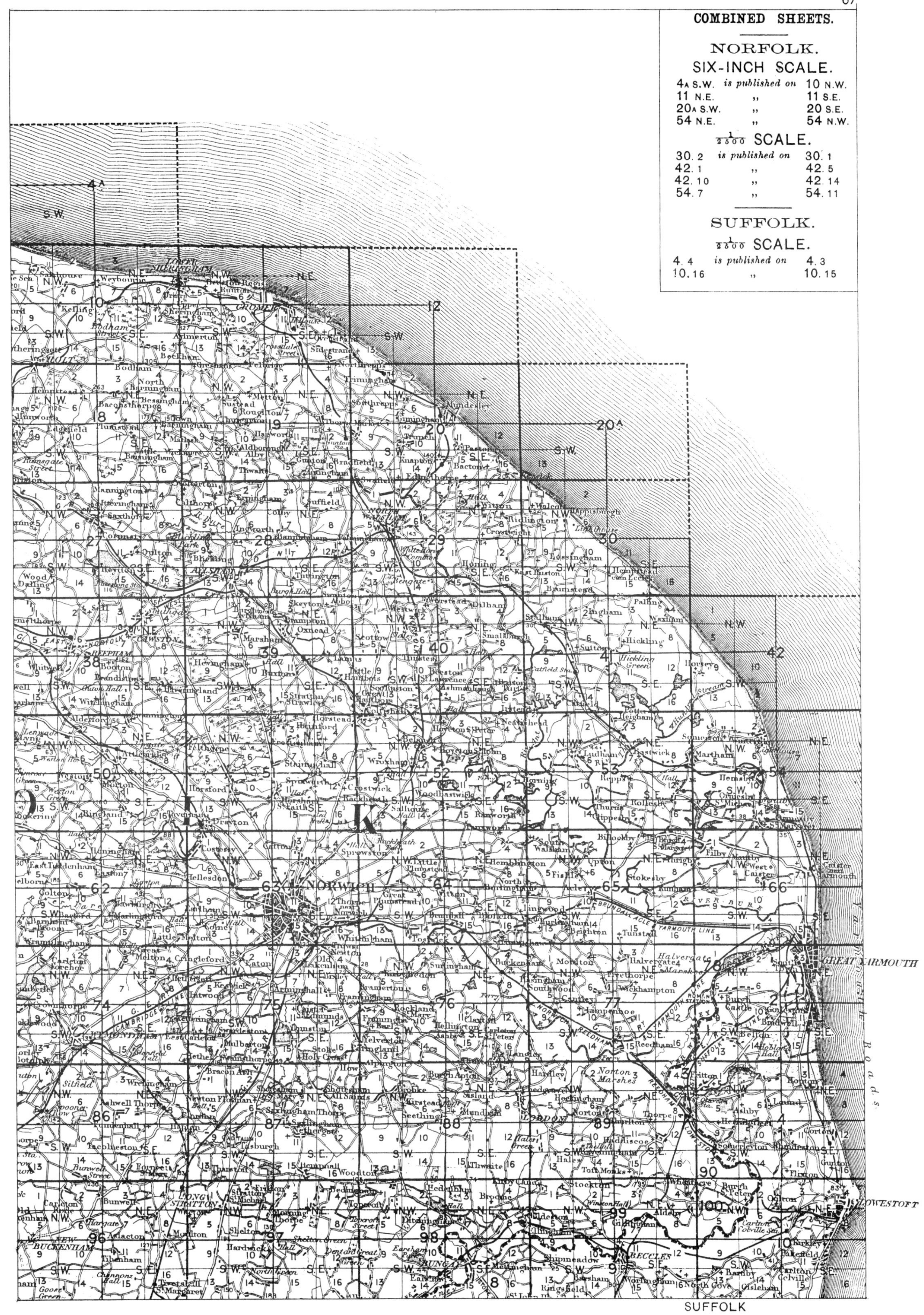
COMBINED SHEETS.
NORFOLK.
SIX-INCH SCALE.
4A S.W. is published on 10 N.W.
11 N.E. „ 11 S.E.
20A S.W. „ 20 S.E.
54 N.E. „ 54 N.W.
1/2500 SCALE.
30. 2 is published on 30. 1
42. 1 „ 42. 5
42. 10 „ 42. 14
54. 7 „ 54. 11
SUFFOLK.
1/2500 SCALE.
4. 4 is published on 4. 3
10. 16 „ 10. 15
NORWICH
GREAT YARMOUTH
LOWESTOFT
CROMER
SUFFOLK

HUNTINGDON

CAMBRIDGE

Huntingdonshire (Det.) is published on the $\frac{1}{2500}$ scale sheets 13.—5, 6, 9, 10, 11, & 14, and Six-inch scale sheets 13 N.W., S.W., *&* S.E., *of Bedfordshire.*

ESSEX

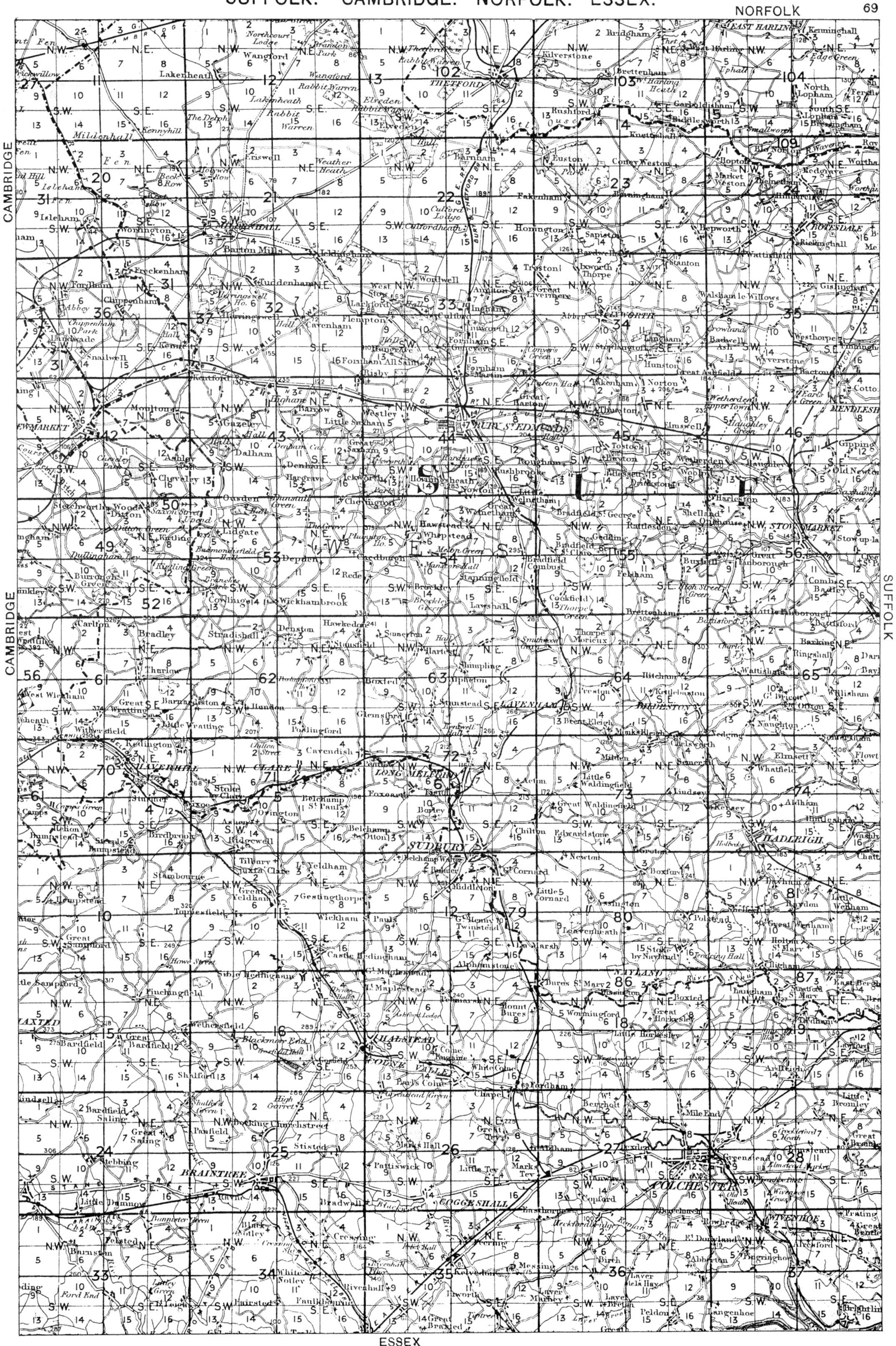
NORFOLK
CAMBRIDGE
SUFFOLK
ESSEX
THETFORD
MILDENHALL
Mildenhall
Lakenheath
Brandon
Elveden
EAST HARLING
Kenninghall
North Lopham
Diss
Botesdale
Ixworth
Bury St. Edmunds
NEWMARKET
STOWMARKET
Mendlesham
Lavenham
Long Melford
HAVERHILL
CLARE
SUDBURY
HADLEIGH
Nayland
HALSTEAD
BRAINTREE
COGGESHALL
COLCHESTER
WIVENHOE
Kelvedon
Witham
Thaxted
Bildeston
Kersey
Cavendish
Wickhambrook
Dalham
Gazeley
Kentford
Chippenham
Freckenham
Ingham
Culford
Fakenham
Euston
Barnham
Hopton
Walsham le Willows
Elmswell
Woolpit
Rattlesden
Cockfield
Glemsford
Boxford
Stoke by Nayland
Bures
Earls Colne
Great Tey
Marks Tey
Stanway
Copford
Rowhedge
Alresford
Langham
Dedham
Ardleigh

ESSEX

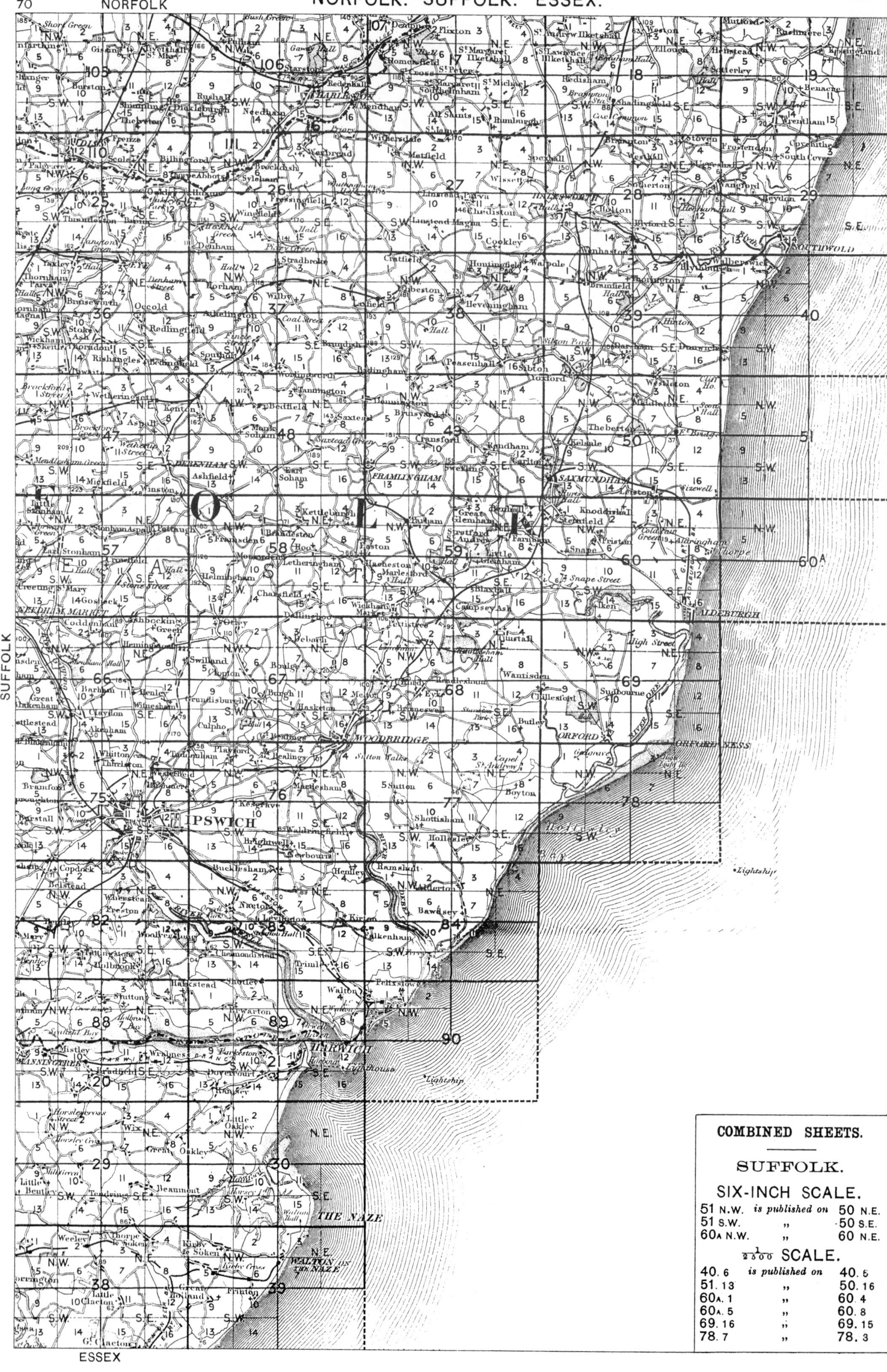
SUFFOLK
HARLESTON
SOUTHWOLD
EYE
FRAMLINGHAM
SAXMUNDHAM
NEEDHAM MARKET
ALDEBURGH
WOODBRIDGE
ORFORD
ORFORD NESS
IPSWICH
Lightship
HARWICH
Lighthouse
Lightship
THE NAZE
WALTON ON THE NAZE
COMBINED SHEETS.
SUFFOLK.
SIX-INCH SCALE.
51 N.W. is published on 50 N.E.
51 S.W. " 50 S.E.
60A N.W. " 60 N.E.
1/2500 SCALE.
40. 6 is published on 40. 6
51. 13 " 50. 16
60A. 1 " 60. 4
60A. 5 " 60. 8
69. 16 " 69. 15
78. 7 " 78. 3

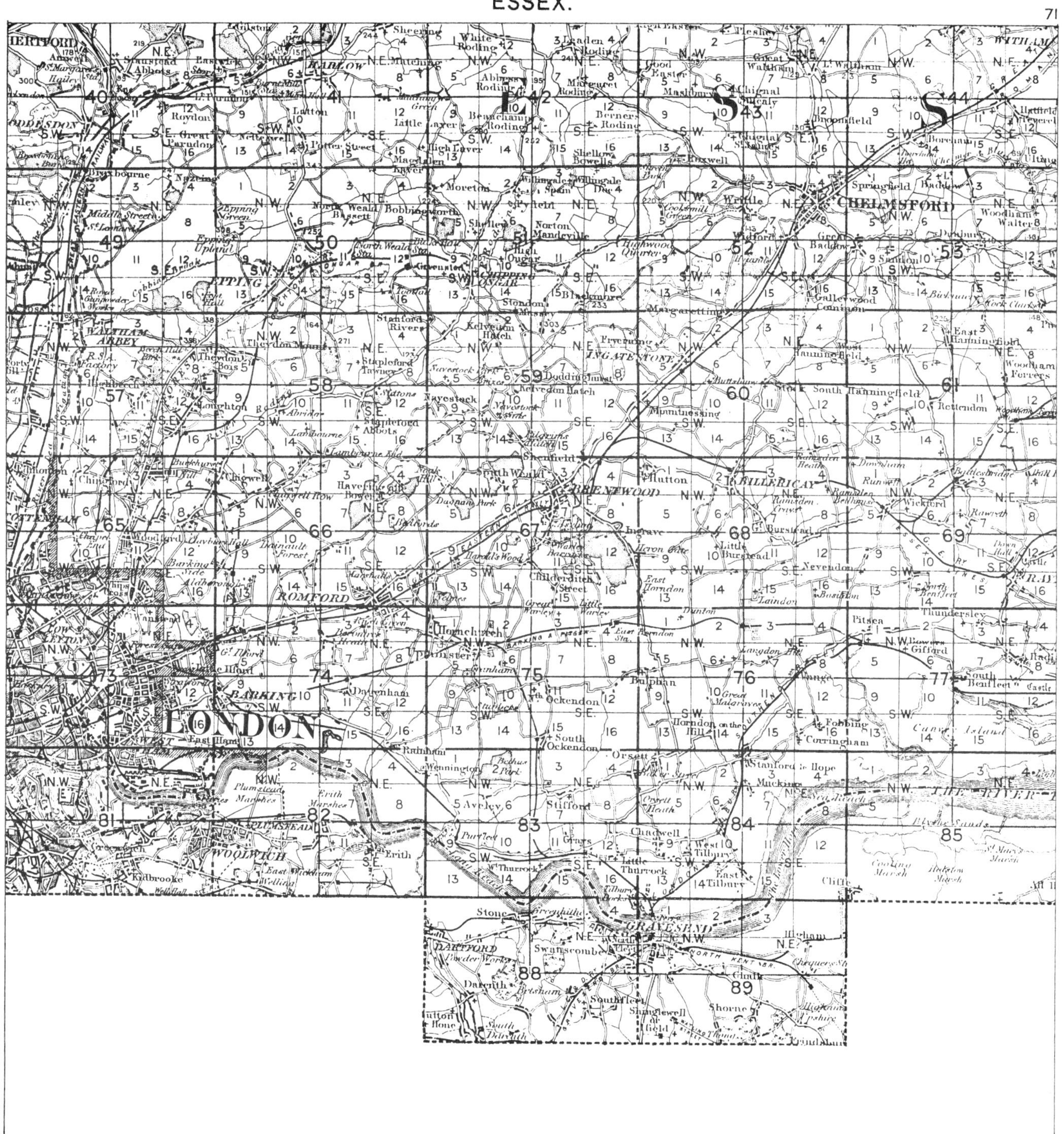

COMBINED SHEETS.

$\frac{1}{2500}$ SCALE.

82. 11	*is published on*	82. 7
84. 12	,,	84. 8

Note—For $\frac{1}{2500}$ scale Maps of the area west of the line marked thus ▨ *see London Index, pages 98 & 99.*

ESSEX.

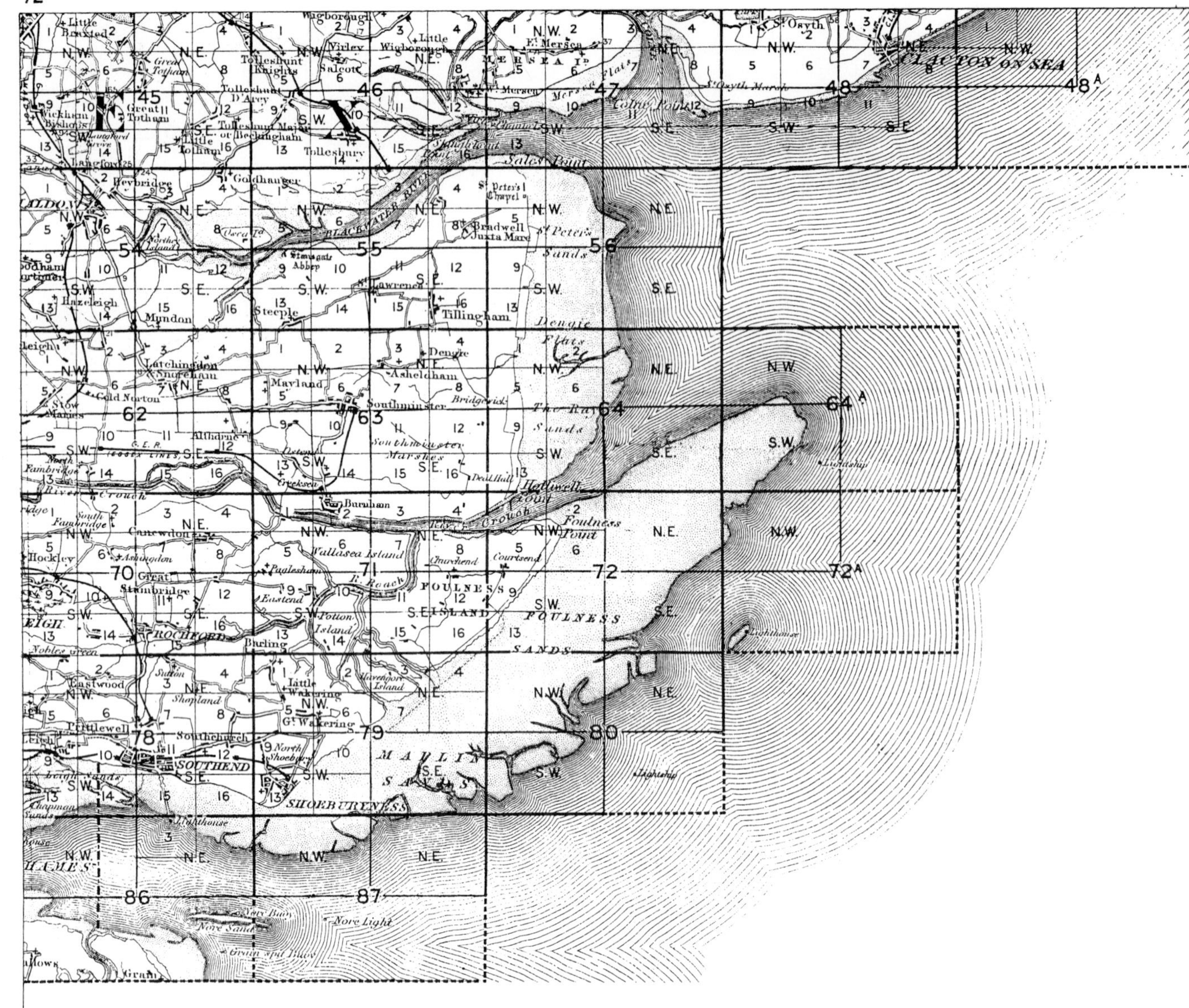

COMBINED SHEETS.

SIX-INCH SCALE.

48 S.E.	*is published on*	48 N.E.
48A N.W.	,,	39 S.W.
64A N.W.	,,	64A S.W.
72A N.W.	,,	72 N.F.

COMBINED SHEETS.

SIX-INCH SCALE.

1 N.E.	*is published on*	1 S.E.
16A N.E.	"	16 N.W.

$\frac{1}{2500}$ SCALE.

1. 7	*is published on*	1. 11
8. 12	"	9. 9
16A. 4	"	16. 1
16A. 8	"	16. 5
20. 1	"	20. 2

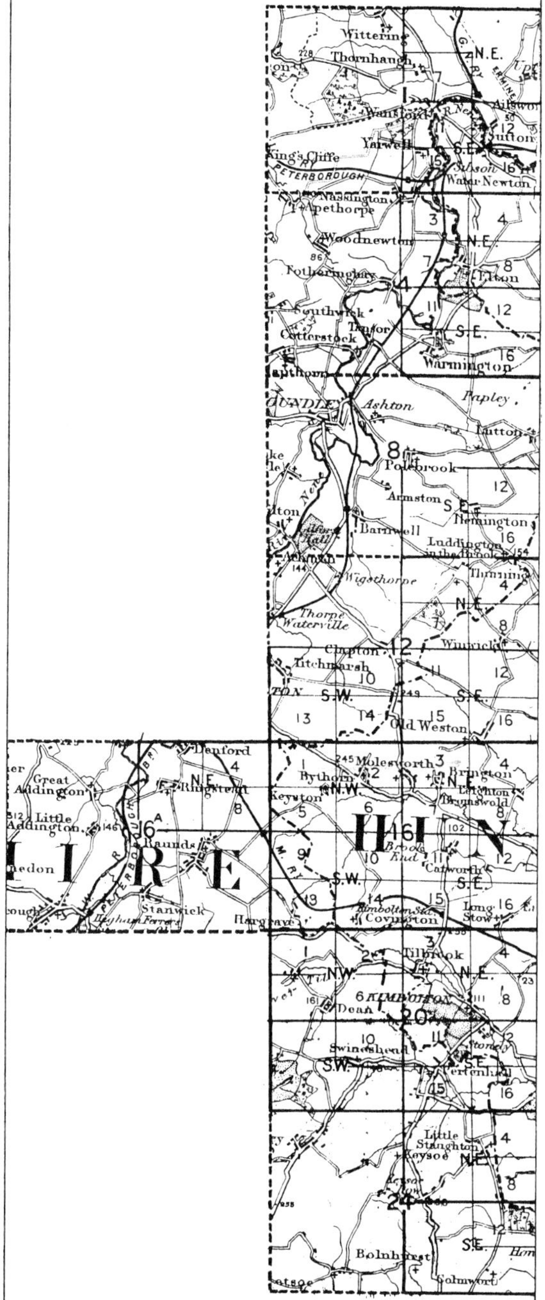

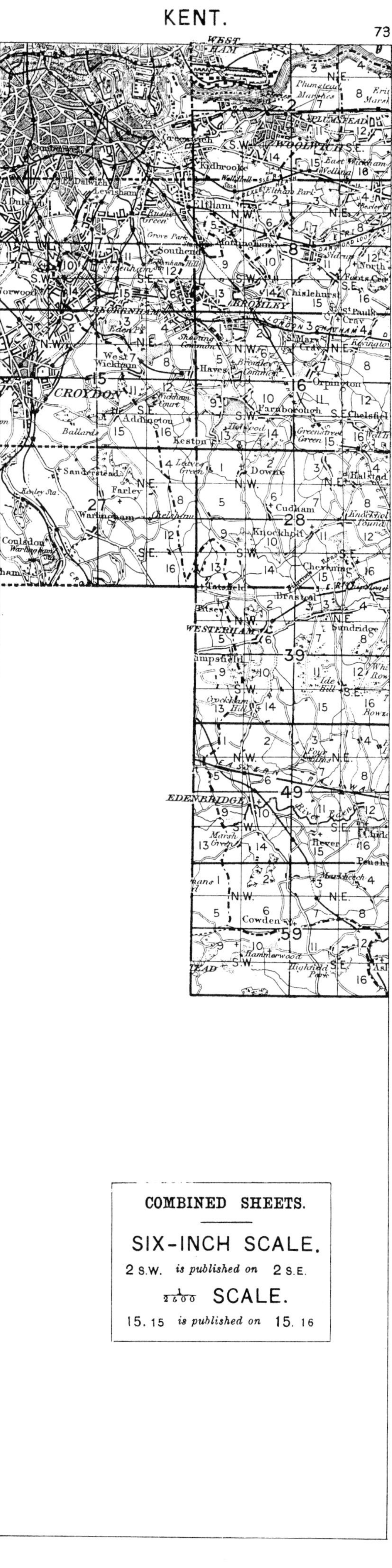

COMBINED SHEETS.

SIX-INCH SCALE.

2 S.W.	*is published on*	2 S.E.

$\frac{1}{2500}$ SCALE.

15. 15	*is published on*	15. 16

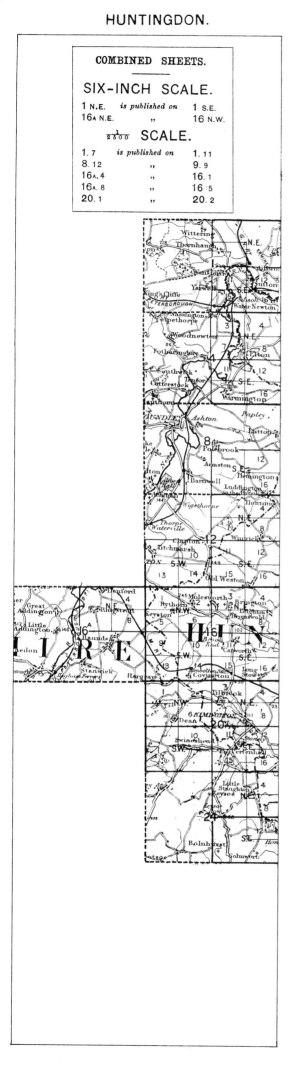

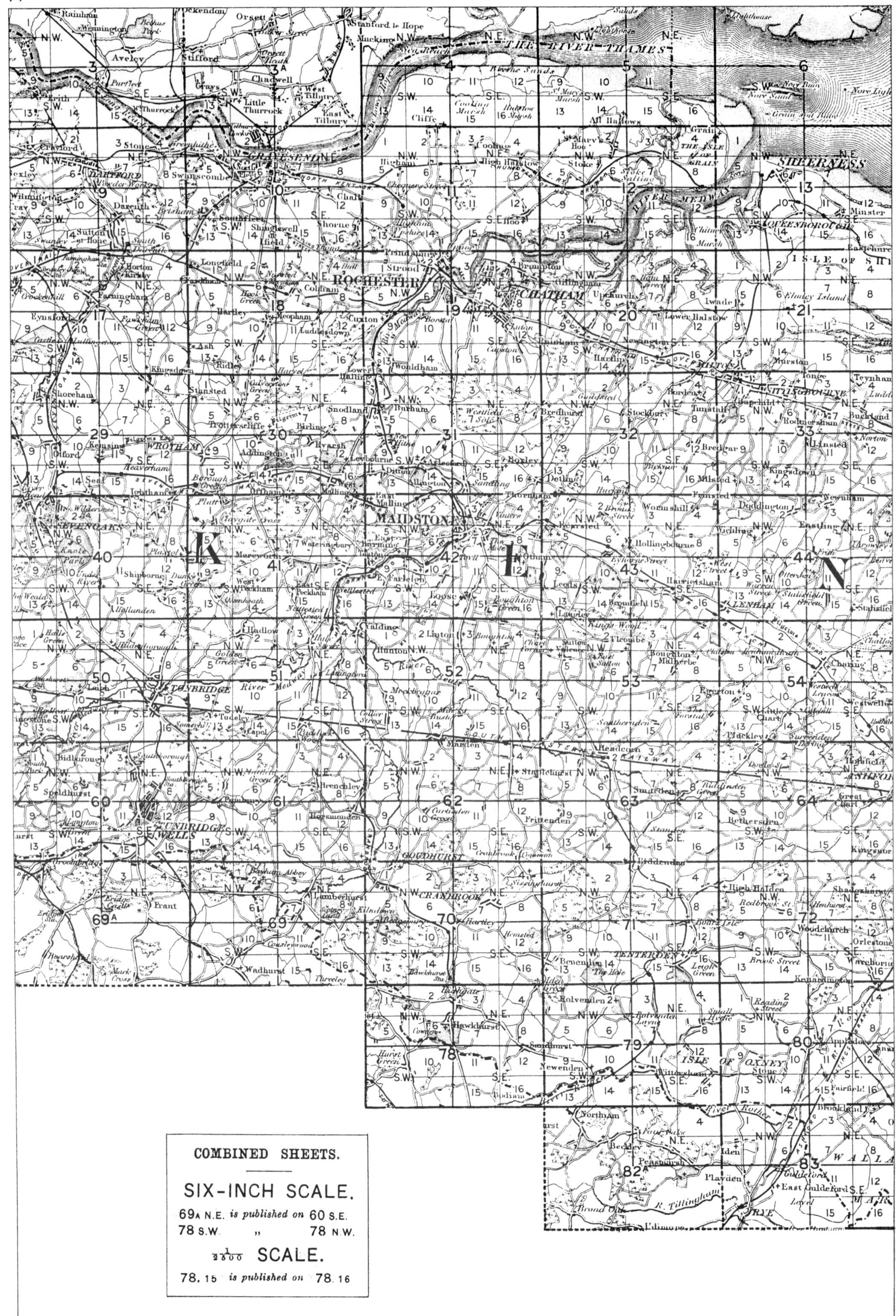
COMBINED SHEETS.
SIX-INCH SCALE.
69A N.E. is published on 60 S.E.
78 S.W. „ 78 N.W.
1/2500 SCALE.
78. 15 is published on 78. 16
K
E
N
ROCHESTER
CHATHAM
MAIDSTONE
GRAVESEND
SHEERNESS
TONBRIDGE
TUNBRIDGE WELLS
SEVENOAKS
CRANBROOK
TENTERDEN
RYE

COMBINED SHEETS.

SIX-INCH SCALE.

23 N.W.	*is published on*	23 S.W.
48A S.W.	,,	48 S.E.
58A N.W.	,,	58 N.E.
58A S.W.	,,	58 S.E.
68A N.W.	,,	68 N.E.
75 S.E.	,,	75 N.E.
86 S.E.	,,	86 N.E.

$\frac{1}{2500}$ SCALE.

23. 7	*is published on*	23. 11
24. 5	,,	24. 6
25. 2	,,	25. 6
26. 2	,,	26. 6
48A. 13	,,	48. 16
58A. 5	,,	58. 8
68. 15	,,	68. 14
68A. 1	,,	68. 4
75. 8	,,	75. 4
82. 13	,,	81. 16
86. 12	,,	86. 11

COMBINED SHEETS.

BEDFORD.

SIX-INCH SCALE.

5 N.E. *is published on* 5 N.W.

5 S.E. „ 5 S.W.

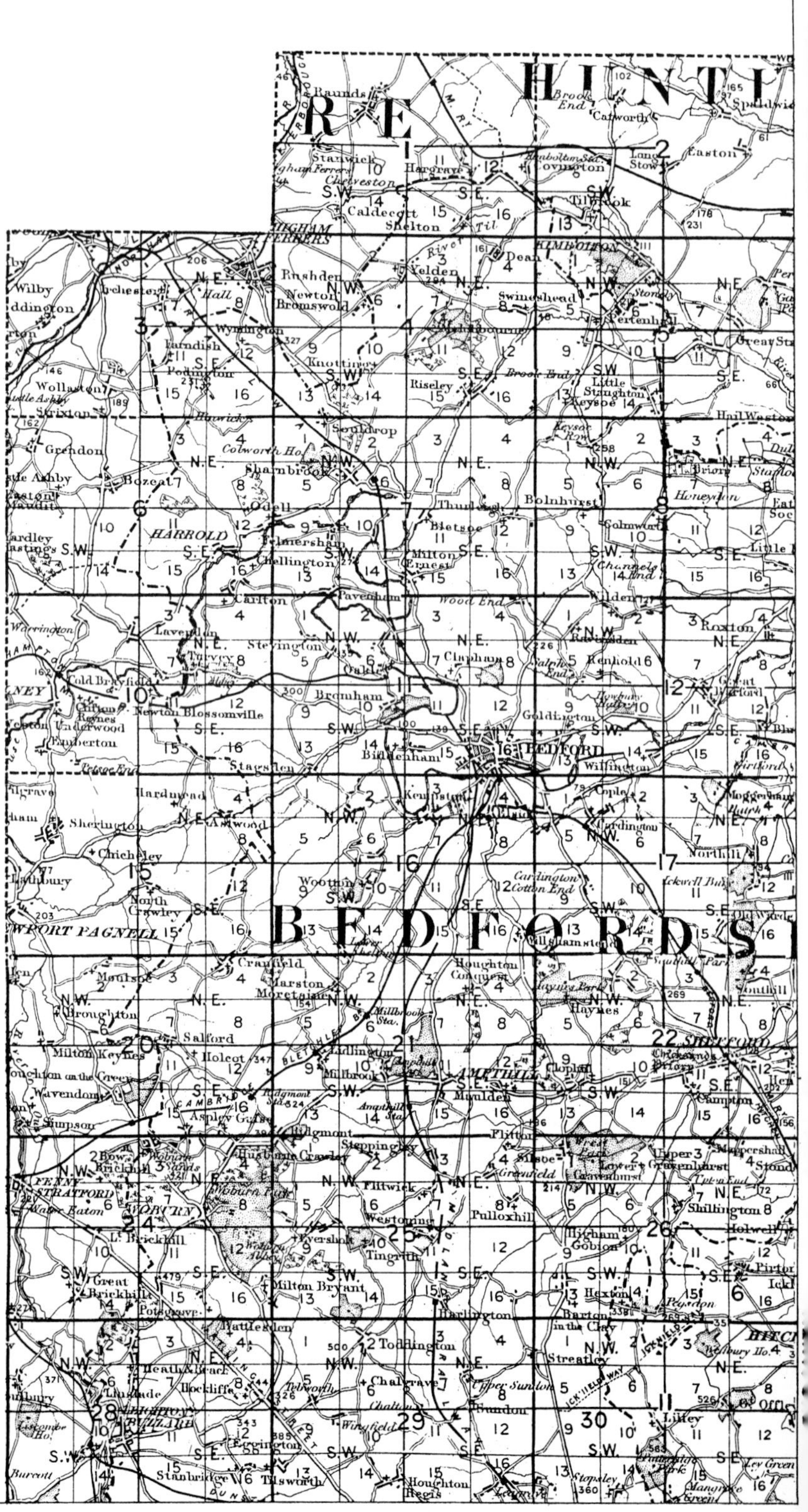

COMBINED SHEETS.

HERTFORD.

SIX-INCH SCALE.

1 S.E.	*is published on*	2 S.W.
15 N.W.	„	14 N.E.
15 S.W.	„	14 S.E.

Huntingdonshire (Det.) is published on the $\frac{1}{2500}$ scale sheets 13.—*5, 6, 9, 10, 11, & 14, and Six-inch scale sheets* 13 N.W., S.W., & S.E., *of Bedfordshire.*

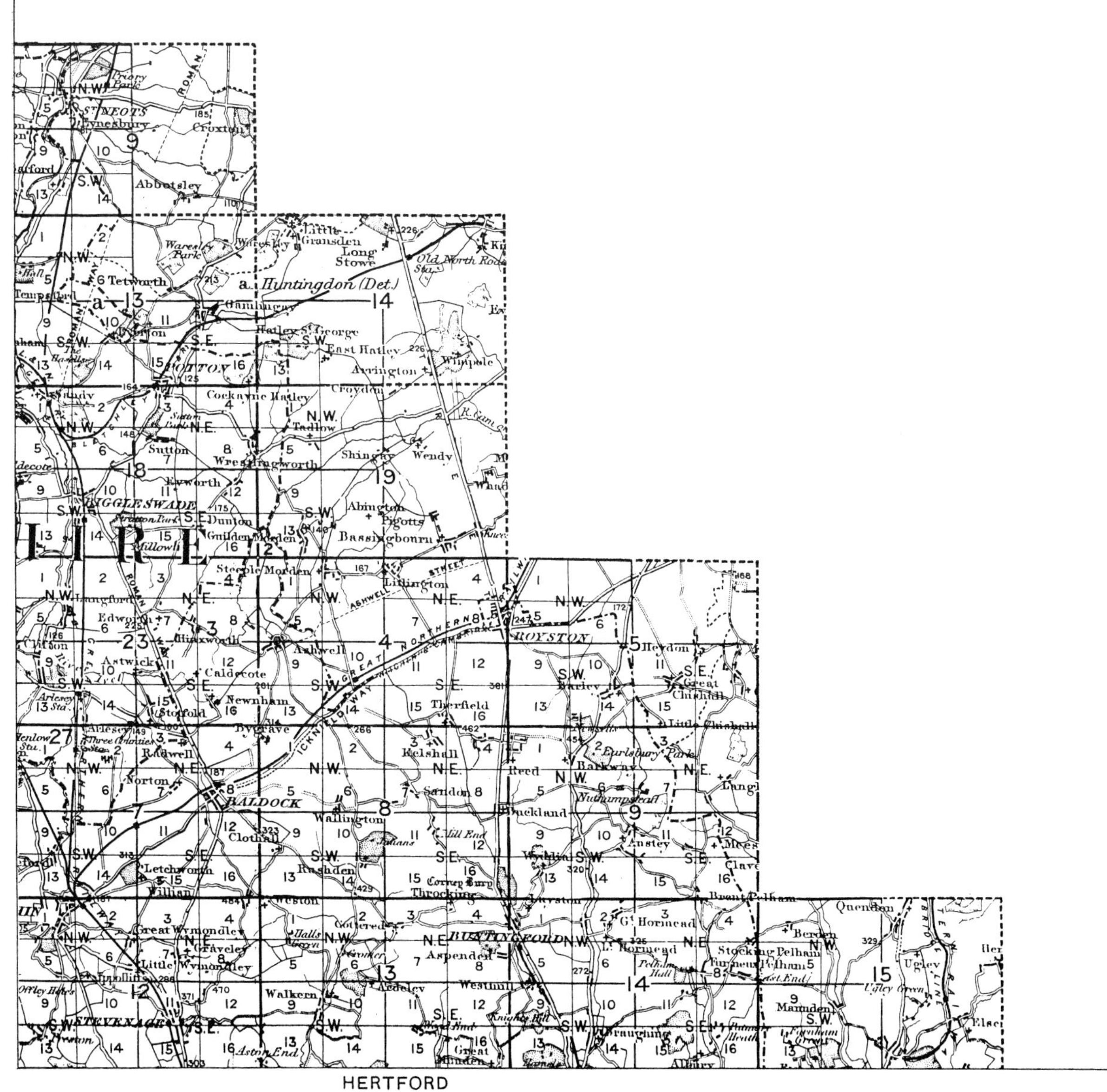

COMBINED SHEETS.

BEDFORD.

SIX-INCH SCALE.

31 S.E. *is published on* 31 N.E.

HERTFORD.

SIX-INCH SCALE.

19 N.W. *is published on* 11 S.W.

$\frac{1}{2500}$ SCALE.

16. 12 *is published on* 17. 9
17. 14 " 17. 13
32. 11 " 32. 12

MIDDLESEX.

$\frac{1}{2500}$ SCALE.

25. 10 *is published on* 25. 6

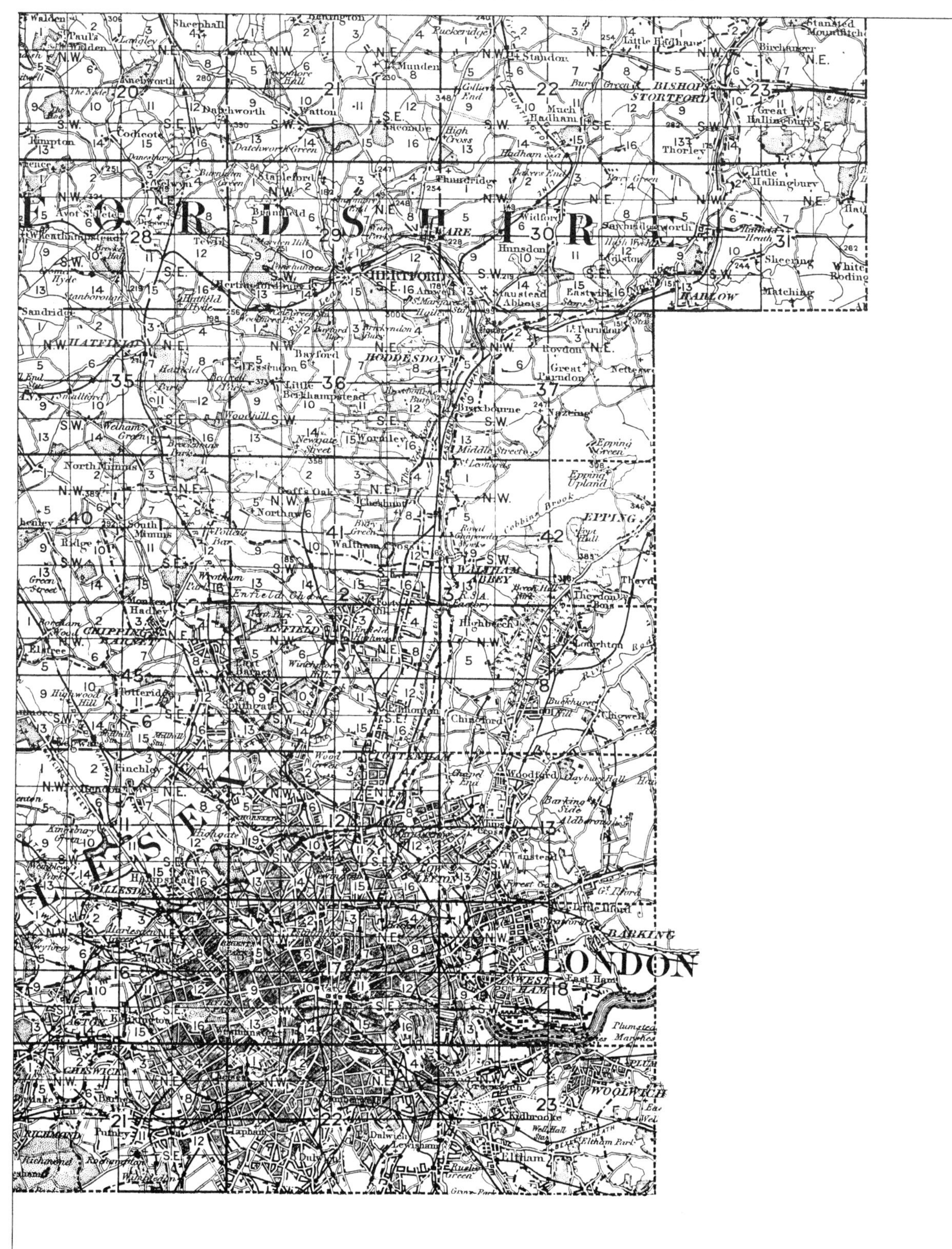

COMBINED SHEETS.

HERTFORD.

SIX-INCH SCALE.

31 N.E. *is published on* 31 N.W.

COMBINED SHEETS.

SIX-INCH SCALE.

5 S.E.	*is published on*	5 S.W.
15 N.W.	,,	15 N.E.
44 N.W.	,,	44 N.E.

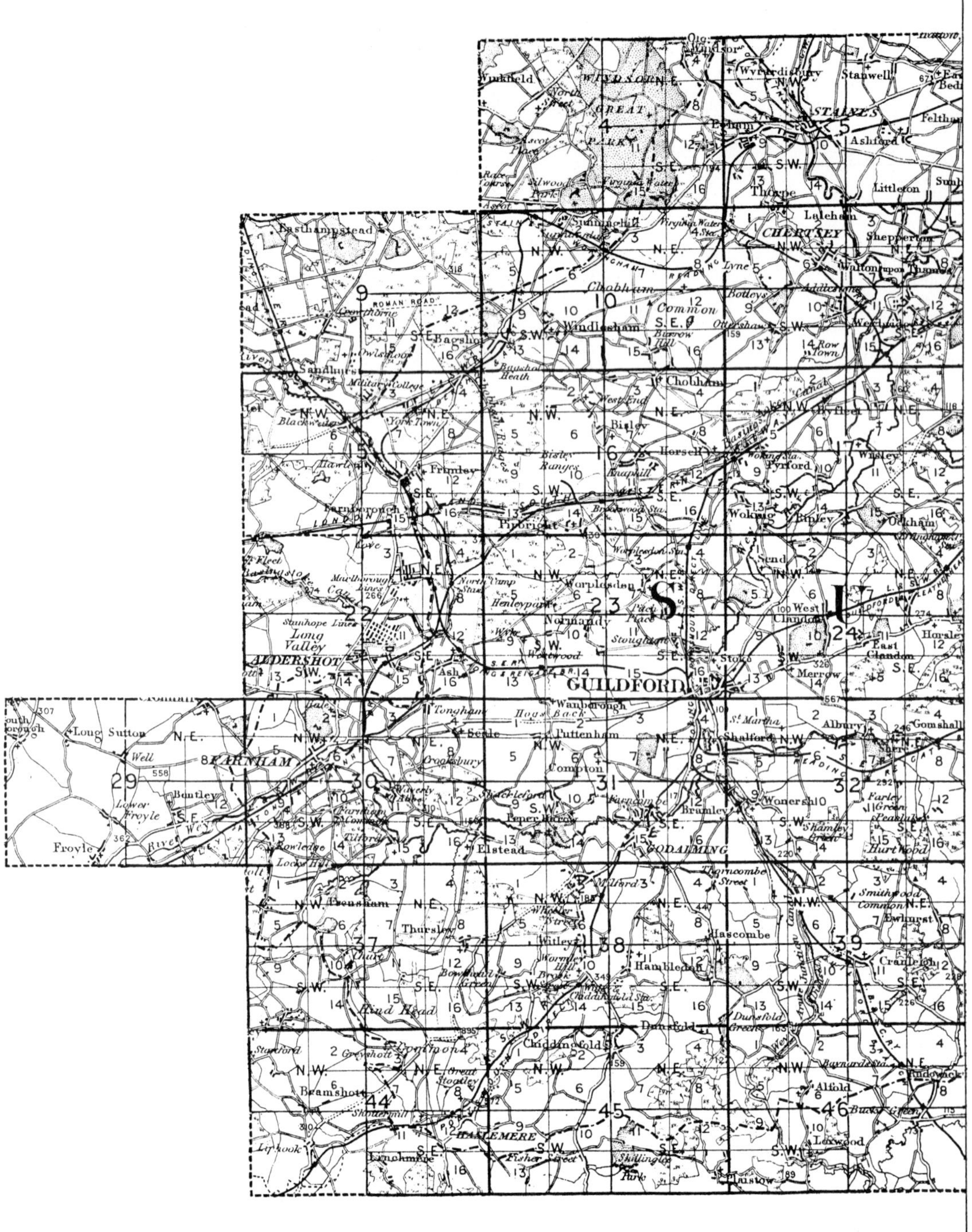

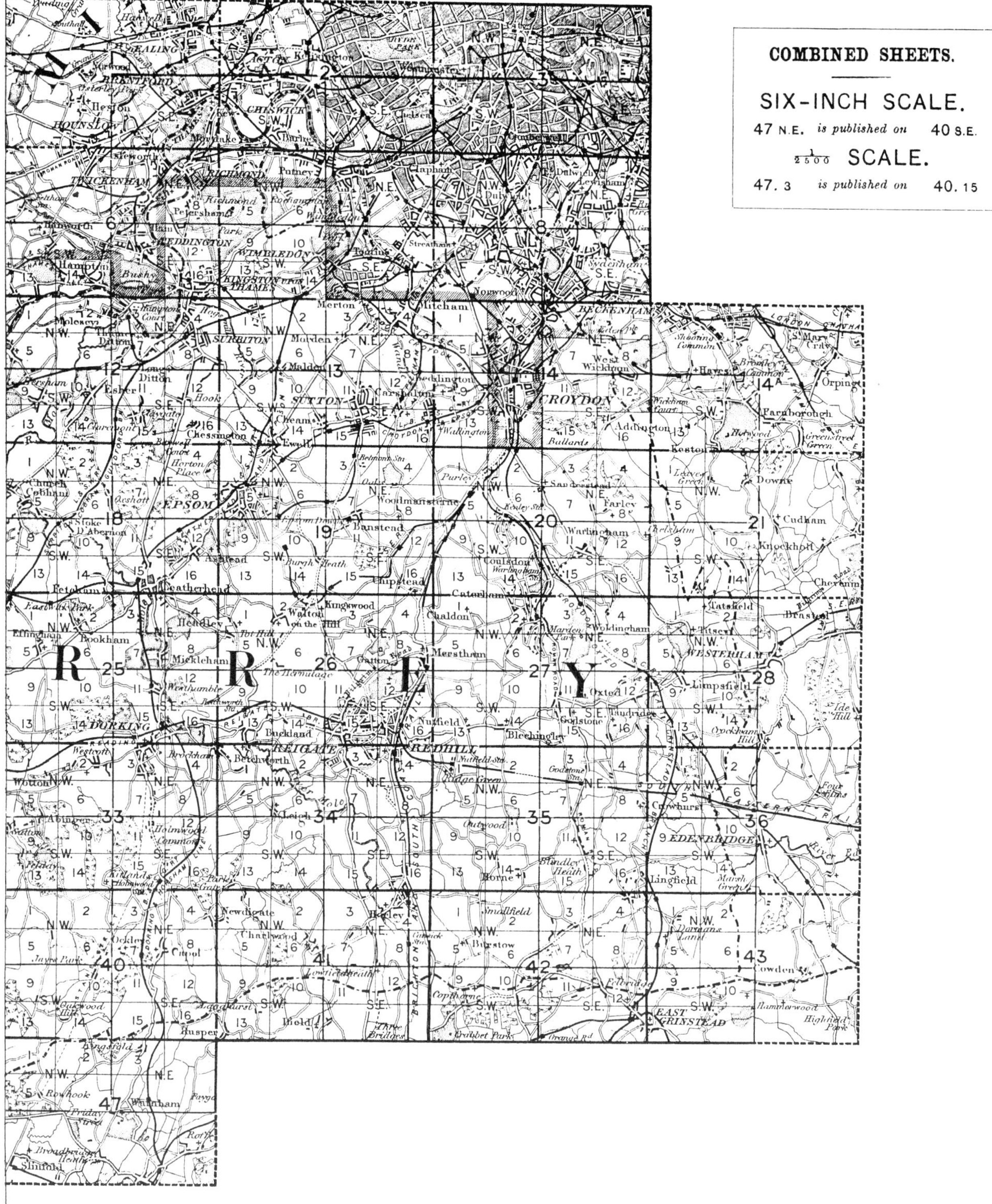

Note.—For $\frac{1}{2500}$ scale Maps north of the line marked thus [hatched line] see London Index, pages 98 & 99.

COMBINED SHEETS.

SIX-INCH SCALE.

74 S.W. *is published on* 74 N.W.

$\frac{1}{2500}$ SCALE.

33. 2	*is published on*	33. 3
72. 16	„	72. 11
73. 16	„	73. 12

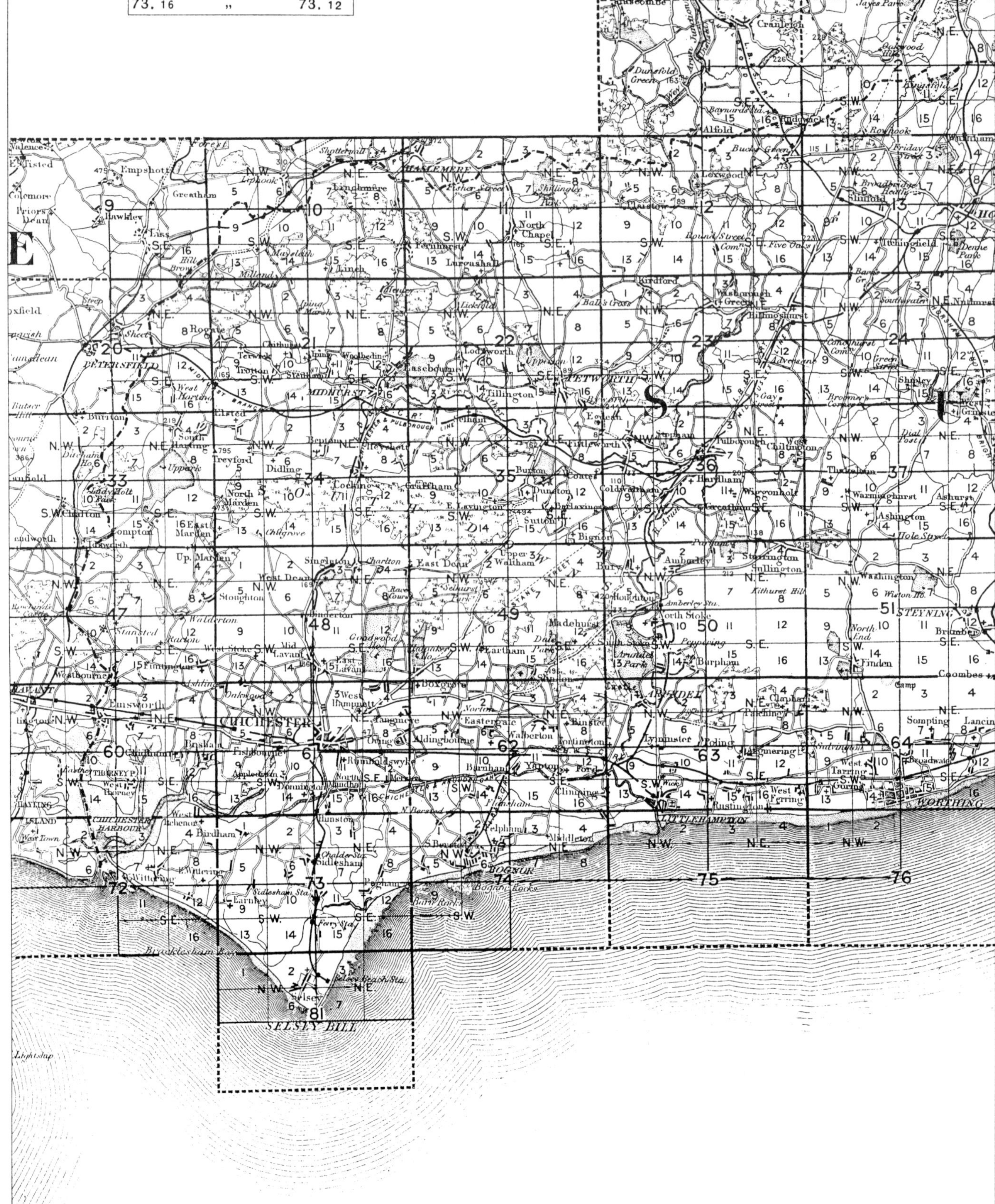

COMBINED SHEETS.

SIX-INCH SCALE.

6 N.E. *is published on* 6 S.E.

$\frac{1}{2500}$ SCALE.

3. 4	*is published on*	3. 3
77. 3	„	77. 4
78. 11	„	78. 7
80. 4	„	80. 3

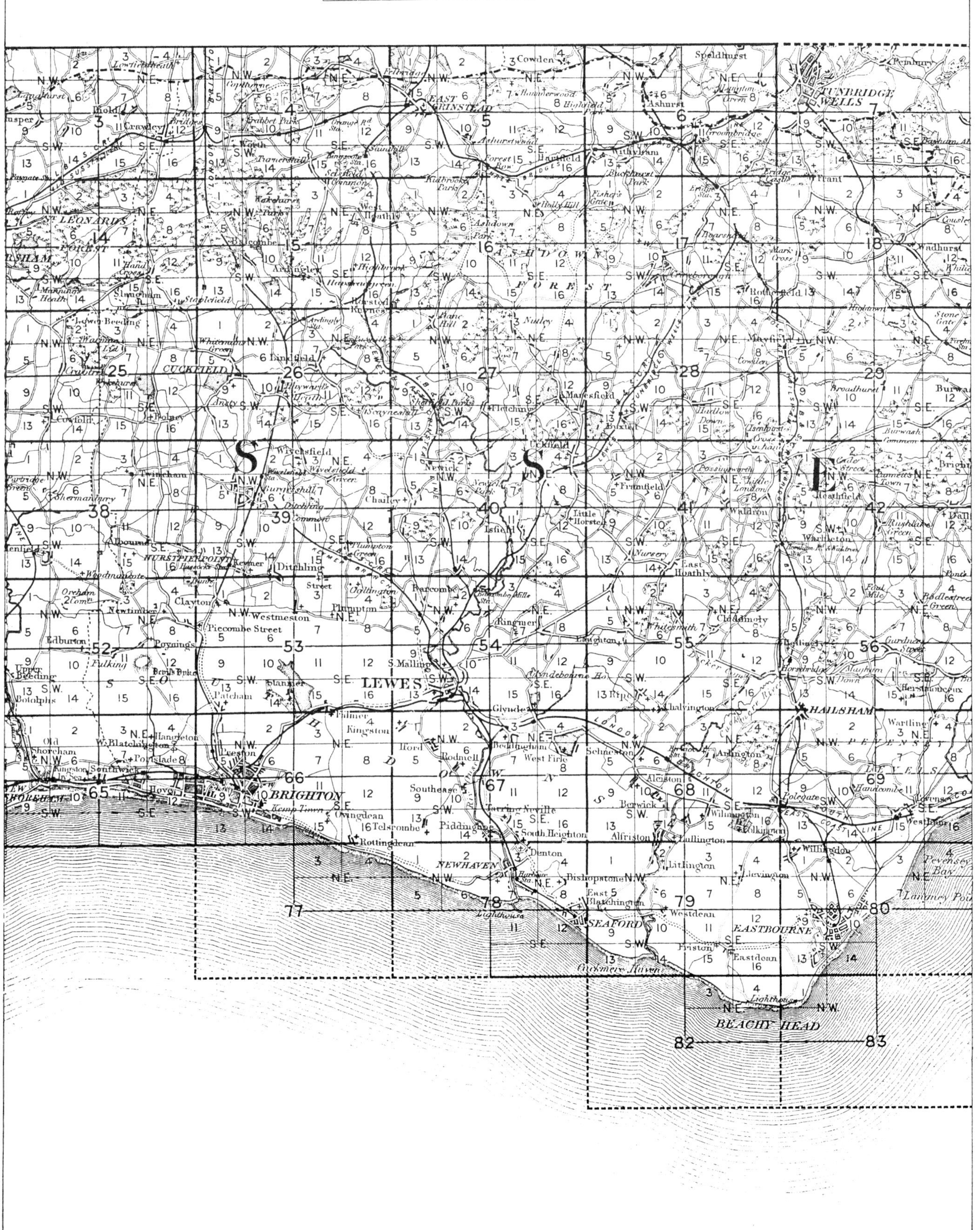

COMBINED SHEETS.

SIX-INCH SCALE.

46 S.E.	*is published on*	46 S.W.
70 S.E.	,,	70 N.E.

$\frac{1}{2500}$ SCALE.

59. 10	*is published on*	59. 9
70. 11	,,	70. 10
71. 4	,,	71. 3

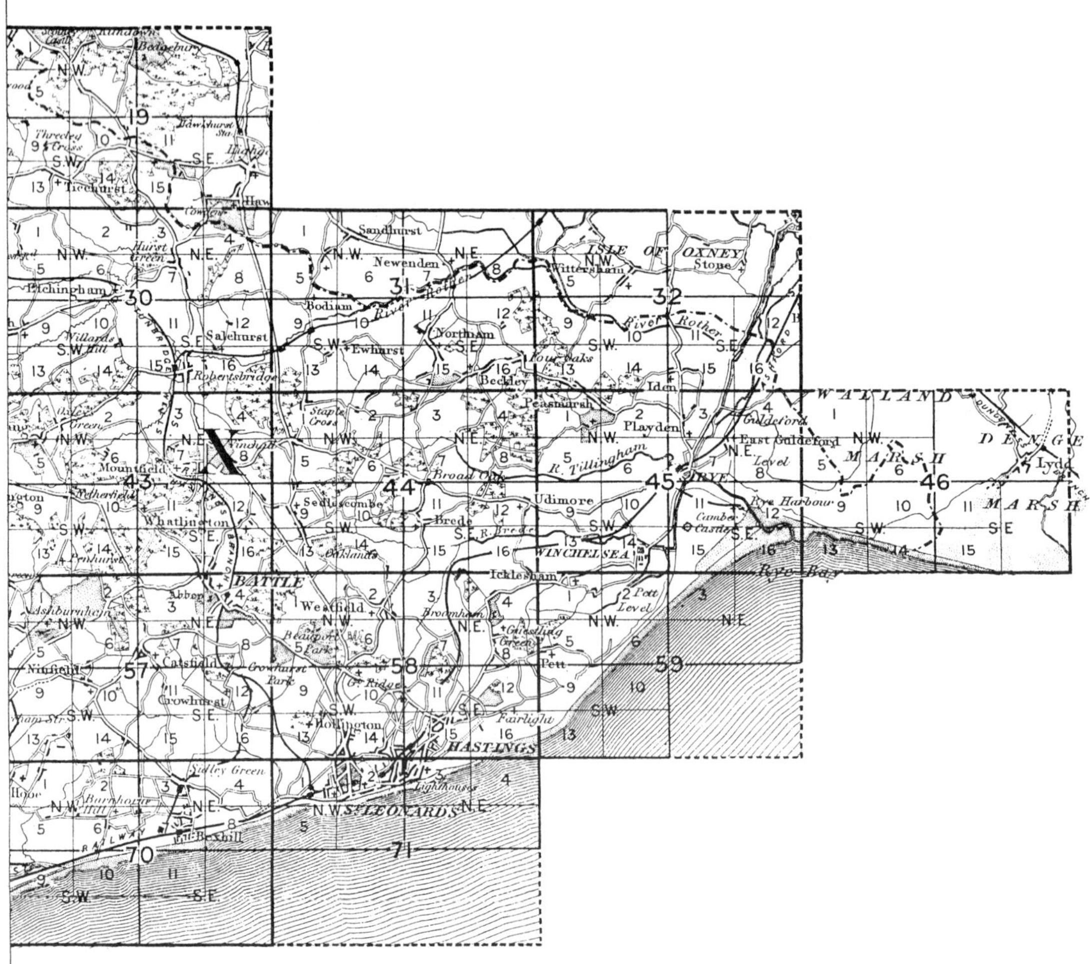

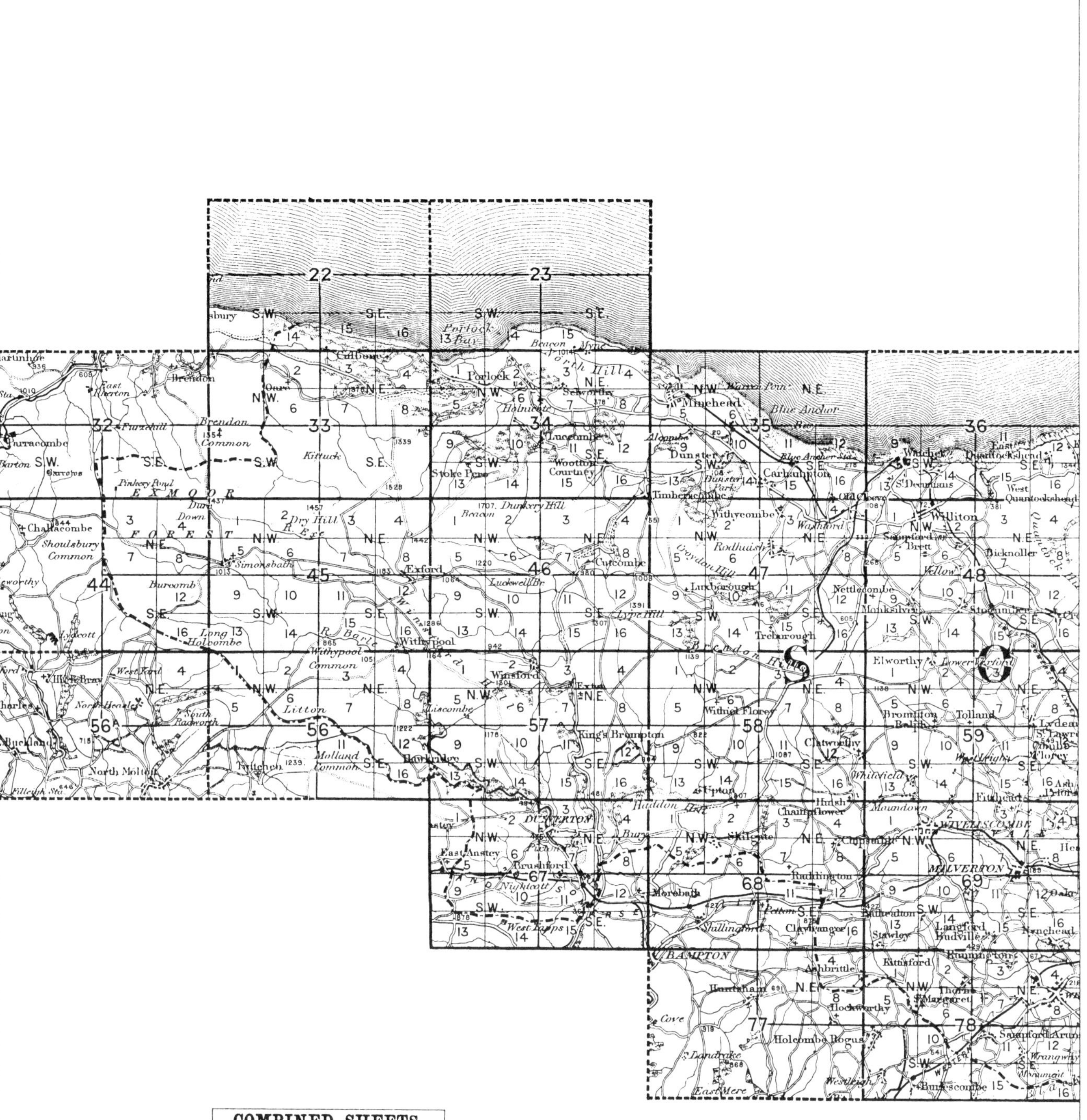

COMBINED SHEETS.

SIX-INCH SCALE.

35 N.E.	*is published on*	35 N.W.
56A N.E.	,,	44 S.E.

$\frac{1}{2500}$ SCALE.

23. 13	*is published on*	22. 16
56A. 4	,,	44. 16
67. 13	,,	67. 9

COMBINED SHEETS.

$\frac{1}{2500}$ SCALE.

15. 3	*is published on*	15. 4
2. 3	,,	GLO'STER 71. 1

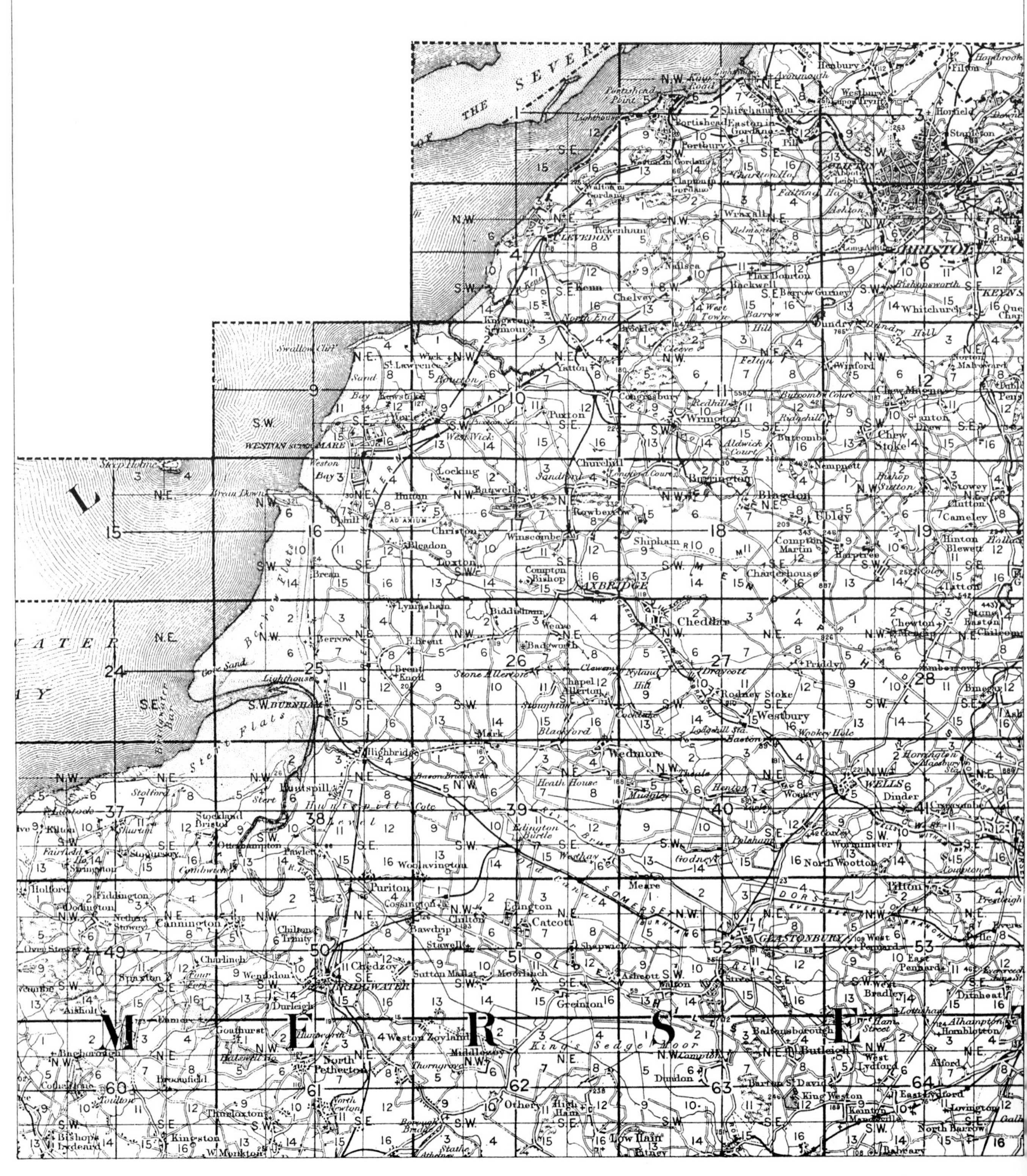

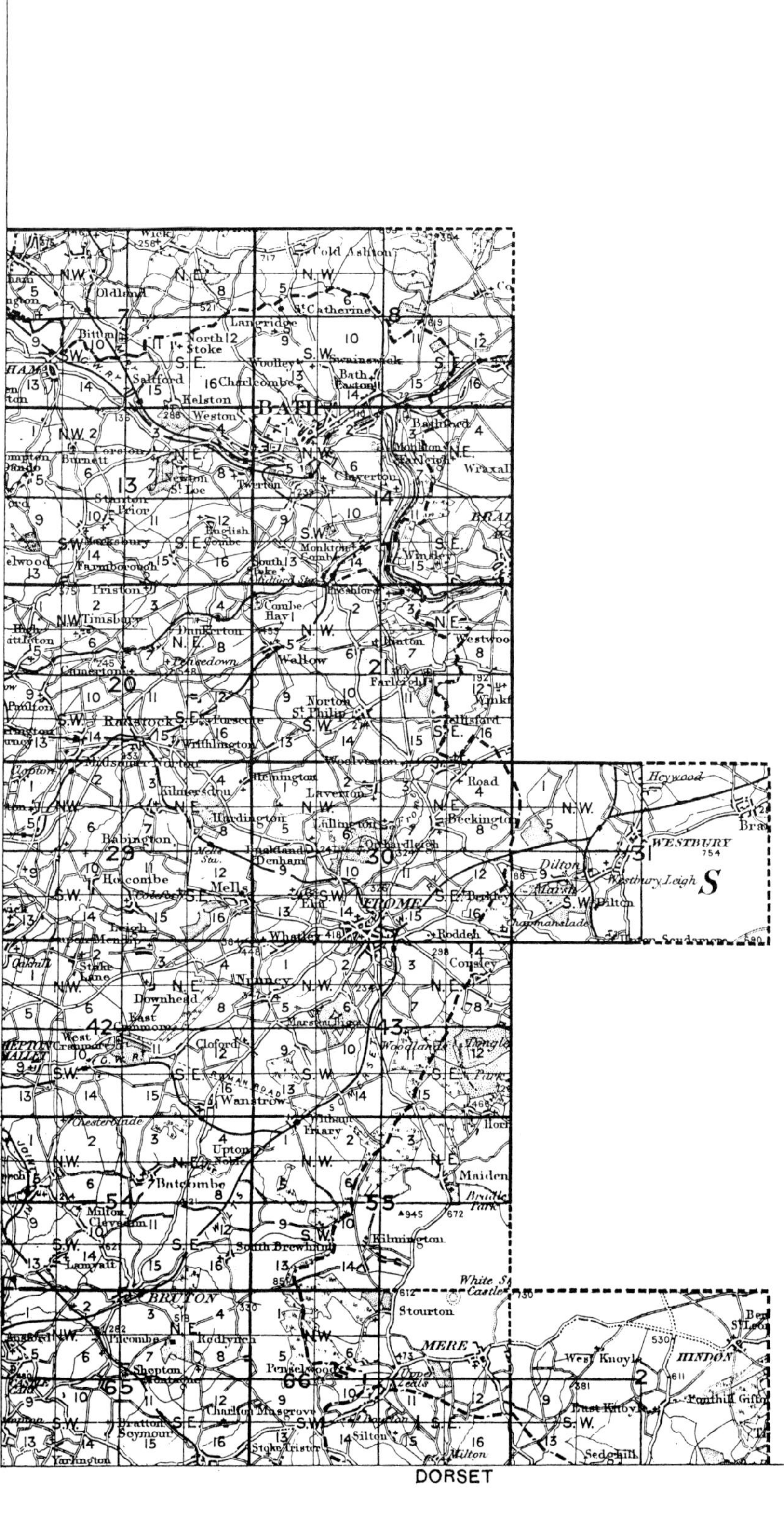
Cold Ashton
St Catherine
Langridge
North Stoke
Woolley
Swainswick
Bitton
Saltford
Charlcombe
Bath Easton
Kelston
Weston
BATH
Batheaston
Corston
Burnett
Newton St. Loe
Twerton
Claverton
Wraxall
Stanton Prior
English Combe
Monkton Combe
Winsley
Farmborough
South Stoke
Priston
Combe Hay
Timsbury
Dunkerton
Wellow
Camerton
Norton St. Philip
Farleigh
Radstock
Writhlington
Woolverton
Road
Hemington
Laverton
Kilmersdon
Hardington
Lullington
Beckington
Babington
Buckland Denham
Orchardleigh
Dilton
WESTBURY
Westbury Leigh
Holcombe
Mells
FROME
Berkley
Chapmanslade
Leigh
Whatley
Rodden
Heywood
Stoke Lane
Nunney
Downhead
East Cranmore
West Cranmore
Marston Bigot
Woodlands
Cloford
Wanstrow
Chesterblade
Trudoxhill
Upton Noble
Batcombe
Maiden Bradley
Milton Clevedon
South Brewham
Kilmington
Lamyatt
Stourton
BRUTON
Pitcombe
Redlynch
MERE
West Knoyle
HINDON
Shepton Montague
Penselwood
Charlton Musgrove
East Knoyle
Fonthill Gifford
Bratton Seymour
Stoke Trister
Silton
Milton
Sedgehill
Yarlington
SOMERSET
DORSET

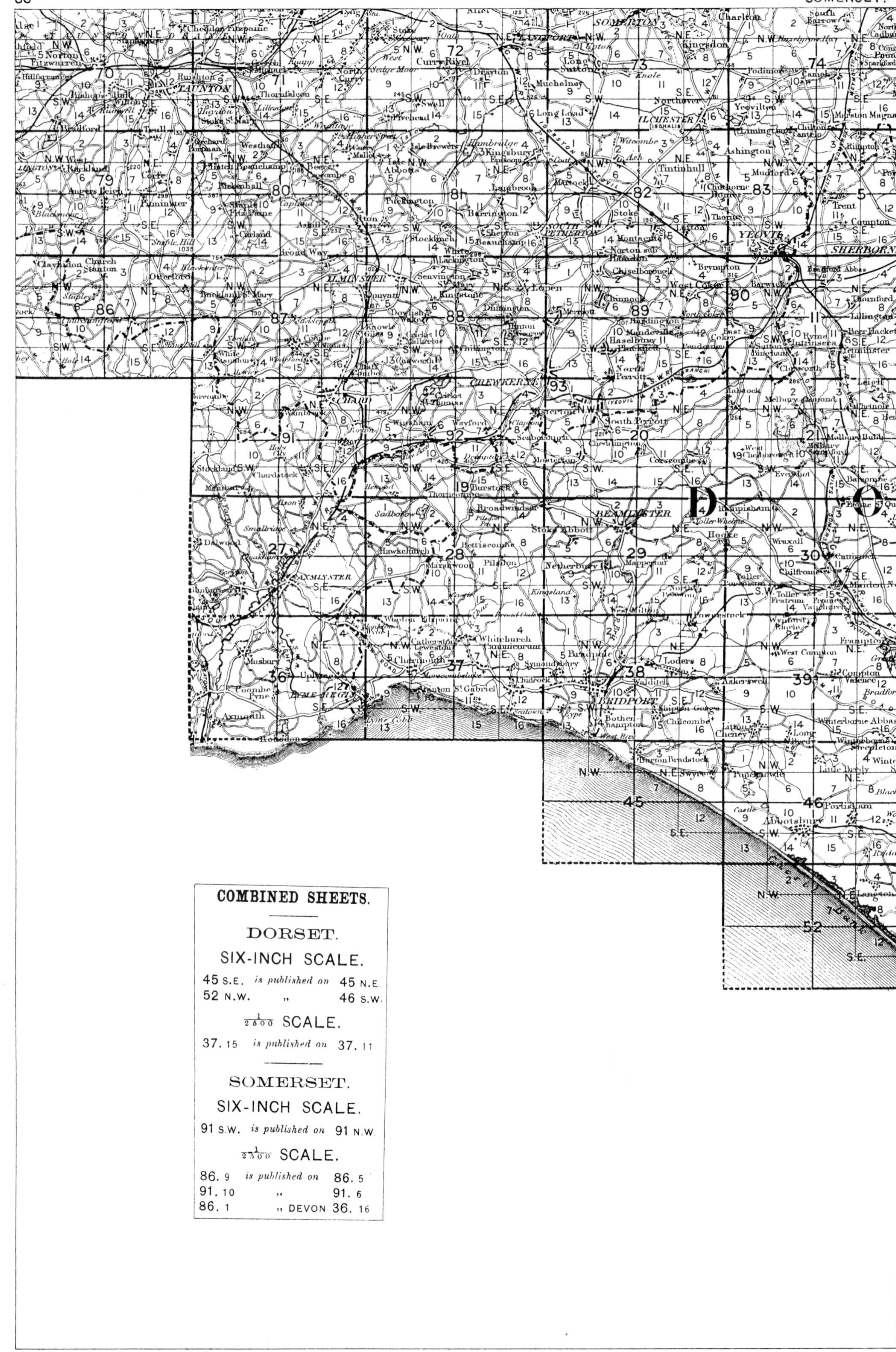
TAUNTON
ILMINSTER
CHARD
CREWKERNE
YEOVIL
SHERBORNE
ILCHESTER
SOMERTON
LANGPORT
SOUTH PETHERTON
AXMINSTER
LYME REGIS
BRIDPORT
BEAMINSTER
D
O
COMBINED SHEETS.
DORSET.
SIX-INCH SCALE.
45 S.E. is published on 45 N.E.
52 N.W. " 46 S.W.
$\frac{1}{2500}$ SCALE.
37. 15 is published on 37. 11
SOMERSET.
SIX-INCH SCALE.
91 S.W. is published on 91 N.W.
$\frac{1}{2500}$ SCALE.
86. 9 is published on 86. 5
91. 10 " 91. 6
86. 1 " DEVON 36. 16

17

COMBINED SHEETS.

DORSET.

SIX-INCH SCALE.

9 N.W.	*is published on*	9 S.W.
51 N.E.	,,	51 N.W.
54 S.E.	,,	54 N.E.
60 N.W.	,,	60 N.E.

$\frac{1}{2500}$ SCALE.

9. 6	*is published on*	9. 10
44. 4	,,	44. 3
57. 10	,,	57. 9
58. 1	,,	58. 2
58. 4	,,	58. 8
60. 2 & 6	,,	60. 7

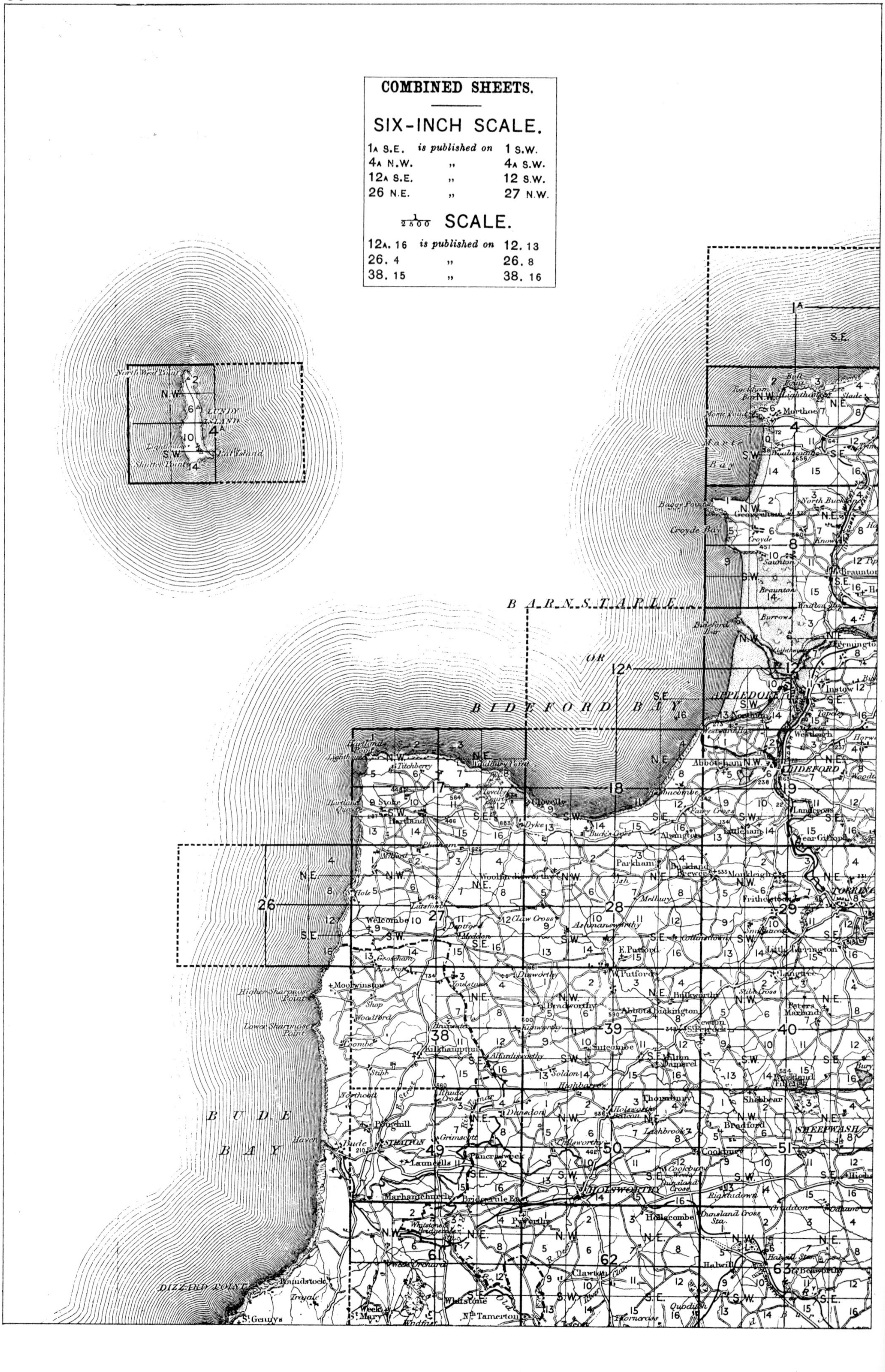

COMBINED SHEETS.

SIX-INCH SCALE.

1A S.E.	*is published on*	1 S.W.
4A N.W.	„	4A S.W.
12A S.E.	„	12 S.W.
26 N.E.	„	27 N.W.

$\frac{1}{2500}$ SCALE.

12A. 16	*is published on*	12. 13
26. 4	„	26. 8
38. 15	„	38. 16

COMBINED SHEETS.

SIX-INCH SCALE.

3 N.W. *is published on* 3 S.W.
3 N.E. „ 3 S.E.

$\frac{1}{2500}$ SCALE.

16.1 *is published on* 16.5

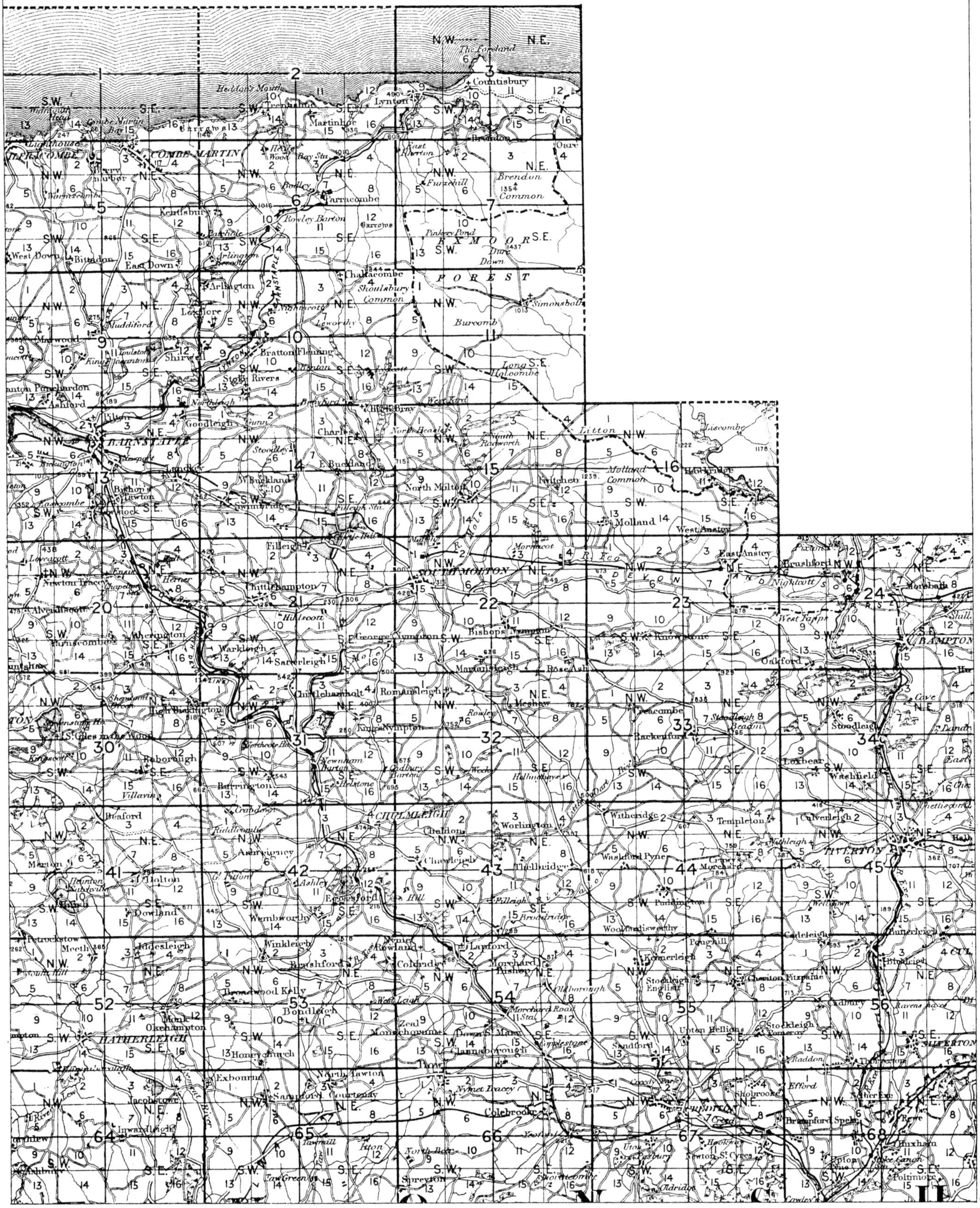

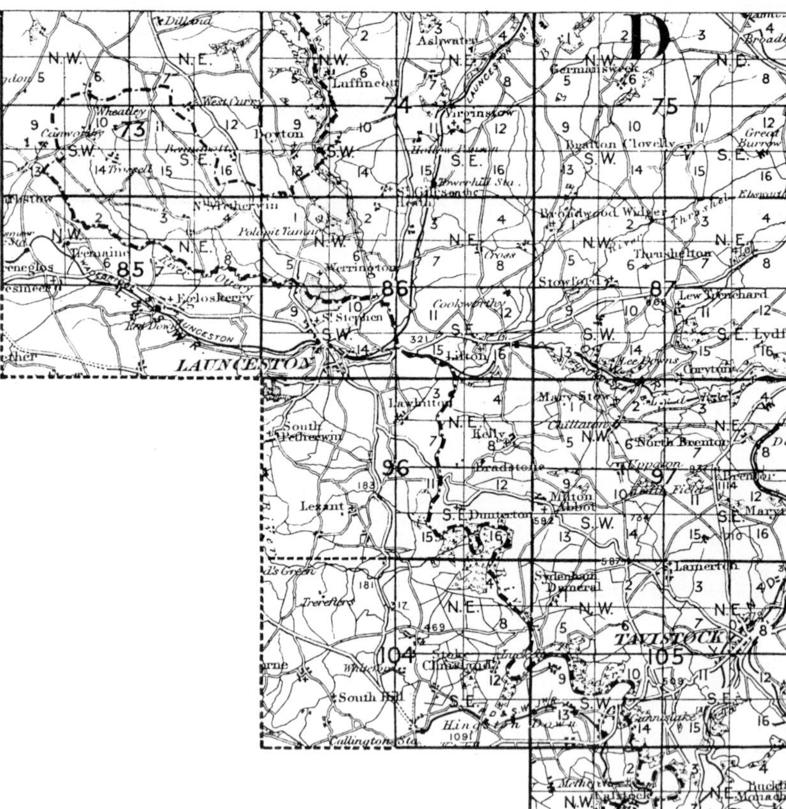

COMBINED SHEETS.

SIX-INCH SCALE.

123 S.W. *is published on* 123 S.E.

$\frac{1}{2500}$ SCALE.

73. 5	*is published on*	73. 6
85. 6	,,	85. 7
111. 5	,,	111. 6
123. 15	,,	123. 16
129. 3	,,	129. 4

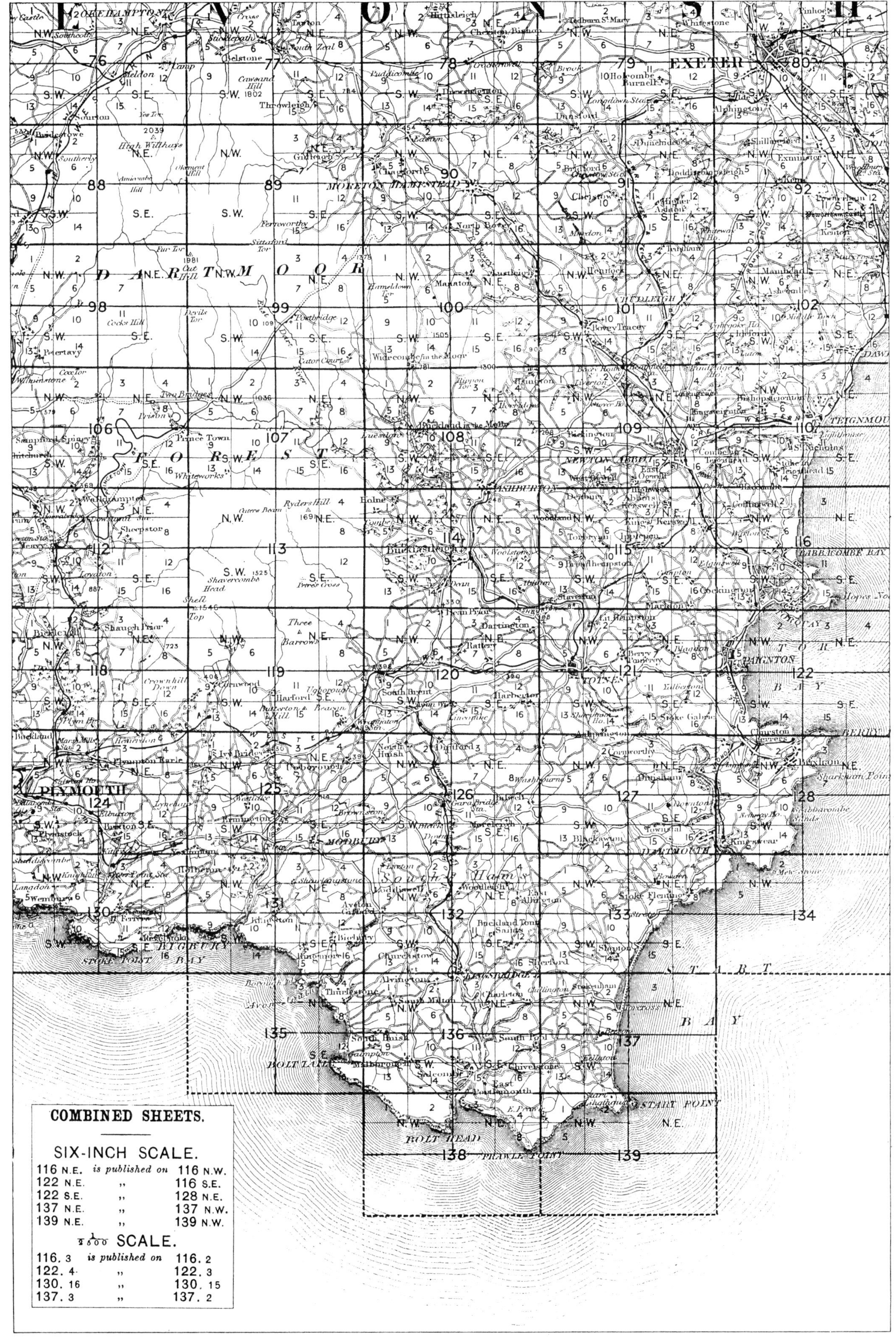
OKEHAMPTON
EXETER
MORETON HAMPSTEAD
DARTMOOR
FOREST
CHUDLEIGH
TEIGNMOUTH
NEWTON ABBOT
ASHBURTON
TOTNES
PAIGNTON
TOR BAY
PLYMOUTH
MODBURY
DARTMOUTH
KINGSBRIDGE
START BAY
BIGBURY BAY
BOLT HEAD
BOLT TAIL
PRAWLE POINT
START POINT
Prince Town
Tavistock
Buckfastleigh
Dartington
Ivy Bridge
Salcombe
Bovey Tracey
Exminster
Dunsford
Chagford
Widecombe in the Moor
Postbridge
Two Bridges
Sheepstor
Shaugh Prior
Cornwood
Harford
South Brent
Kingsteignton
Bishopsteignton
Stoke in Teignhead
Cockington
Marldon
Berry Pomeroy
Harberton
Churston Ferrers
Brixham
Kingswear
Stoke Fleming
Blackawton
Slapton
Chivelstone
Thurlestone
South Milton
Malborough
Aveton Gifford
Churchstow
Kingston
Yealmpton
Plympton Earle
Plymstock
Wembury
High Willhays
Hameldown Tor
Three Barrows
Shell Top
78
79
80
88
89
90
91
92
98
99
100
101
102
106
107
108
109
110
112
113
114
115
116
118
119
120
121
122
124
125
126
127
128
130
131
132
133
134
135
136
137
138
139
COMBINED SHEETS.
SIX-INCH SCALE.
116 N.E. is published on 116 N.W.
122 N.E. ,, 116 S.E.
122 S.E. ,, 128 N.E.
137 N.E. ,, 137 N.W.
139 N.E. ,, 139 N.W.
1/2500 SCALE.
116. 3 is published on 116. 2
122. 4 ,, 122. 3
130. 16 ,, 130. 15
137. 3 ,, 137. 2

COMBINED SHEETS.

SIX-INCH SCALE.

25 S.E.	*is published on*	35 N.E.
84 S E.	,,	84 N.E.
95 N.W.	,,	83 S.W.
95 N.E.	,,	83 S.E.
103 S.W.	,,	103 N.W.
103A N.W.	,,	103 N.E.

$\frac{1}{2500}$ SCALE.

48. 2	*is published on*	48. 3
103A. 1	,,	103. 4

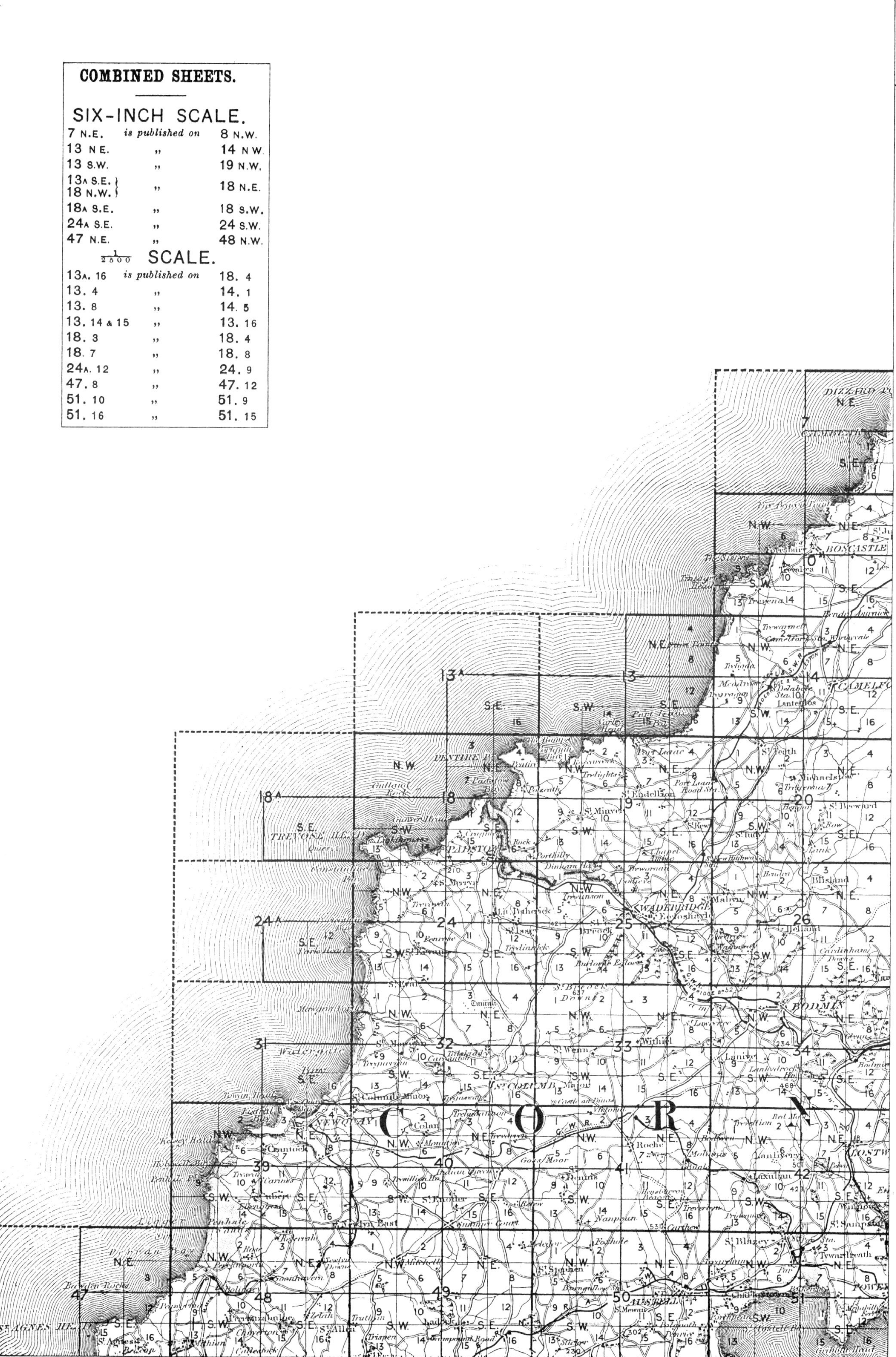

COMBINED SHEETS.

SIX-INCH SCALE.

7 N.E.	*is published on*	8 N.W.
13 N.E.	„	14 N.W.
13 S.W.	„	19 N.W.
13A S.E. } 18 N.W. }	„	18 N.E.
18A S.E.	„	18 S.W.
24A S.E.	„	24 S.W.
47 N.E.	„	48 N.W.

$\frac{1}{2500}$ SCALE.

13A. 16	*is published on*	18. 4
13. 4	„	14. 1
13. 8	„	14. 5
13. 14 & 15	„	13. 16
18. 3	„	18. 4
18. 7	„	18. 8
24A. 12	„	24. 9
47. 8	„	47. 12
51. 10	„	51. 9
51. 16	„	51. 15

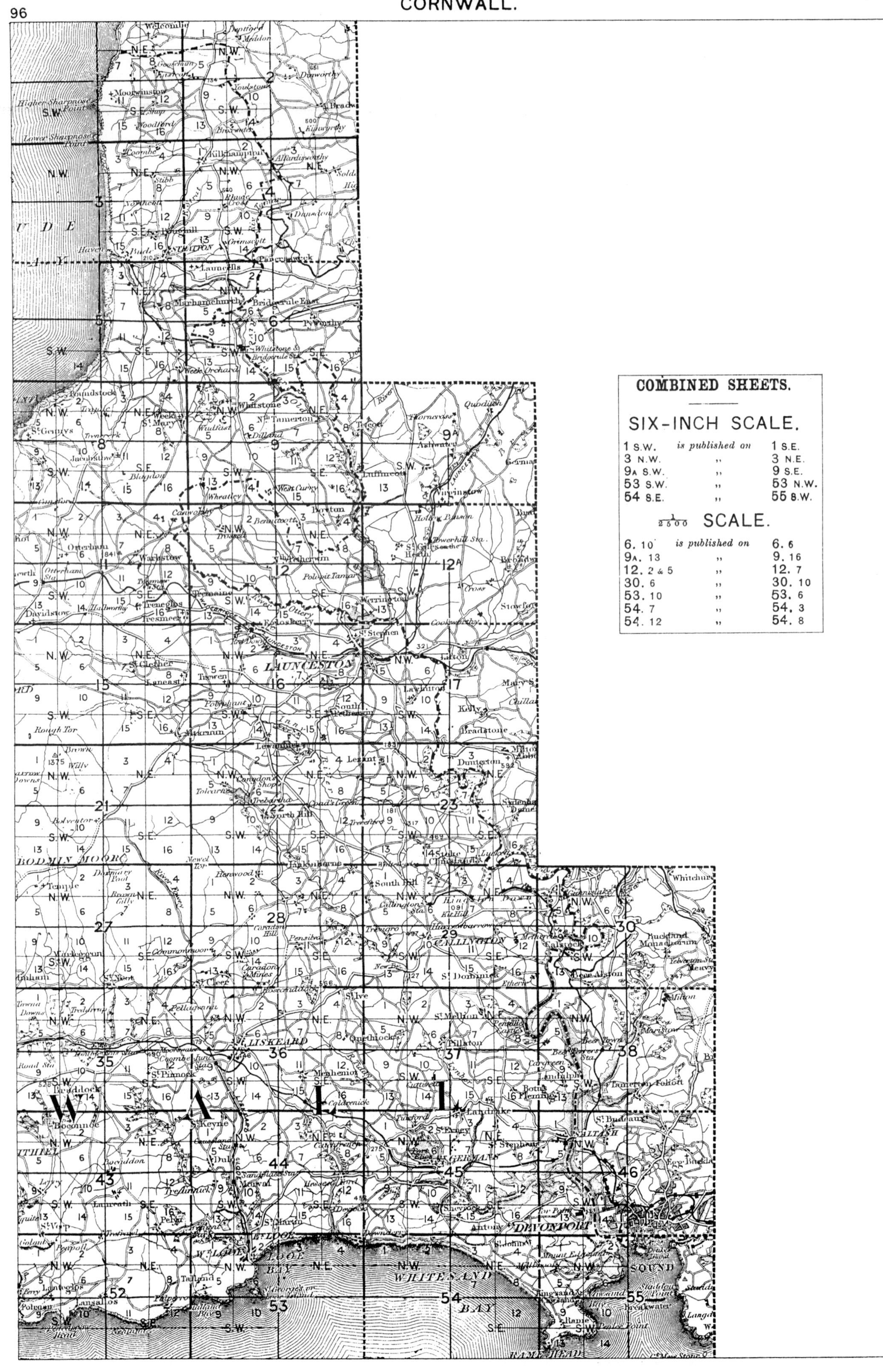
COMBINED SHEETS.
SIX-INCH SCALE.
1 S.W. is published on 1 S.E.
3 N.W. ,, 3 N.E.
9A S.W. ,, 9 S.E.
53 S.W. ,, 53 N.W.
54 S.E. ,, 55 S.W.
1/2500 SCALE.
6. 10 is published on 6. 6
9A. 13 ,, 9. 16
12. 2 & 5 ,, 12. 7
30. 6 ,, 30. 10
53. 10 ,, 53. 6
54. 7 ,, 54. 3
54. 12 ,, 54. 8
LAUNCESTON
LISKEARD
DEVONPORT
BODMIN MOOR
WHITESAND BAY
RAME HEAD

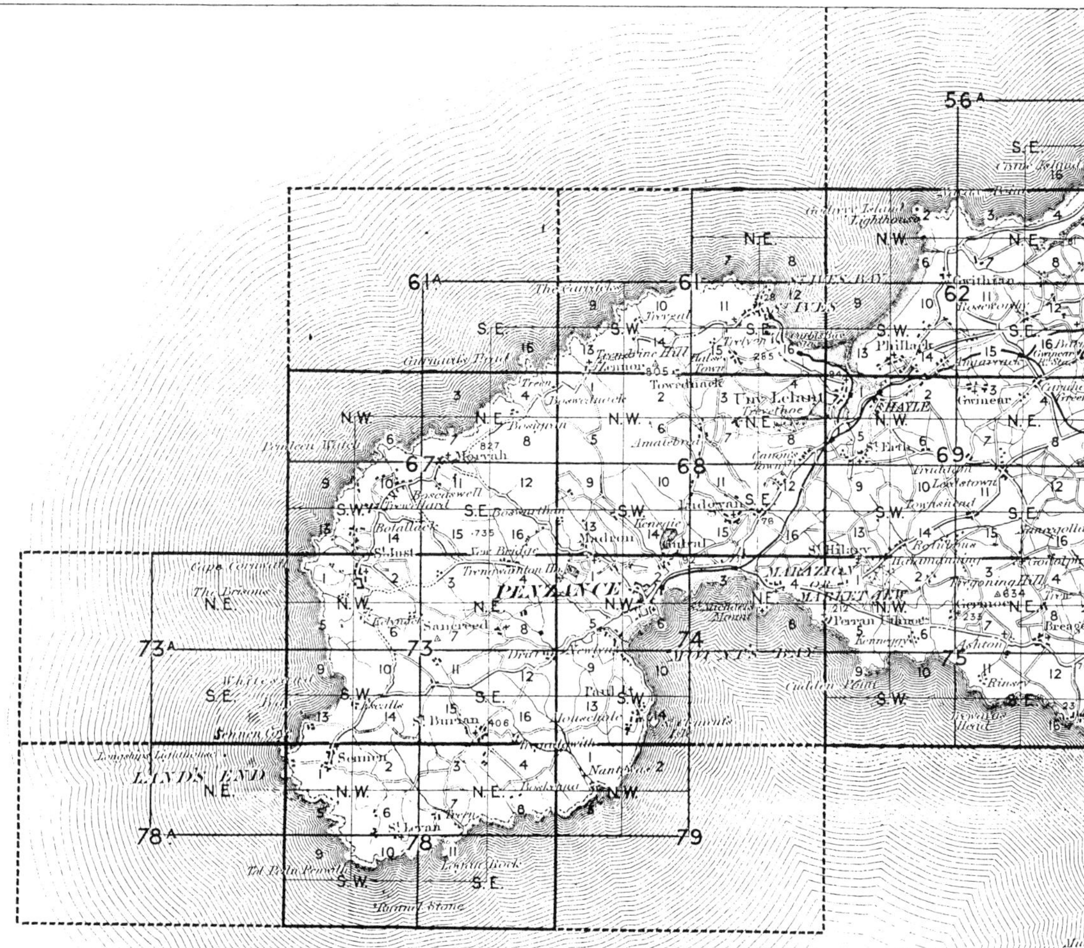

Note.—The Isles of Scilly lie 28 miles S.W. of Lands End, Cornwall. They are not shown in position on this Index.

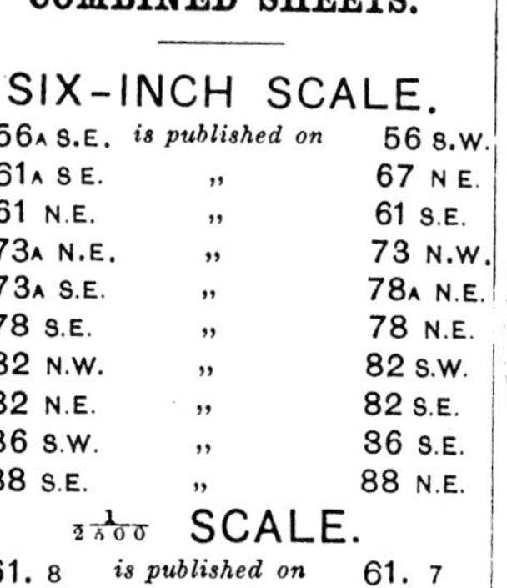

COMBINED SHEETS.

SIX-INCH SCALE.

56A S.E.	*is published on*	56 S.W.
61A S.E.	,,	67 N.E.
61 N.E.	,,	61 S.E.
73A N.E.	,,	73 N.W.
73A S.E.	,,	78A N.E.
78 S.E.	,,	78 N.E.
82 N.W.	,,	82 S.W.
82 N.E.	,,	82 S.E.
86 S.W.	,,	86 S.E.
88 S.E.	,,	88 N.E.

$\frac{1}{2500}$ SCALE.

61. 8	*is published on*	61. 7
62. 9	,,	62. 13
82. 6	,,	82. 10

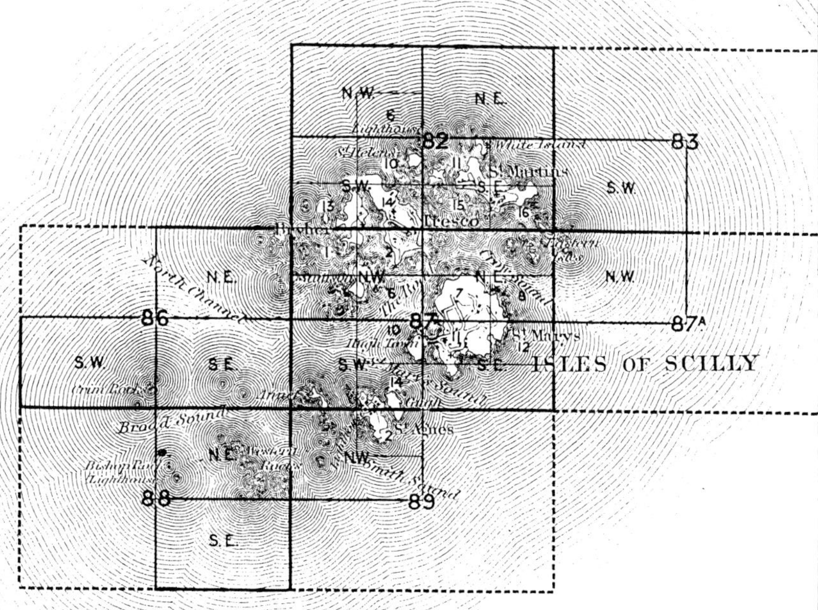

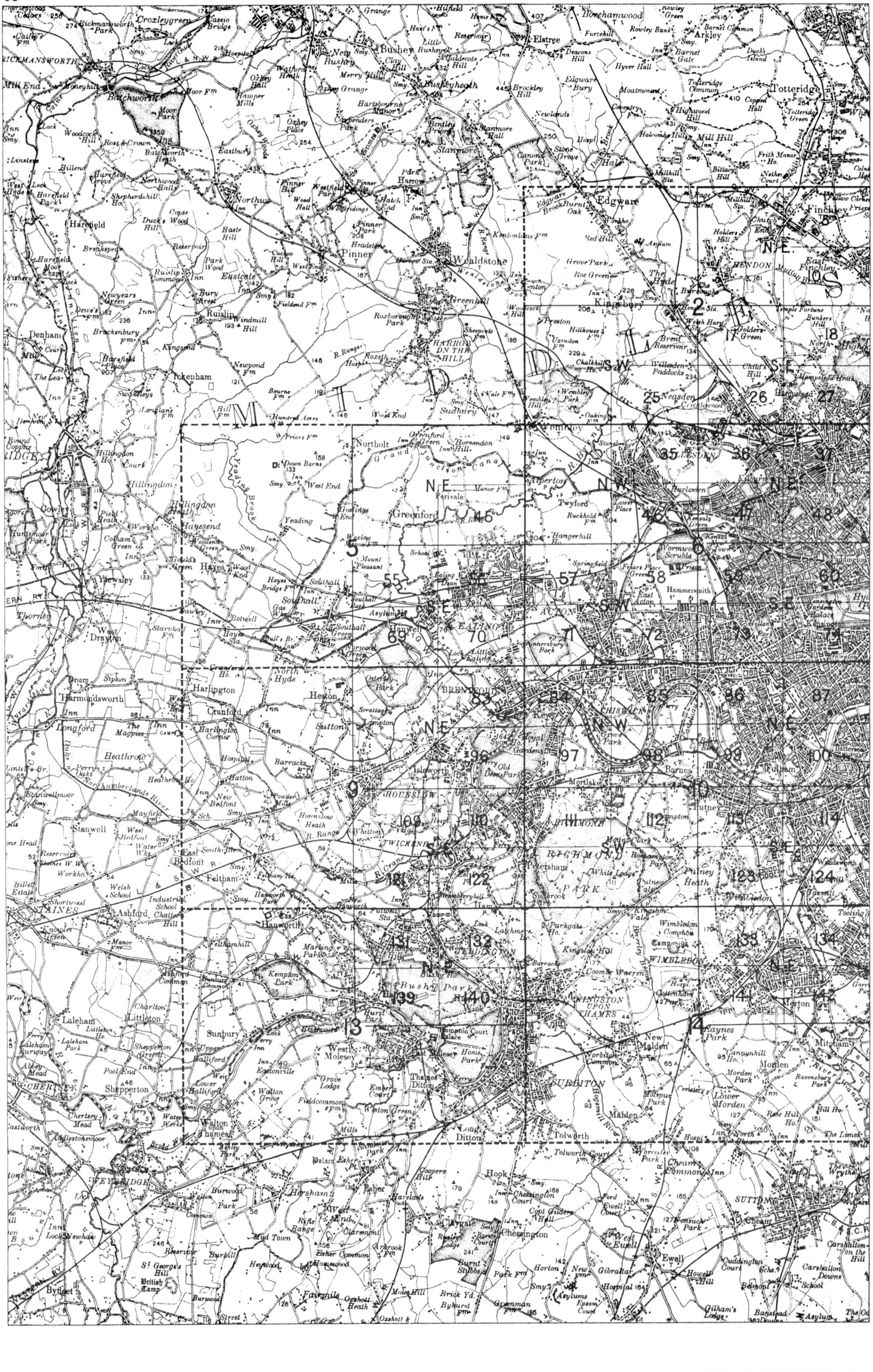

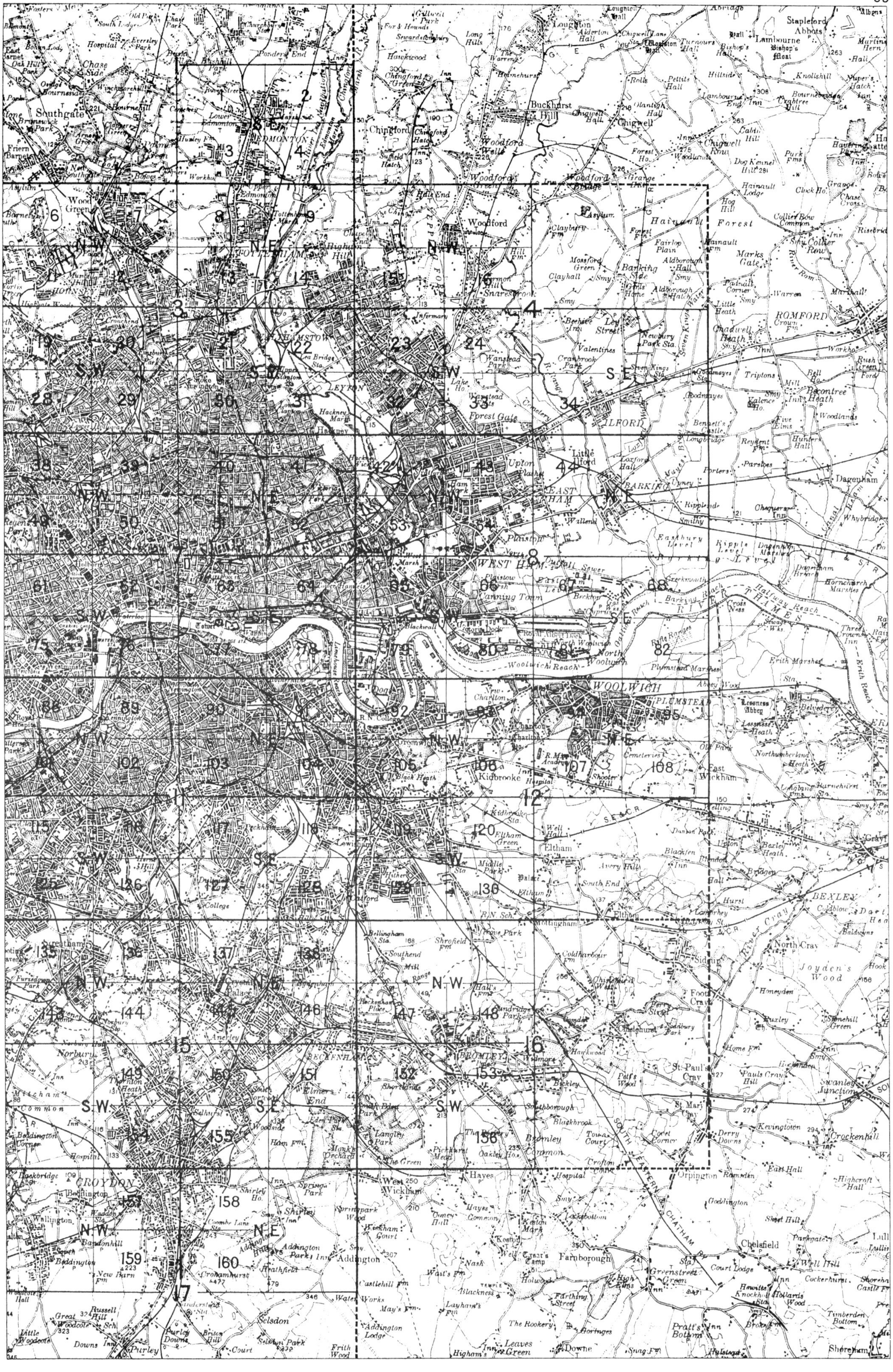

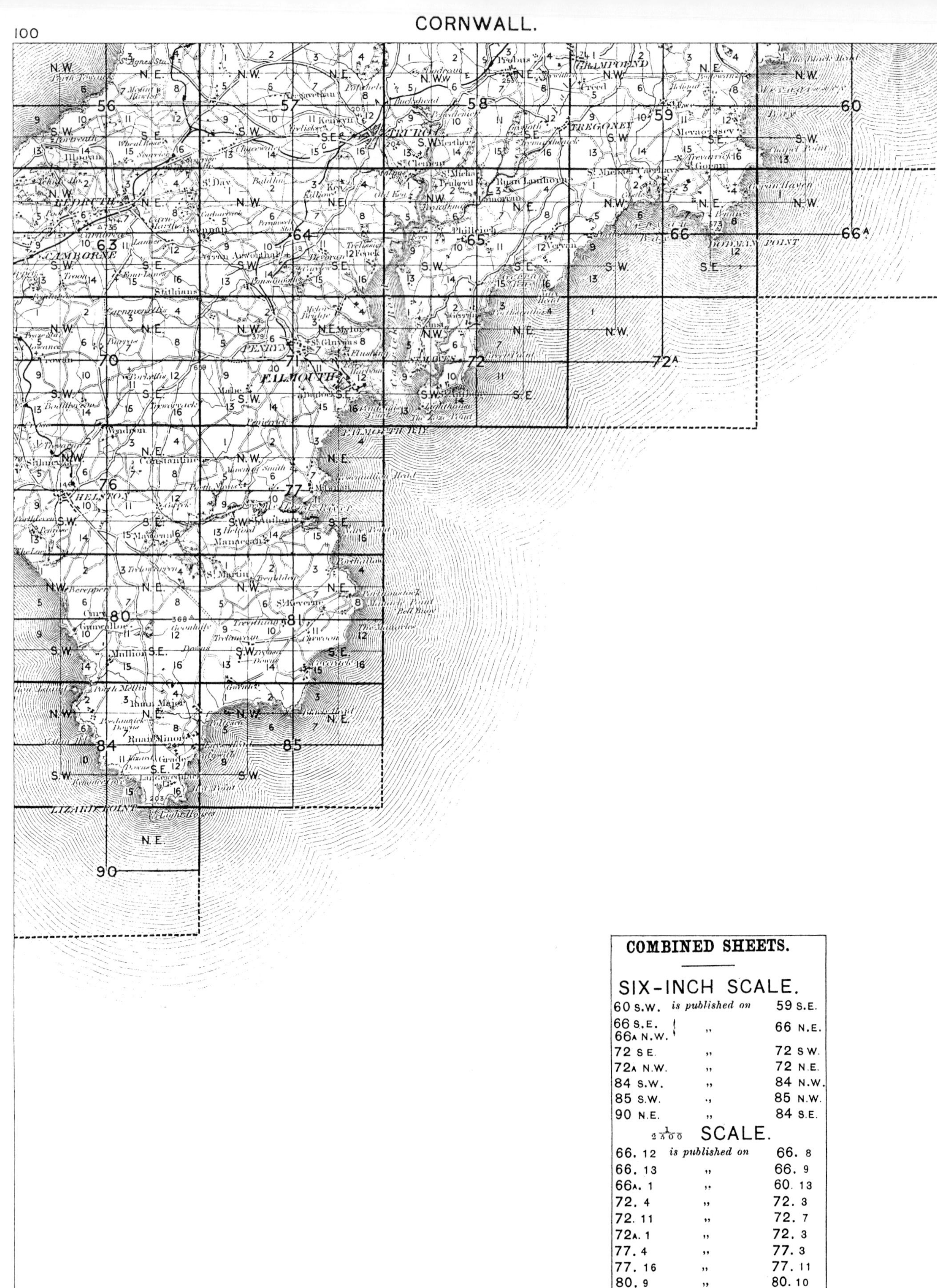

COMBINED SHEETS.

SIX-INCH SCALE.

60 S.W.	*is published on*	59 S.E.
66 S.E. / 66A N.W.	"	66 N.E.
72 S.E.	"	72 S.W.
72A N.W.	"	72 N.E.
84 S.W.	"	84 N.W.
85 S.W.	"	85 N.W.
90 N.E.	"	84 S.E.

$\frac{1}{2500}$ SCALE.

66. 12	*is published on*	66. 8
66. 13	"	66. 9
66A. 1	"	60. 13
72. 4	"	72. 3
72. 11	"	72. 7
72A. 1	"	72. 3
77. 4	"	77. 3
77. 16	"	77. 11
80. 9	"	80. 10
81. 16	"	81. 12
85. 6 & 7	"	85. 3
85. 9	"	85. 5

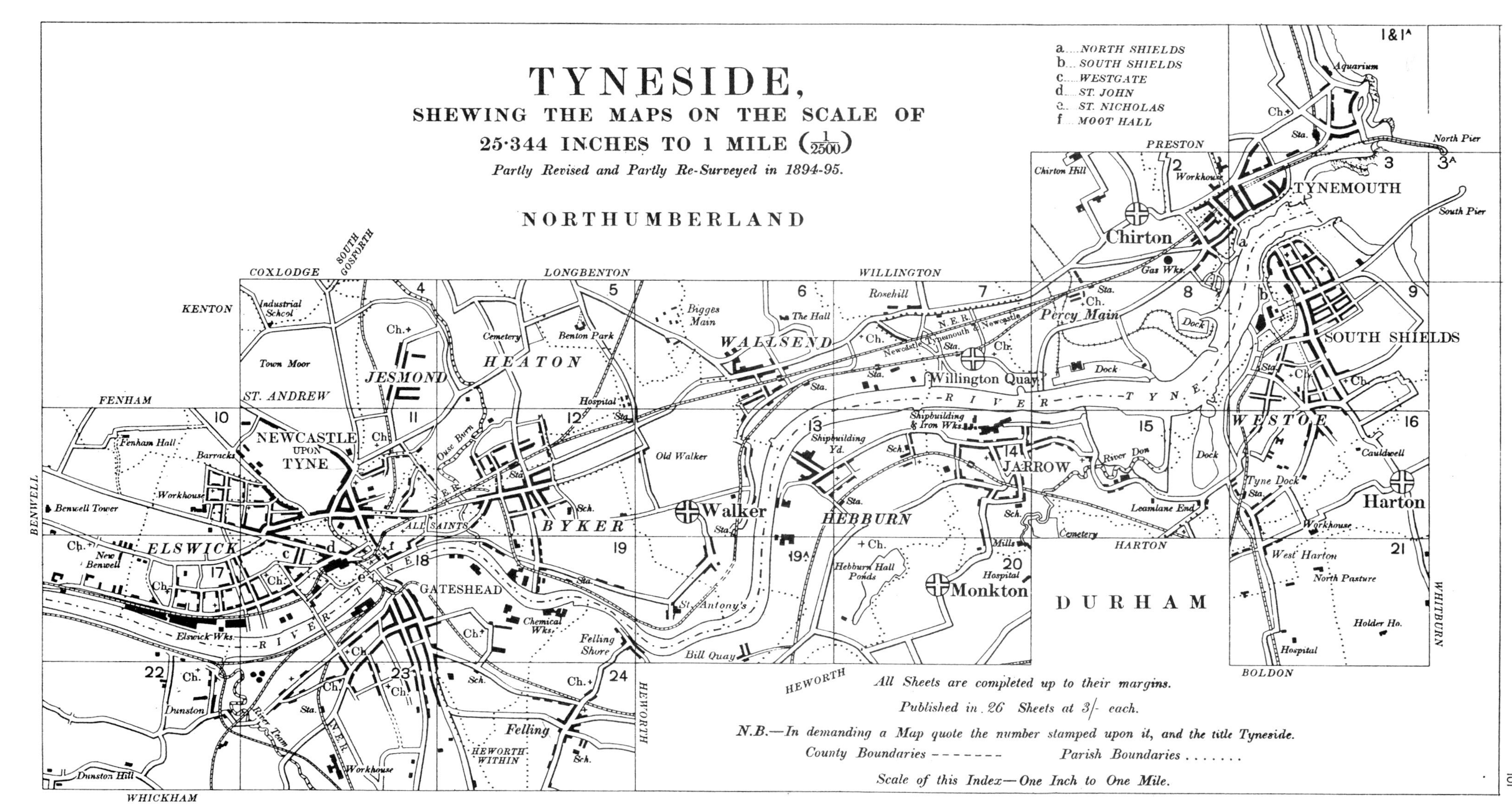
TYNESIDE,
SHEWING THE MAPS ON THE SCALE OF
25·344 INCHES TO 1 MILE (1/2500)
Partly Revised and Partly Re-Surveyed in 1894-95.
NORTHUMBERLAND
DURHAM
a....NORTH SHIELDS
b....SOUTH SHIELDS
c....WESTGATE
d....ST. JOHN
e....ST. NICHOLAS
f....MOOT HALL
All Sheets are completed up to their margins.
Published in 26 Sheets at 3/- each.
N.B.—In demanding a Map quote the number stamped upon it, and the title Tyneside.
County Boundaries - - - - - - -
Parish Boundaries . . . .
Scale of this Index—One Inch to One Mile.
TYNEMOUTH
SOUTH SHIELDS
Chirton
Harton
WESTOE
JARROW
HEBBURN
Monkton
Walker
WALLSEND
Willington Quay
Percy Main
HEATON
JESMOND
BYKER
NEWCASTLE UPON TYNE
GATESHEAD
ELSWICK
Felling
RIVER TYNE
North Pier
South Pier
Aquarium
PRESTON
WILLINGTON
LONGBENTON
COXLODGE
SOUTH GOSFORTH
KENTON
FENHAM
BENWELL
WHICKHAM
HEWORTH
HARTON
BOLDON
WHITBURN
ST. ANDREW
ALL SAINTS
HEWORTH WITHIN
Town Moor
Industrial School
Benton Park
Biggs Main
Rosehill
The Hall
Old Walker
St. Antony's
Bill Quay
Felling Shore
Chemical Wks.
Elswick Wks.
Dunston
Dunston Hill
River Team
New Benwell
Benwell Tower
Fenham Hall
Barracks
Workhouse
Hospital
Cemetery
Ouse Burn
Shipbuilding Yd.
Shipbuilding & Iron Wks.
Hebburn Hall Ponds
River Don
Leamlane End
Tyne Dock
Cauldwell
West Harton
North Pasture
Holder Ho.
Chirton Hill
Gas Wks.
Dock
Mills
N.E.R.
Newcastle Tynemouth & Newcastle
1&1A
2
3
3A
4
5
6
7
8
9
10
11
12
13
14
15
16
17
18
19
19A
20
21
22
23
24

ESSEX
(NEW SERIES)

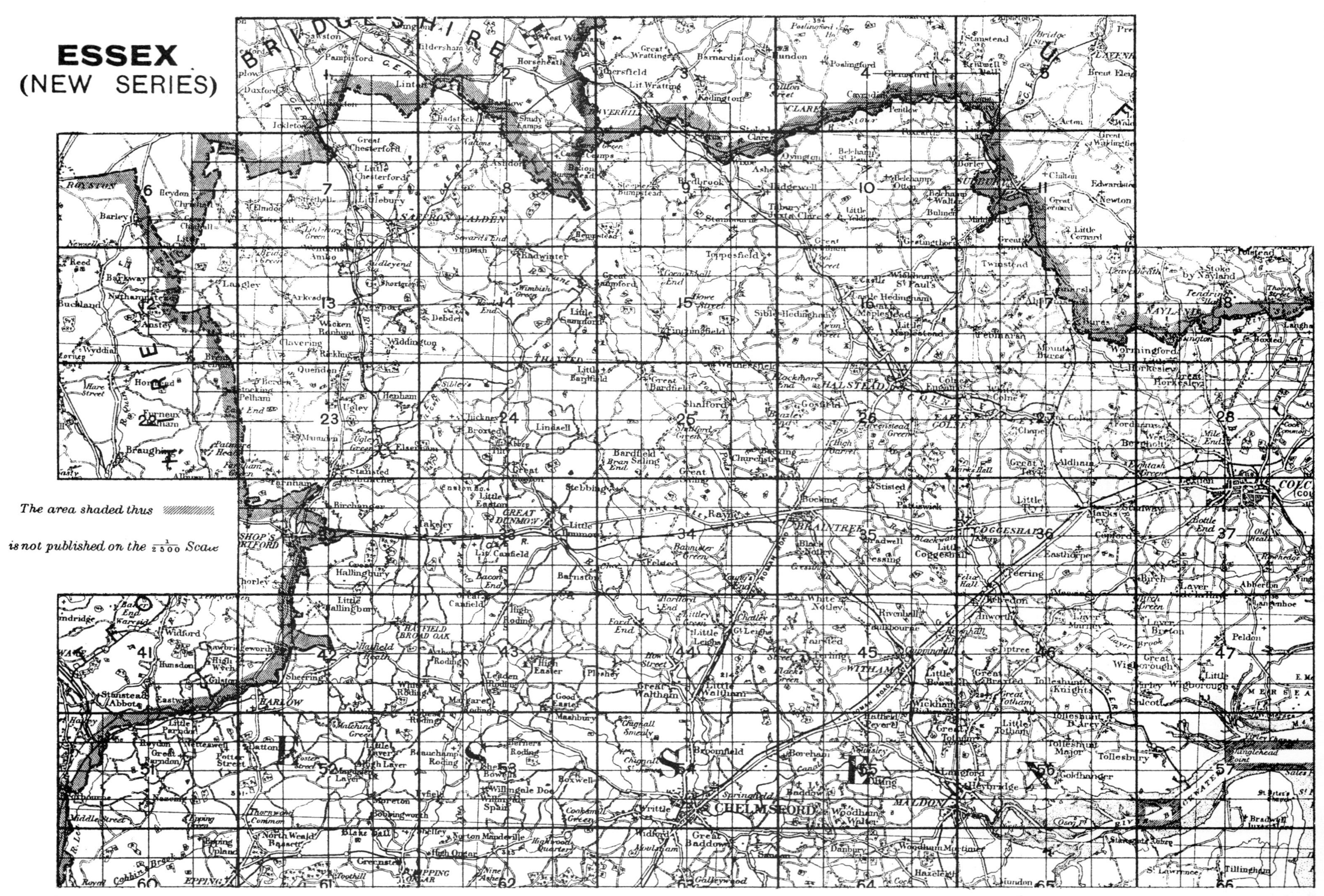

The area shaded thus ▨ *is not published on the* $\frac{1}{2500}$ *Scale*

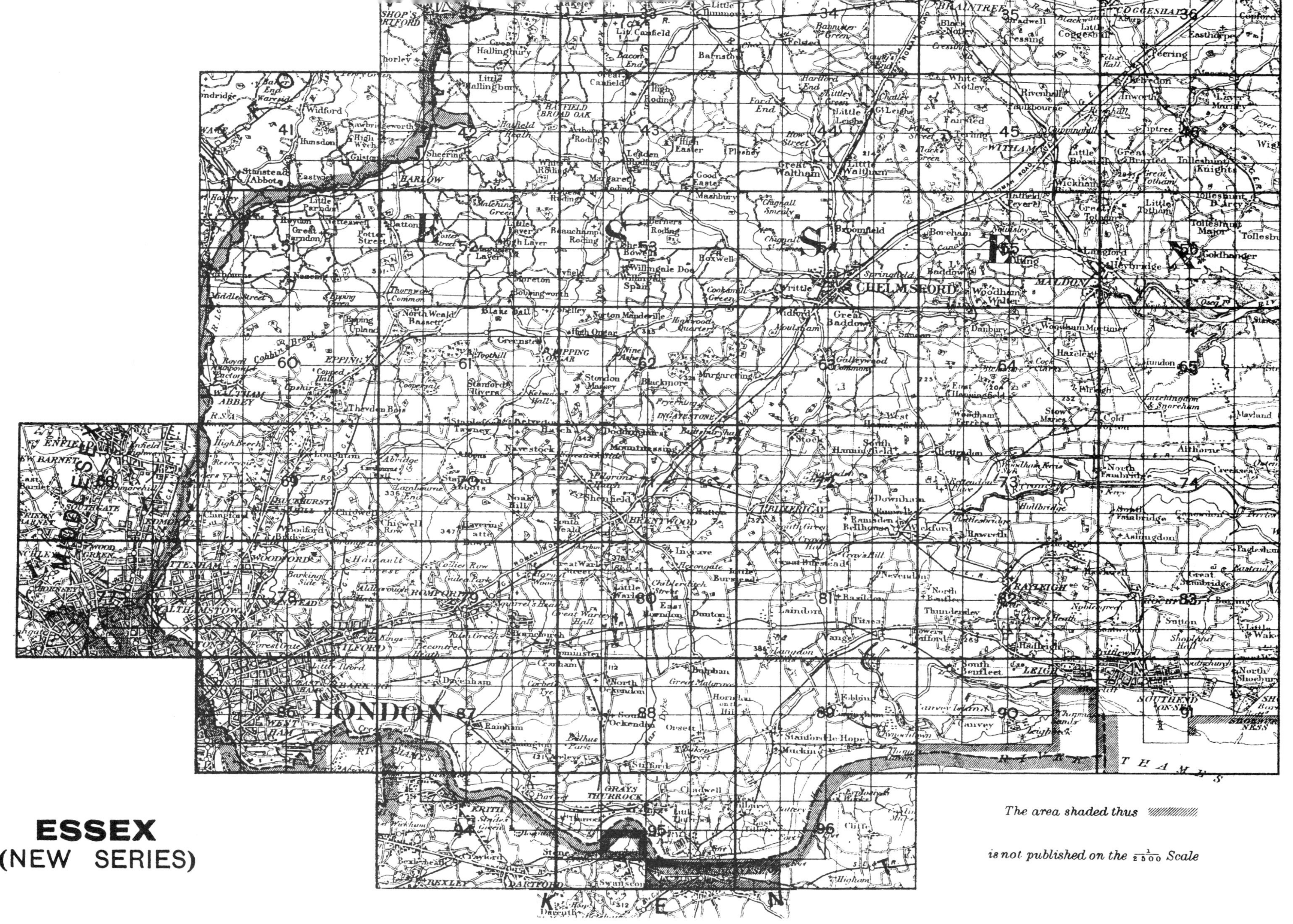

ESSEX
(NEW SERIES)

The area shaded thus

is not published on the $\frac{1}{2500}$ Scale

ESSEX
(NEW SERIES)

COMBINED SHEETS.

SIX INCH SCALE.

N. 93. *is published on* N. 92.

$\frac{1}{2500}$ SCALE.

N. 2. 10.	*is published on*	N. 2. 9.
N. 17. 3.	,,	N. 17. 7.
N. 17. 12.	,,	N. 18. 9.
N. 40. 14.	,,	N. 40. 13.
N. 59. 2.	,,	N. 59. 1.
N. 96. 3.	,,	N. 96. 2.

The area shaded thus *is not published on the* $\frac{1}{2500}$ *Scale*

NORTHUMBERLAND
(NEW SERIES)

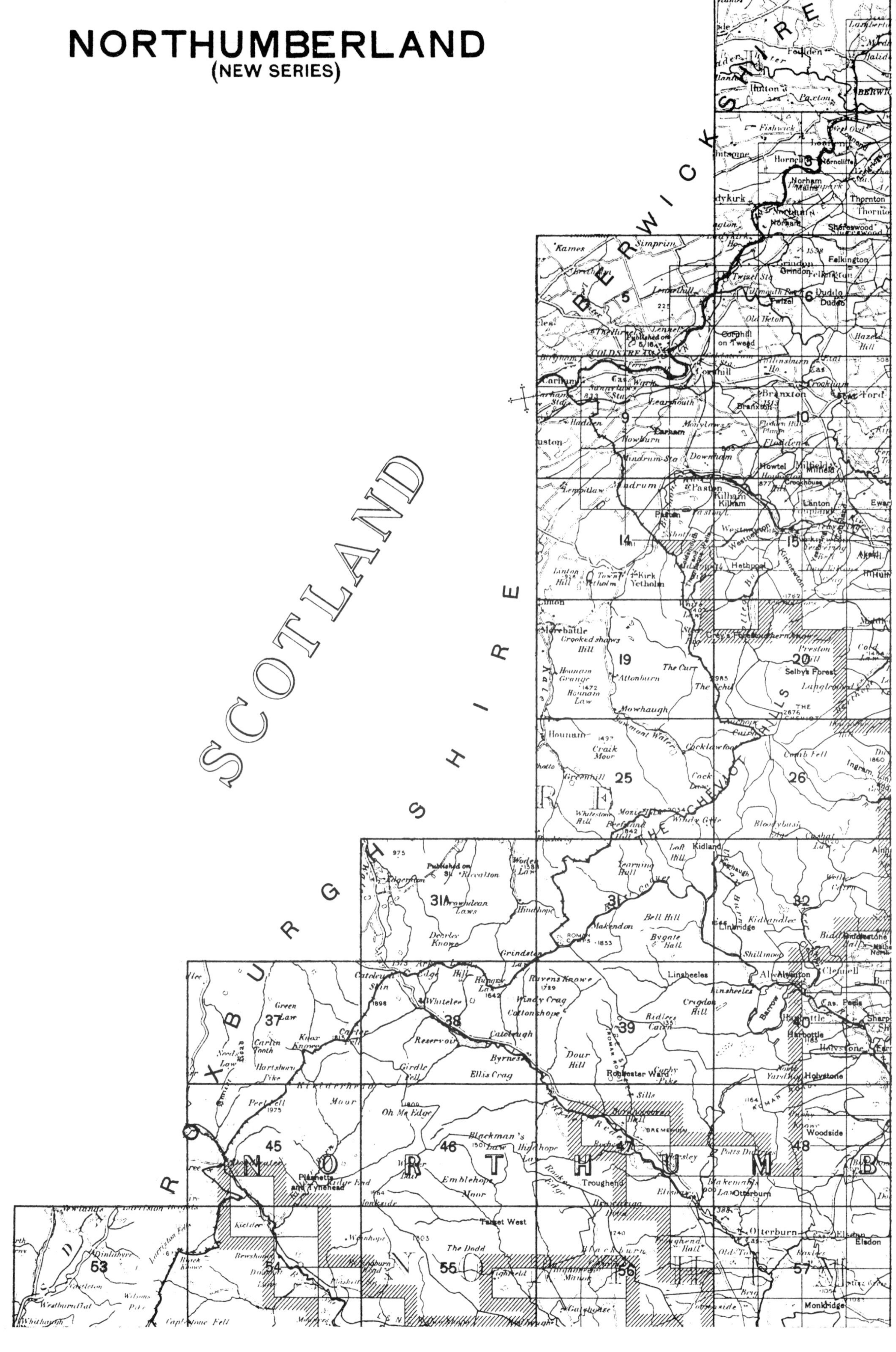

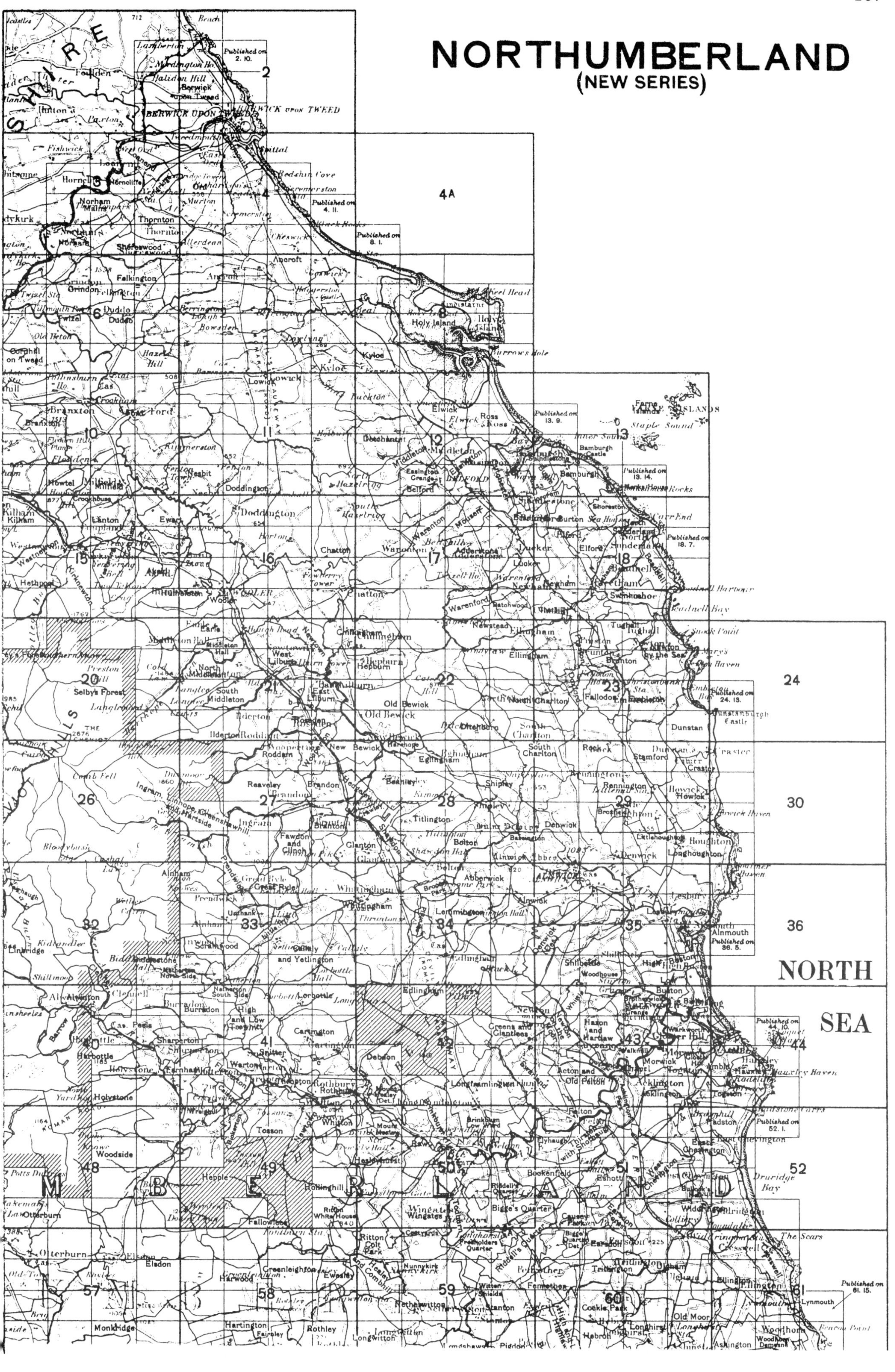
NORTHUMBERLAND
(NEW SERIES)
2
4
4A
6
8
10
11
12
13
15
16
17
18
20
21
22
23
24
26
27
28
29
30
32
33
34
35
36
40
41
42
43
44
48
49
50
51
52
57
58
59
60
61
Published on 2. 10.
Published on 4. 11.
Published on 8. 1.
Published on 13. 9.
Published on 13. 14.
Published on 18. 7.
Published on 24. 13.
Published on 36. 5.
Published on 44. 10.
Published on 52. 1.
Published on 61. 15.
NORTH
SEA
BERWICK UPON TWEED
Holy Island
Lowick
Wooler
Alnwick
Rothbury
Alnmouth
Amble
Warkworth
Bamburgh
Belford
Otterburn
Elsdon
Morpeth
Lynmouth
Ashington

NORTHUMBERLAND
(NEW SERIES)

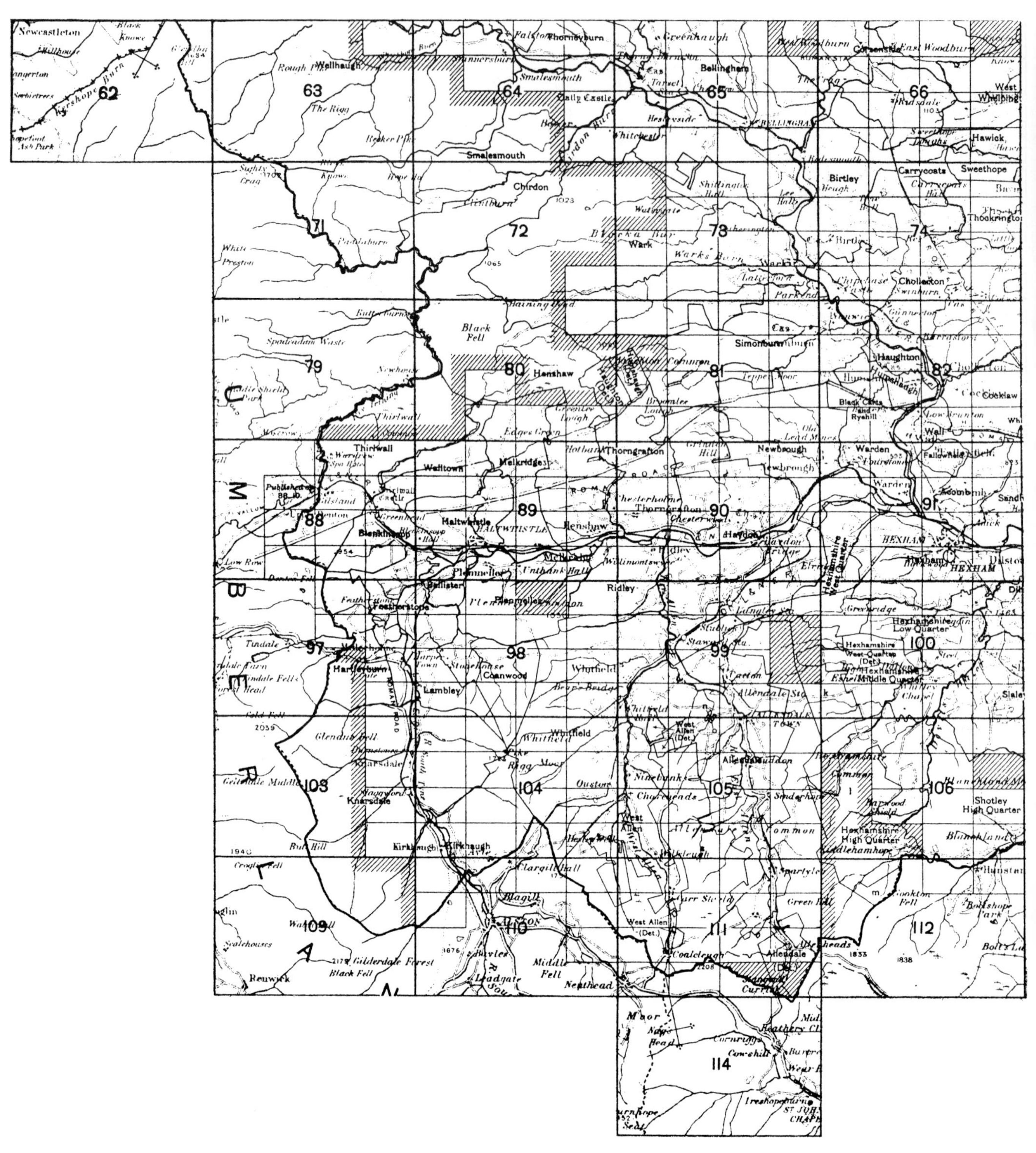

NORTHUMBERLAND
(NEW SERIES)

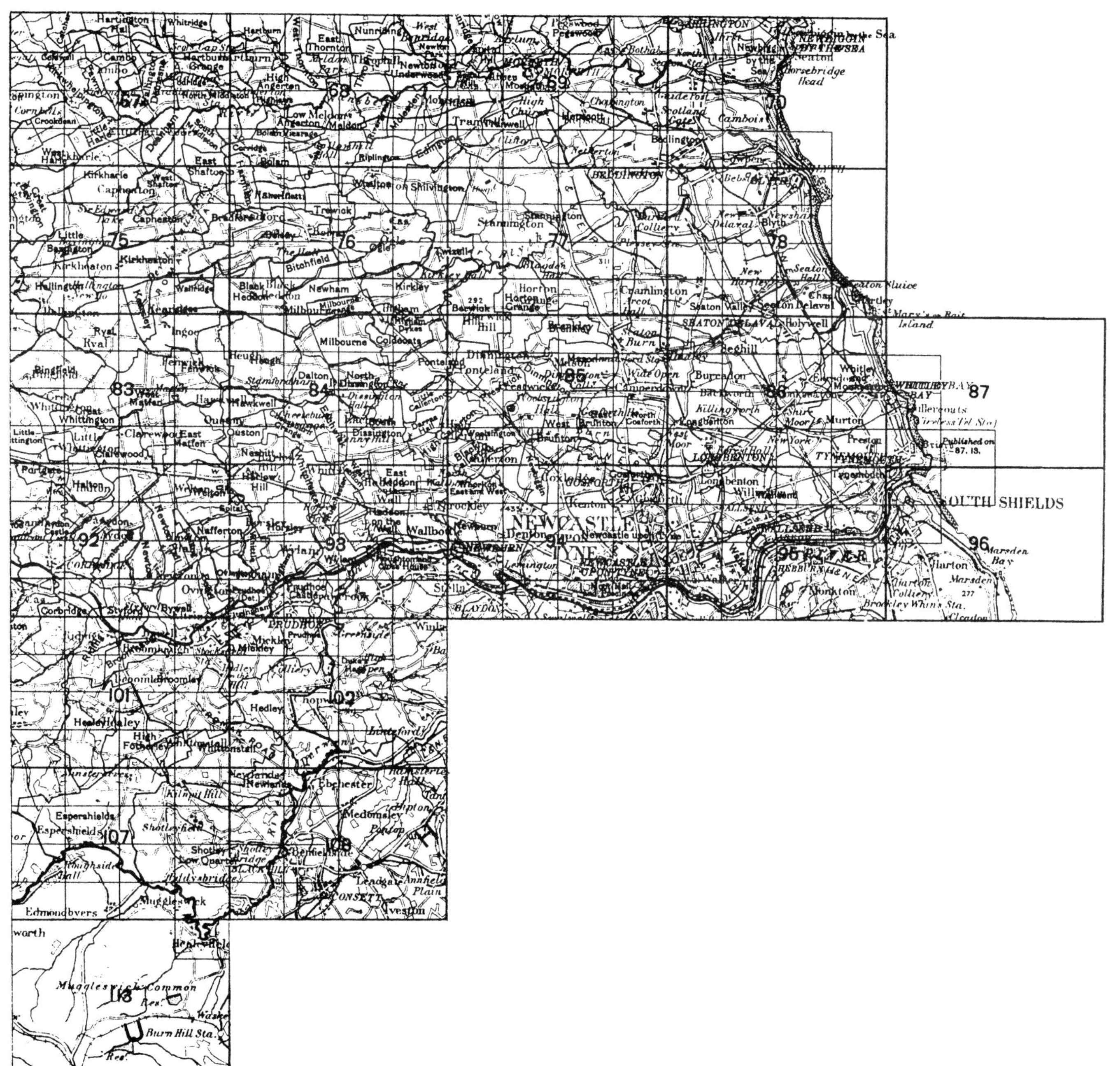

CONVENTIONAL SIGNS AND WRITING

Used on the $\frac{1}{2500}$ Plans of the

ORDNANCE SURVEY.

BOUNDARIES

Counties

County & Civil Ph.

Ridings & Quarter Sessional Div^ns.

County Boroughs. (England) — Co. Boro. Bdy.

County Burghs (Scotland) — Co. Burgh Bdy.

Municipal Wards — Ward Bdy.

Urban Districts — U.D. Bdy.

Police Burghs (Scotland) — Burgh. Bdy.

Parliamentary County Divisions — Parly. Div. Bdy.

Poor Law Unions — Union Bdy.

Parliamentary Boroughs — Parly. Boro. Bdy.

Div^ns. of Parly. Boroughs — Div. of Parly. Boro. Bdy

Municipal Boroughs — Munl. Boro. Bdy.

Rural Districts — R.D. Bdy.

Civil Parishes

Method of shewing the Boundaries in connection with the Detail.

The initials are placed where a change occurs in the nature of the Boundaries, as referred to a road, wall, stream, drain, or fence, and the symbol ...... is used for marking the extent of the Boundary to which the initials refer.

1. *Centre of Stream* — C.S. C.S.
2. *Centre of Track of Stream* — C. Tk. S. Tk. S.
3. *Centre of Road* — C.R.

Side of Stream or Drain

4. S.S.
5. S.D. S.D. — *Drain or Stream Straight, Boundary changes Sides*
6. S.S. S.S. — *Boundary Straight, Stream or Drain changes Sides*

7. *Track of Hedge* — Tk. H. Tk. H.
8. *Root of Hedge, Face of Cop, Side of Fence* — R.H. R.H.
9. *Face of Wall* — F.W.

4 feet from Root of Hedge or Fence &c.

10. 4 ft. R.H.
11. 4 ft. R.H. 4 ft. R.H. — *Fence Straight, Boundary changes Sides*
12. 4 ft. R.H. 4 ft. R.H. — *Boundary Straight, Fence changes Sides*
13. 4 ft. R.H. — *Stream on the Boundary side of Fence*
14. 4 ft. R.H. 4 ft. R.H. — *Boundary Straight, Fence changes Sides*

15. *Centre of Fence, Top of Cop, Centre of Wall &c.* — C.F. T.C. C.W.
16. *Defaced or Undefined, Track of Stream, Drain, or Fence* — Def. Tk. S. Und.

From 4 to 9 the dots should be in contact with the line which represents the Side of Stream or Drain, Root of Hedge, Face of Cop, Side of Fence, Face of Wall.

From 10 to 14 the dots should not be in contact with the line which represents the Hedge or Fence, &c.

No. 15 The dots should be on the continuous line representing Centre of Fence, Top of Cop, Centre of Wall, &c.

WRITING

Counties .... } C
Ridings & Quarter Sessional Div^ns .... }

County Boroughs (England) .... } C
County Burghs (Scotland) .... }

Parliamentary County Div^ns .... P

Poor Law Unions .... P

Parliamentary Boroughs .... P

Divisions of Parly. Boroughs .... D

Municipal Boroughs .... M

Municipal Wards .... W

Urban Districts .... } U
Police Burghs (Scotland) .... }

Rural Districts .... R.D.

Civil Parishes .... *P*

Towns (other than the above) .... *T*

Districts (Close) in Towns & Suburbs .... *D*

Districts (Open) in Towns & Suburbs .... *D*

Parish Churches & Villages

Other Villages

PARKS & DEMESNES

Gentlemen's Seats

Manufactories, Mines, Farms, Locks

Workhouses

Bridges *(On Main Roads)*, Bridges *(Other)*

Isolated Houses

BAYS & HARBOURS

NAVIGABLE RIVERS & CANALS

Small Rivers & Brooks

BOGS, MOORS & FORESTS

Woods & Copses

RANGES OF HILLS

Parts of Ranges

Single Hill Features

Antiquities:— ROMAN, Pre-historic or Saxon, Norman *or Subsequent*

RAILWAYS. *RAILWAYS (Mineral).* Stations.

These Examples must vary in size and extent according to the importance of the Districts they refer to.

AREAS

...ry parcel is numbered thus 27

...area is given underneath in Acres, thus .... 4·370

Braces, indicating that the spaces so connected are .... }
included in the same reference number and area .... }

ALTITUDES *(in Feet)*

...face Levels along roads, and of Trig^l Stations, obtained by Spirit levelling, are written thus 326+, the cross shewing the spot at which the altitude is taken.

The Altitudes are above the assumed mean level of the Sea at Liverpool.

...tudes with the letters B.M. marked ↑ against them, refer to marks made on Buildings, Walls, Milestones &c., (Bench Marks).

CONVENTIONAL SIGNS

Mile Stone ...... M.S
Pump ...... P
Signal Post ...... S.P
Guide Post ...... G.P
Letter Box ...... L.B
Sun Dial ...... S.D

Foot Bridge ...... F.B.
Foot Path ...... F.P.
Bridle Road ...... B.R.
Electricity Pylon . E.P
Telephone Call Box . T.C.B
Police —„— . P.C.B

Antiquities (Site of)
Arrow denotes flow of water

W.D. Boundary Stone ...... B.S. W↑D
Adm^{y} Dep^{t} —„— —„— A⚓D

Sluice ...... Sl.
Trough ...... Tr.
Spring ...... Sp
Well ...... W
Mooring Ring ...... M.R

Trig^{l} Station ...... △
Altitude at Trig^{l} Station ...... 507 △
Bench Mark ...... B.M. 325·9 ↑
Surface Level ...... 342 .

Boundary Stone ...... B.S
—„— *Post* ...... B.P

High or Low Water Mark of Ordinary Tides ...... H.or L.W.M.
—„— *Spring* —„— H.or L.W.M.

Wood, Deciduous

Marsh

Reeds

Fir

Mixed Wood

Brushwood

Osiers

Orchard

Bush

Furze

Rough Pasture

Ford

Ferry

Sloping Masonry

Flat Rock

Stepping Stones

Lock

Waterfall

Fences, Walls, Buildings &c.

20

Railway crossing River or Canal

Railway crossing Road

Quarry

Sand Pit

Embankment

Level Crossi

Refuse Heap

Shingle

Cutting

Road crossing Railway

Open Country

27
4·220

28
·190

30
·270

29
3·670

F.P

Gravel Pit

Clay Pit

Road over single stream

B.R.

Road over River or Canal

CONVENTIONAL SIGNS AND WRITING

Used on the Six Inch Maps of the ORDNANCE SURVEY

BOUNDARIES

Parliamentary County Divisions .... Parly. Div. Bdy.

Poor Law Unions .... Union Bdy.

Parliamentary Boroughs .... Parly. Boro. Bdy.

Divns of Parly. Boroughs .... Div. of Parly. Boro. Bdy

Municipal Boroughs .... Munl. Boro. Bdy.

Urban Districts .... U.D. Bdy.

Police Burghs (Scotland) .... Burgh Bdy.

Rural Districts .... R.D. Bdy.

Civil Parishes ....

Counties ....

County & Civil Ph. ....

Ridings & Quarter Sessional Divns ....

County Boroughs (England) .... Co. Boro. Bdy.

County Burghs (Scotland) .... Co. Burgh. Bdy.

ALTITUDES *(in Feet)*

The Altitudes are above the mean level of the Sea at Liverpool. *The Contour altitudes are written thus* .200

...tudes along roads, and of Trig! Stations obtained by Spirit Levelling, are written thus 317 ·, the dot showing the spot at which the altitude is taken.

Altitudes with the letters B.M. marked ↑ against them, refer to marks made on Buildings, Walls, Milestones, &c., (Bench Marks).

The large figures under the Parish name thus CLAUGHTON *represent its area in Acres.*
Acres 3785·525

The Latitudes are given on the margin to every 30 seconds, & the Longitudes to every minute.

WRITING

Counties	C		*Municipal Boroughs*	M
Ridings & Quarter Sessional Div^{ns}			*Urban Districts*	U
County Boroughs (England)	C		*Police Burghs (Scotland)*	
County Burghs (Scotland)			*Rural Districts*	R.D.
Parliamentary County Div^{ns}	P		*Civil Parishes*	*P*
Poor Law Unions	P		*Towns (Other than the above)*	*T*
Parliamentary Boroughs	P		*Districts (Close) in Towns & Suburbs*	*D*
Divisions of Parly. Boroughs	D		*Districts (Open) in Towns & Suburbs*	*D*

Parish Churches & Villages

Other Villages

PARKS & DEMESNES

Gentlemen's Seats

Manufactories, Mines, Farms, Locks

Workhouses

Bridges *(On Main Roads), Bridges (Other)*

Isolated Houses

BAYS & HARBOURS

NAVIGABLE RIVERS & CANALS

Small Rivers & Brooks

BOGS, MOORS & FORESTS

Woods & Copses

RAILWAYS, *RAILWAYS (Mineral)* Stations

RANGES OF HILLS
Separate parts of Ranges
Single Features

Antiquities { ROMAN / Pre-historic or Sax / Norman *or Subseq*

These Examples must vary in size and extent according to the importance of the Districts they refer to.

CONVENTIONAL SIGNS

Symbol shewing direction of flow of water ....>

Antiquities, Site of ....+

Trigonometrical Station ....

Bench Mark (B.M.) ....

Pump, Guide Post, Signal Post ....

Well, Spring, Boundary Post ....

Surface Level ....·285

Double Lines of Railway

Single — do — & Tramways

Fenced — *M.S (Mile Stone)* — *Main Roads* — *Unfenced*

Fenced — *Minor — do —* — *Unfenced*

CONTOURS

In Red or Blue — *Instrumental* 200

In Red or Blue — *Sketched* 225

In Black — *Instrumental* 200

In Black — *Sketched* 225

Before 1895 all contours were shewn by dotted lines

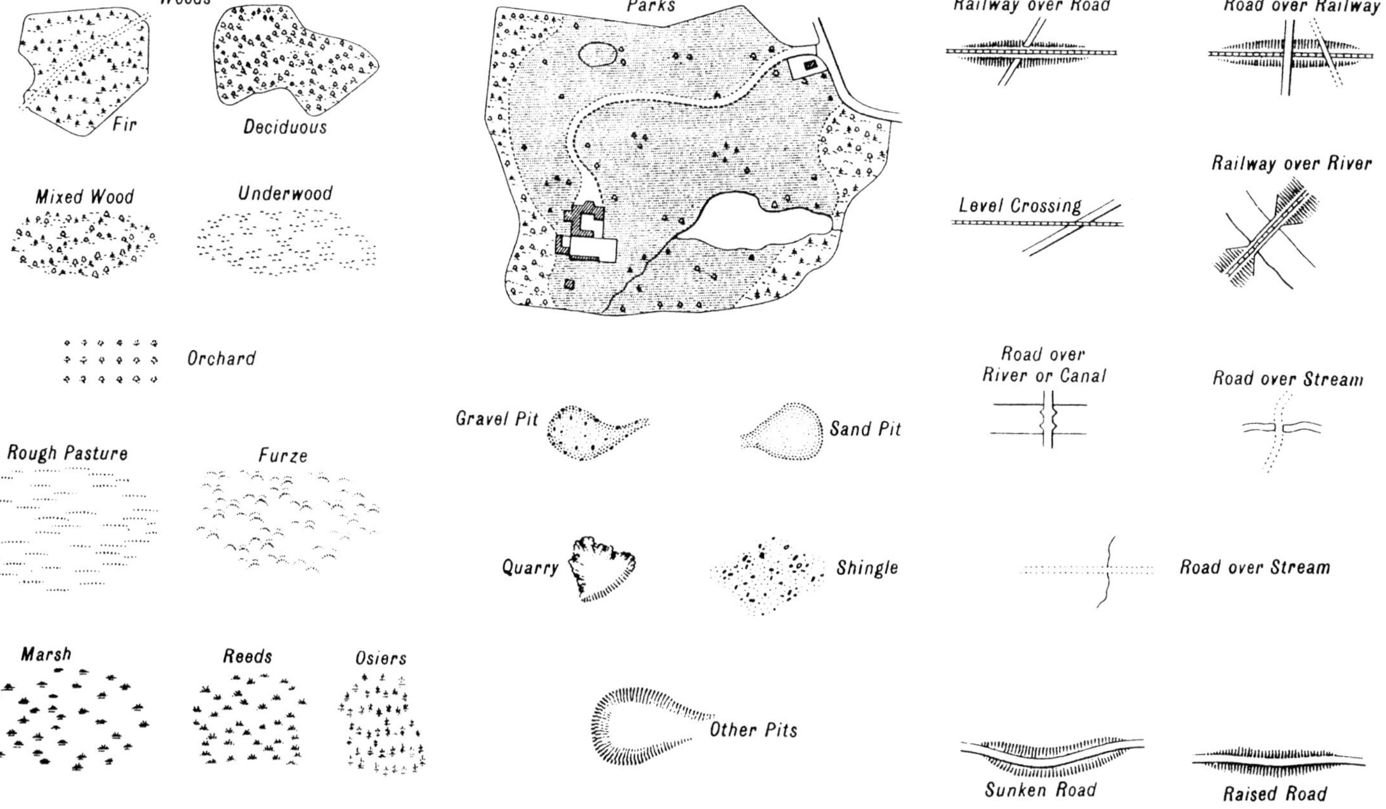

Conversion chart for 1:2500 sheets of London

The numbering of the 1:2500 mapping of London is uniquely complicated, and this chart has been prepared in the hope of lessening the confusion. The position in summary is that in the first edition of the 1:2500 (surveyed c.1862-72) the sheets covering built-up or semi-built-up London were numbered in a single sequence from 1 to 89; adjoining areas were mapped variously as parts of Middlesex, Essex, Surrey, or Kent; as the Middlesex sheets were on the same county origin as the London sheets, their numbers are given here. In the second edition ('Edition of 1894-6') built-up London was covered by 160 sheets, a sequence which included the 89 London sheets of the first edition, all of which were renumbered. It is this 160-sheet layout which is illustrated on atlas pages 98 and 99; the 'large' numbers (1 to 17) are the framework for the 1:1056 mapping of London. In the third edition (revised 1912-15) the sheets were again renumbered, as 14 full sheets, some of which doubled up as full sheets of Middlesex or Essex, although some parts of Surrey and Kent treated as 'London' in the second edition were once again mapped only as parts of these counties in the third edition. Thus in the chart, sheet 62 in the second edition was sheet 35 in the first edition, and sheet 5.10 in the third edition; it also bore the number Middlesex 17.10.

Mx	17.10
1	35
2	62
3	5.10

					Mx 11.4 2 5
					Mx 11.8 2 10
				Mx 11.11 2 17	Mx 11.12 1 2 2 18 3 2.12
			Mx 11.14 2 25	Mx 11.15 2 26 3 2.15	Mx 11.16 1 7 2 27 3 2.16
			Mx 16.2 2 35	Mx 16.3 1 14 2 36 3 4.3	Mx 16.4 1 15 2 37 3 4.4
	Mx 15.8 2 45		Mx 16.6 1 22 2 46 3 4.6	Mx 16.7 1 23 2 47 3 4.7	Mx 16.8 1 24 2 48 3 4.8
Mx 15.11 2 55	Mx 15.12 2 56	Mx 16.9 2 57	Mx 16.10 1 31 2 58 3 4.10	Mx 16.11 1 32 2 59 3 4.11	Mx 16.12 1 33 2 60 3 4.12
Mx 15.15 2 69	Mx 15.16 2 70	Mx 16.13 2 71	Mx 16.14 1 40 2 72 3 4.14	Mx 16.15 1 41 2 73 3 4.15	Mx 16.16 1 42 2 74 3 4.16
	Mx 20.4 2 83	Mx 21.1 2 84	Mx 21.2 1 51 2 85 3 8.2	Mx 21.3 1 52 2 86 3 8.3	Mx 21.4 1 53 2 87 3 8.4
	Mx 20.8 2 96	Mx 21.5 2 97	Mx 21.6 1 62 2 98 3 8.6	Mx 21.7 1 63 2 99 3 8.7	Mx 21.8 1 64 2 100 3 8.8
Mx 20.11 2 109	Mx 20.12 2 110	2 111	1 72 2 112 3 8.10	Mx 21.9 1 73 2 113 3 8.11	Mx 21.10 1 74 2 114 3 8.12
Mx 20.15 2 121	Mx 20.16 2 122			1 82 2 123 3 8.15	1 83 2 124 3 8.16
Mx 25.3 2 131	Mx 25.4 2 132			2 133	2 134
Mx 25.7 2 139	Mx 25.8 2 140			2 141	2 142

A Herts 44 Middx 5	B Herts 45 Middx 6	C Essex 68 Herts 46 Middx 7	D Essex 69 Middx 8
E Middx 10	F Lon 1 Middx 11	G Essex 77 Lon 2 Middx 12	H Essex 78 Lon 3
I Middx 15	J Lon 4 Middx 16	K Lon 5	L Essex 86 Lon 6
M Middx 20	N Lon 8 Middx 21	O Lon 9	P Lon 10
Q Middx 25	R Lon 12	S Lon 13	T Lon 14

The third edition 1:10,560 mapping of London

This was arranged as a block of twenty 'full' sheets, identified by letter, as shewn in the diagram above. Some of these sheets doubled as part of the Essex, Middlesex and Hertfordshire series, as well as corresponding to the 'full' numbered sheets (1 to 14) of the London 1:2500 third edition.

		Mx 7.11 2 1	Mx 7.12 2 2				
		Mx 7.15 2 3	Mx 7.16 2 4				
Mx 12.1 2 6	Mx 12.2 2 7	Mx 12.3 2 8	Mx 12.4 2 9				
Mx 12.5 2 11	Mx 12.6 2 12	Mx 12.7 1 1 2 13	Mx 12.8 2 14	2 15 3 Ex 78.5	2 16 3 Ex 78.6		
Mx 12.9 1 3 2 19 3 2.9	Mx 12.10 1 4 2 20 3 2.10	Mx 12.11 1 5 2 21	Mx 12.12 1 6 2 22	2 23 3 Ex 78.9	2 24 3 Ex 78.10		
Mx 12.13 1 8 2 28 3 2.13	Mx 12.14 1 9 2 29 3 2.14	Mx 12.15 1 10 2 30 3 2.15	Mx 12.16 1 11 2 31	Mx 13.13 1 12 2 32 3 Ex 78.13	1 13 2 33 3 Ex 78.14	2 34 3 Ex 78.15	
Mx 17.1 1 16 2 38 3 5.1	Mx 17.2 1 17 2 39 3 5.2	Mx 17.3 1 18 2 40 3 5.3	Mx 17.4 1 19 2 41 3 5.4	Mx 18.1 1 20 2 42 3 Ex 86.1	1 21 2 43 3 Ex 86.2	2 44 3 Ex 86.3	
Mx 17.5 1 25 2 49 3 5.5	Mx 17.6 1 26 2 50 3 5.6	Mx 17.7 1 27 2 51 3 5.7	Mx 17.8 1 28 2 52 3 5.8	Mx 18.5 1 29 2 53 3 Ex 86.5	1 30 2 54 3 Ex 86.6		
Mx 17.9 1 34 2 61 3 5.9	Mx 17.10 1 35 2 62 3 5.10	Mx 17.11 1 36 2 63 3 5.11	Mx 17.12 1 37 2 64 3 5.12	Mx 18.9 1 38 2 65 3 Ex 86.9	1 39 2 66 3 Ex 86.10	2 67 3 Ex 86.11	2 68 3 Ex 86.12
Mx 17.13 1 43 2 75 3 5.13	Mx 17.14 1 44 2 76 3 5.14	Mx 17.15 1 45 2 77 3 5.15	Mx 17.16 1 46 2 78 3 5.16	Mx 18.13 1 47 2 79 3 6.13	1 48 2 80 3 Ex 86.14	1 49 2 81 3 Ex 86.15	1 50 2 82 3 6.16
1 54 2 88 3 9.1	1 55 2 89 3 9.2	1 56 2 90 3 9.3	1 57 2 91 3 9.4	1 58 2 92 3 10.1	1 59 2 93 3 10.2	1 60 2 94 3 10.3	1 61 2 95 3 10.4
1 65 2 101 3 9.5	1 66 2 102 3 9.6	1 67 2 103 3 9.7	1 68 2 104 3 9.8	1 69 2 105 3 10.5	1 70 2 106 3 10.6	1 71 2 107 3 10.7	2 108 3 10.8
1 75 2 115 3 9.9	1 76 2 116 3 9.10	1 77 2 117 3 9.11	1 78 2 118 3 9.12	1 79 2 119 3 10.9	1 80 2 120 3 10.10		
1 86 2 125 3 9.13	1 87 2 126 3 9.14	1 88 2 127 3 9.15	1 89 2 128 3 9.16	2 129 3 10.13	2 130 3 10.14		
2 135 3 13.1	1 88 2 136 3 13.2	1 89 2 137 3 13.3	2 138 3 13.4				
2 143 3 13.5	2 144 3 13.6	2 145 3 13.7	2 146 3 13.8	2 147 3 14.5	2 148		
	2 149	2 150	2 151	2 152	2 153		
	2 154	2 155			2 156		
	2 157	2 158					
	2 159	2 160					

Specimen — 6 Inch Scale. $\frac{1}{(10560)}$
Town.

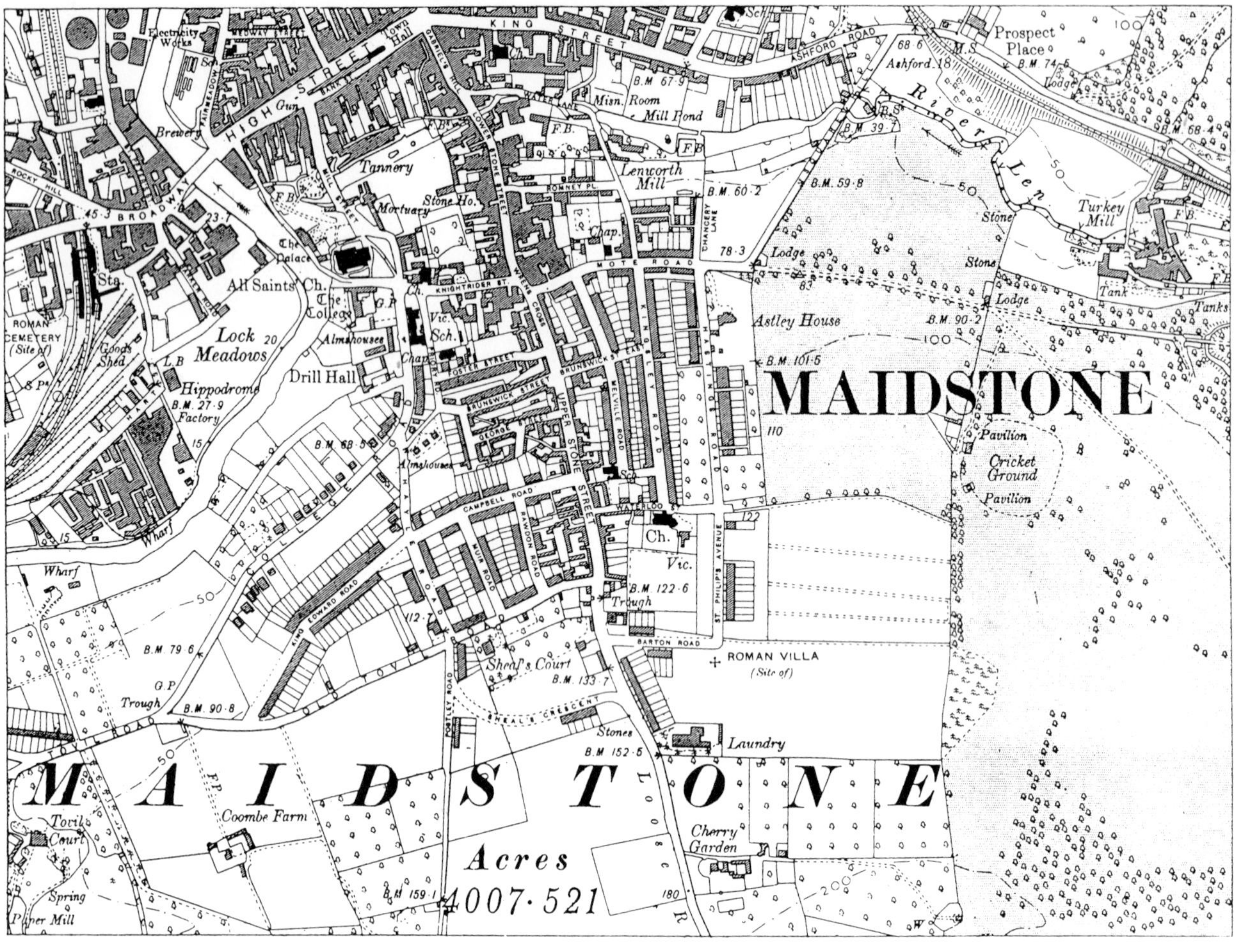

Specimen — 25 Inch Scale $\frac{1}{(2500)}$

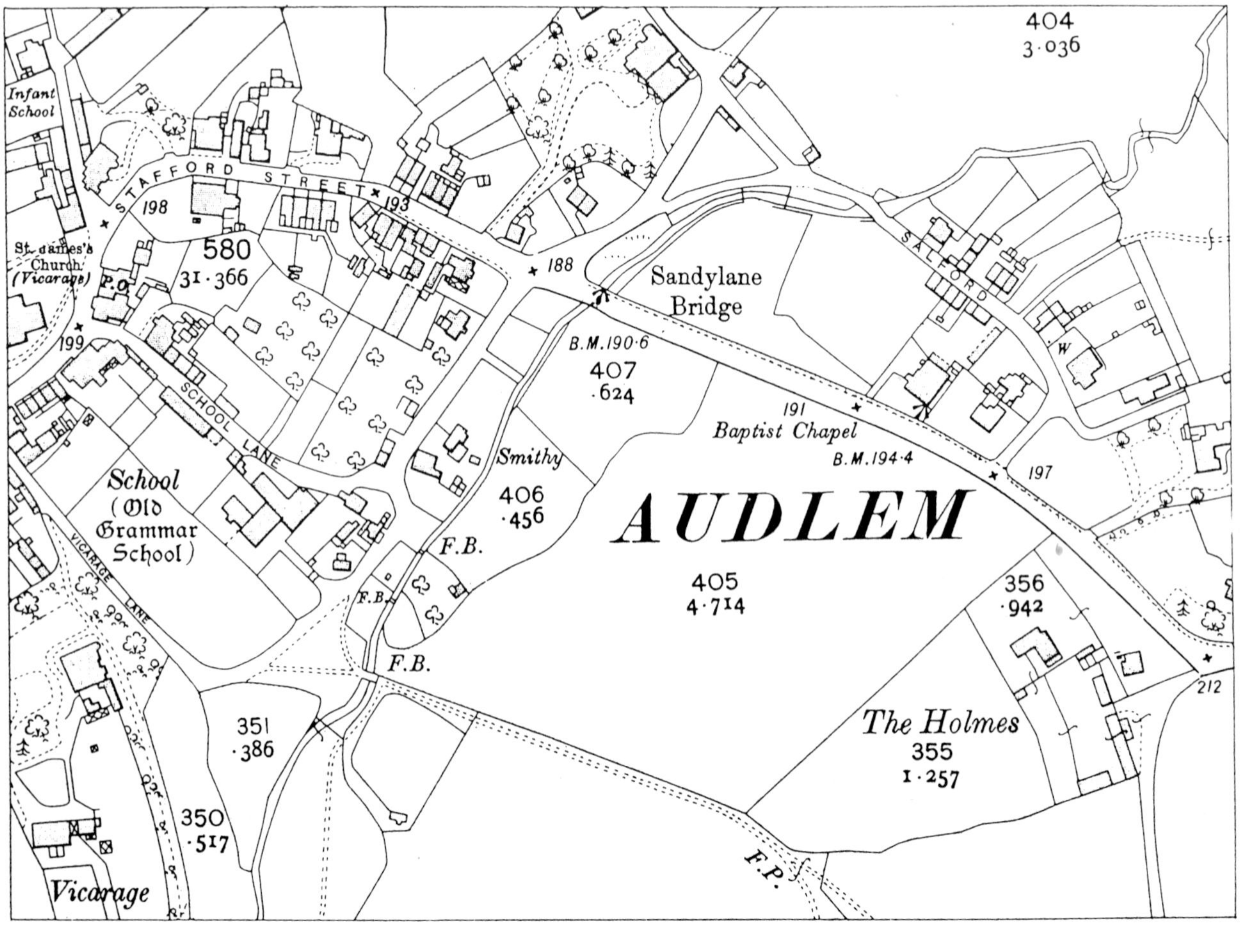